RAF BOMBER COMMAND
Reflections of War

RAF BOMBER COMMAND
Reflections of War

Volume 5
Armageddon
(27 September 1944–May 1945)

Martin W Bowman

Pen & Sword
AVIATION

First Published in Great Britain in 2013 by
Pen & Sword Aviation
an imprint of
Pen & Sword Books Ltd
47 Church Street, Barnsley, South Yorkshire S70 2AS

Copyright © Martin W Bowman, 2013

ISBN 978-1-84884-496-4

Typeset in 10/12pt Palatino by
Concept, Huddersfield

Printed and bound in England by
CPI Group (UK) Ltd, Croydon, CRO 4YY

Pen & Sword Books Ltd incorporates the imprints of Pen & Sword
Archaeology, Atlas, Aviation, Battleground, Discovery, Family History,
History, Maritime, Military, Naval, Politics, Railways, Select, Social History,
Transport, True Crime, and Claymore Press, Frontline Books, Leo Cooper,
Praetorian Press, Remember When, Seaforth Publishing and Wharncliffe.

For a complete list of Pen & Sword titles please contact
PEN & SWORD BOOKS LIMITED
47 Church Street, Barnsley, South Yorkshire, S70 2AS, England
E-mail: enquiries@pen-and-sword.co.uk
Website: www.pen-and-sword.co.uk

Contents

Acknowledgements

Gebhard Aders; Harry Andrews DFC; Frau Anneliese Autenrieth; Mrs Dorothy Bain; Günther Bahr; Charlie 'Jock' Baird; Harry Barker; Irene Barrett-Locke; Raymond V Base; Don Bateman; Steve Beale; A D 'Don' Beatty; Jack Bennett; Andrew Bird; Peter Bone; Alfons Borgmeier; Jack Bosomworth; Len Browning; Don Bruce; George Burton; Jim Burtt-Smith; Maurice Butt; Philip J Camp DFM; City of Norwich Aviation Museum (CONAM); Bob Collis; Jim Coman; B G Cook; John Cook DFM; Rupert 'Tiny' Cooling; Dennis Cooper; Ray Corbett; Coen Cornelissen; Leslie Cromarty DFM; Tom Cushing; Hans-Peter Dabrowski; Rob de Visser; Dr. Karl Dörscheln; J Alan Edwards; Wolfgang Falck; David G Fellowes; Elwyn D Fieldson DFC; Karl Fischer; Søren C Flensted; Vitek Formanek; Stanley Freestone; Ian Frimston; Prof. Dr Ing. Otto H Fries; Air Vice Marshal D J Furner CBE DFC AFC; Ken Gaulton; Jim George; Margery Griffiths, Chairman, 218 Gold Coast Squadron Association; Group Captain J R 'Benny' Goodman DFC* AFC AE; Alex H Gould DFC; Hans Grohmann; Charles Hall; Steve Hall; Jack F Hamilton; Eric Hammel; Erich Handke; James Harding; Frank Harper; Leslie Hay; Gerhard Heilig; Bob Hilliard; Peter C Hinchliffe; Neville Hockaday RNZAF; Werner 'Red' Hoffmann; Ted Howes DFC; Air Commodore Peter Hughes DFC; John Anderson Hurst; Zdenek Hurt; Ab A Jansen; Karl-Ludwig Johanssen; Wilhelm 'Wim' Johnen; Arthur 'Johnnie' Johnson; John B Johnson; Graham B Jones; Hans-Jürgen Jürgens; Erich Kayser; George Kelsey DFC; Les King; Christian Kirsch; Hans Krause; Reg Lawton; J R Lisgo; Chas Lockyer; Günther Lomberg; Peter Loncke; George Luke; Ian McLachlan; Nigel McTeer; B L Eric Mallett RCAF; Len Manning; The Honourable Terence Mansfield; Eric Masters; Bernard 'Max' Meyer DFC; Cyril Miles; Colin Moir; Frank Mouritz; Friedrich Ostheimer; Maurice S Paff; Simon Parry; Path Finder Association; Wing Commander David Penman DSO OBE DFC; Richard Perkins; Peter Petrick; Karl-Georg Pfeiffer; Eric Phillips; Vic Poppa; John Price; Stan Reed; Ernie Reynolds; Peter Richard; Albert E Robinson; Heinz Rökker; Squadron Leader Geoff Rothwell DFC; Fritz Rumpelhardt;

David M Russell; Kees Rijken; Eric Sanderson; Klaus J Scheer; Dr. Dieter Schmidt-Barbo; Karl-Heinz Schoenemann; Jerry Scutts; Johan Schuurman; Group Captain Jack Short; Leslie R Sidwell; Don L Simpkin; SAAF Assn; Albert Spelthahn; Dr Ing. Klaus Th. Spies; Dick Starkey; Squadron Leader Hughie Stiles; Mike 'Taff' Stimson; Ted Strange DFC; Maurice Stoneman; Ken Sweatman; Paul Todd; Fred Tunstall DFC; Hille van Dieren; George Vantilt; Bob Van Wick; Andreas Wachtel; Georg Walser; David Waters; H Wilde; John Williams; H J Wilson; Henk Wilson; Geoffrey and Nick Willatt; Dennis Wiltshire; Louis Patrick Wooldridge DFC; Fred Young DFM; Cal Younger.

I am particularly grateful to my friend and colleague Theo Boiten, with whom I have collaborated on several books, for all of the information on the *Nachtjagd* or German night fighter forces contained herein. And, aviation historians everywhere owe a deep sense of gratitude to his and all the other valuable sources of reference listed in the end notes; in particular, those by the incomparable W R 'Bill' Chorley, Martin Middlebrook and Chris Everitt and Oliver Clutton-Brock. Finally, all of the late authors' books, as listed, who are beyond compare. This book and its companion volumes are dedicated to their memory.

CHAPTER 1

Beating The Life Out Of Germany

'Hell's bells', yelled Skipper. 'Mac, get us outta here!'

The first intimation that anything was wrong came suddenly, when anti-aircraft shells began to burst all around us. I can still see the port wing dissecting a hideous ball of black smoke tinged with wicked orange flame and I can still smell the cordite. But, with the roar of our engines in my ears, it was like watching with the sound turned off.

I'd become used to being scared but this was different. This was real fear and there was nothing I could do. The next few seconds would be in the hands of our pilot. It was our twelfth op – eighteen more to go.

Peter Bone, Lancaster mid-upper gunner, 626 Squadron

'It seems rather a makeshift place, out in the wilderness but I guess we'll get used to it' Ernest Peter Bone noted rather gloomily in his diary on the night of 27 September 1944. The bomb aimer and the rest of Squadron Leader Richard Lane's crew had just been posted to 626 Squadron at Wickenby, about ten miles north-east of Lincoln. In time they did more than just get used to Wickenby; in the ensuing nine months they would become part of it. Peter Bone recalls:

Wickenby had been carved out of farmland in September 1942 to accommodate 12 Squadron, veteran of the Battle of France but latterly based at nearby Binbrook. A year later its 'C' flight had, like Adam's rib, been taken away to form the nucleus of a new squadron, number 626. Its first operation had been on the night of 10/11 November 1943 when 313 Lancasters bombed railway yards on the main line to Italy at Modane in Southern France. Wickenby was typical of many wartime bomber squadrons, appearing like mushrooms almost over-night in the flat countryside of Eastern England. With two squadrons, each comprising of two flights of eight Lancasters apiece, flown

1

by a total of 224 aircrew, it was serviced by hundreds of ground personnel of both sexes, working in shifts on aircraft maintenance, air traffic control, motor transport, parachute packing and, not least in importance, in the cookhouse, because as Napoleon once observed, an army marches on its stomach. Not for Wickenby the imposing red brick buildings of the pre-war bases. We made do with prefabricated huts. But it was to be our home for the time being.

But what circuitous chain of circumstances had conspired to put the former junior reporter behind two Browning .303in machine guns in a Lancaster bomber at the age of twenty-two and sit in a gun turret on 25 bombing operations, 16 by night and nine by day? Once back in England after his training in Canada, Peter Bone's immediate destination had been Harrogate in West Yorkshire.

We were billeted for a few days in a requisitioned girls' college, during which time we were issued the flying kit we would begin using at our next base, an Operational Training Unit 'somewhere in England'. To remind the more thoughtless of us, we were given a talk on security. It was all too easy, we were warned, especially after a few beers, to let slip information that could jeopardize the forthcoming invasion of occupied Europe. Then we were all given three weeks' leave; our first opportunity to see our loved ones at home for about a year. There were long cycle rides with Geoff and sometimes with my sister and brother, boating on the Thames, movies to see locally with my girlfriend and plays to see in London. The high spot was seeing my favourite dance band at a music hall in North London.

But early in May I received a telegram to return to Harrogate forthwith. I learned I was to be posted to 83 OTU at a place called Peplow in Shropshire, not far from where I had spent an uncomfortable week or so under canvas nearly two years before. Then I had been a lowly AC2 – Aircraftsman Second Class – a rookie, the butt of good-natured ribbing from the old hands. But, now I was a sergeant with the half-wing of an air gunner on my tunic and quite, at home in this, the youngest of the three services and, in the eyes of the public, the most glamorous. Not for nothing were we dubbed 'The Brylcreem Boys' by envious sailors and soldiers. I was very proud to be a member of the Royal Air Force. Frank Broome, whom I had got to know well since the Gunnery course in Canada, was also posted to Peplow and as the train drew into the station, we caught sight of black-painted bombers on the airfield across the fields. They were Wellington bombers and that meant – Bomber Command. Fleeting dismay – perhaps I was thinking of the disastrous Nürnburg operation just five weeks earlier, was soon forgotten as we scrambled off the train with all our kit. A rather sharp-faced Flight Lieutenant seemed to appear from nowhere and briskly took charge. A transport took us to the airfield. Next morning, the Station Commander addressed us. We were several hundred would-be pilots, navigators, bomb-aimers, wireless operators and gunners. 'Right chaps, you see that big hangar over there? I want you all to go there every day until you've sorted yourselves into crews. Take your time and choose your companions carefully, because you'll be flying together, with luck, for the next year. Off you go!' It all seemed very casual and it wasn't until the end of the two months course that I really understood the wisdom that lay behind this exercise in democracy.

Frank and I agreed that we might as well stick together as we seemed to hit it off quite well and we set out to find a pilot. Frank had little luck with the several flight-sergeants he approached. They already had gunners. It was after noticing that a flight lieutenant pilot and flying officer navigator were still standing around on their own that we realized that the pilot was the sharp-faced officer who had taken charge of the new intake at the railway station. Frank and I looked dubiously at each other. An officer pilot was heady stuff indeed but a *Flight Lieutenant*? I decided to take the plunge, Frank hard behind me. Saluting smartly, I asked him if he was still looking for a crew, in particular, two gunners. His stern features broke into a grin. 'I was beginning to think no-one would ask', he replied. Frank and I introduced ourselves. 'I'm Dick Lane' was the rejoinder 'and this is my navigator Freddie Dirs'.

Flight Lieutenant Lane's tunic bore some ribbons. 'I've done one tour in Coastal Command' he went on 'and I don't want to break my neck on this one.' We said that went for us too. 'How did you do at gunnery school then?' he asked. 'We both had average assessments' we replied. 'Well, all I'm looking for right now is keenness,' said Flight Lieutenant Lane. We were feeling keener by the second to fly with this obviously experienced officer and hoped we exuded the keenness that he was looking for. 'Skill will come later. That's what we are all here for, isn't it?' Completely bowled over, we chorused 'Yessir.' 'Well, we've still got to find a bomb-aimer and a wireless operator, so we'll see you here tomorrow, then – Cheerio!'

Cheerio! No officer had spoken to us in such familiar terms before! Our pride knew no bounds in the mess that evening. Next day we spotted a short round figure whose battledress bore the half-wing of a bomb-aimer. He was standing apart from the crowd with a rather diffident expression on his face. He looked older than most of us. 'Well, I was hoping to get a few days leave to see the wife and kids,' he admitted 'but I'll join you.' Freddy Till, it turned out, was 33 and probably could have been exempted from military service because he was a master plumber. His quiet Sussex burr however, masked a fierce independence and determination. He had already teamed up with a wireless operator-air gunner, Bert Bray, a 20-year old Hereford lad with a shock of unruly black hair and a friendly grin that exposed some broken teeth. Bert had done some boxing in his time. Although he had worked on the land, he proved to be no slouch when it came to radio and electronics.

For operational flying on four-engined Lancasters and Halifaxes, our team was not yet complete. We wouldn't pick up a flight engineer until our next course. But for the purposes of our training here on the twin-engined Wellington bombers, now almost obsolete, we were a team, an aircrew. We practised dinghy drill, watched as Skipper became disoriented from lack of oxygen in a compression chamber and learned how to activate a parachute. I had expected, with considerable trepidation, to have to do some jumps but, as they told us reassuringly, all we needed to know was 'It don't mean a thing if you don't pull that string.'

When we started our flying exercises, long cross country flights up and down England, our navigator was hampered by air sickness and had to be replaced. His successor was a Canadian flight sergeant who, however, didn't meet the high standard demanded by Skipper, himself no mean navigator. So he too went. While we waited for a replacement, we all went on leave, an unexpected bonus. It was the middle of June, just a week after D-Day and there was great excitement everywhere at the news that the landings in Normandy had been successful. But what the British public didn't know was that for a year the Germans had been experimenting with what Hitler called his 'Vengeance Weapons', designed partly to retaliate for our increasingly heavy air attacks on their industrial cities by American Flying Fortresses and Liberators by day and Bomber Command of the RAF by night, and partly to disrupt the flow of supplies to the Allied armies arriving in Northern France. The first of these unmanned missiles, the V-1s, began to arrive in Southern England on 12 June. About the size of a fighter aircraft, it was made of steel and had a one-tonne explosive warhead. It was programmed to exhaust its fuel somewhere over London, whereupon it dived to earth, on whatever happened to lie beneath.

I arrived home on the evening of 14 June. On the following night I was awakened in the early hours by what sounded like a harsh motorcycle engine just above the house accompanied by an eerie orange light that lit up the room I was sharing with my brother. Then there was a flash and a deafening explosion. Glass flew everywhere and ceilings came down. The flying bomb – we quickly dubbed it the Buzz-bomb or the doodlebug – had hit the hut in the field behind our house, killing the night watchman whose job it was to guard the 'Dig for Victory' allotments that had been tennis courts in happier days. About one hundred houses in our street were damaged. Some of the residents, including my father, were slightly injured. As she had done on countless nights during the *Blitz*, my mother made a pot of tea and everyone went back to work as usual next morning. For perhaps the first time I realized that my parents, my sister and my brother were as much in the front line, if not more so, than I would soon be. It was a sobering thought. About 5,800 V-1s fell on Southern England from now until six weeks before the war ended.

Back at OTU Skipper's rank now came in useful. He was able to choose the most skilled navigator in the new intake that had just arrived. Duncan MacLean, a 21-year-old Scotsman, turned out to be just the man Skipper was looking for. Mac was rather taciturn, not very tidy and never happier than when he was gambling in the mess with a bottle of beer at his elbow. When we knew we wouldn't be flying the next day, he was sometimes wheeled back from the mess in a wheelbarrow; but he never let beer interfere with his work. He proved to be a first-rate navigator and was cheerfully unruffled under stress, as we were to find out.

The training exercises were designed to give each crew member an introduction to the equipment he would be using on operations. Skipper of course was a second tour man but even he had to learn new techniques. Mac, in his curtained-off cubicle immersed himself in the complexities of electronic navigational aids which were now standard equipment. Although extremely useful, they were subject to gremlins, those mythical hobgoblins that were the bane of the lives of all fliers in World War II. Freddy, lying full-length in the nose of the Wellington, concentrated on his bomb-sight in practice bombing with twenty-five pounders on the bombing range. Bert, in his cubicle, busied himself receiving and transmitting messages on his receiver, while Frank and I practised air-to-air and air-to-sea firing.

The air-to-air exercises entailed the use of a camera gun while a single-engined fighter plane simulated attacks from the rear. Frank and I learned just when to order Skipper to take appropriate evasive action by throwing the Wellington into a corkscrew manoeuvre, to port or starboard depending on which side the attack was coming from but always on the side of the attack so that the fighter would, in theory, fly right over the bomber and be lost in the darkness. So when Frank or I ordered Skipper to 'Corkscrew port' for example, he would without a second's hesitation thrust the bomber into a steep dive to port for a thousand feet, making sure that he didn't exceed a certain speed, because above that speed the wings would break off. Then, Skipper would level off, climb steeply for a thousand feet and then, if necessary, repeat the manoeuvre until it seemed certain the attacker had been thrown off.

The force of gravity was of course very great during this manoeuvre. On the descent one would be pinioned to the dome of the turret and on the ascent one would be pressed to the floor and in each case it was almost impossible to move. To make matters worse, for me at any rate, in the Corkscrew manoeuvre each gunner had to use the rear turret, which, by virtue of its position, was, even in straight and level flying, subject to a considerable see-sawing motion, which my stomach objected to pretty quickly. The Corkscrew manoeuvre, therefore, made me violently sick and I would invariably end up sliding around miserably in my own vomit. I was greatly relieved when Frank, well aware of my discomfort, opted for the rear turret in our fledgling aircrew and I became the mid-upper gunner. But as the Wellington had no mid-upper turret, I kept watch through the astrodome, normally used by the navigator for taking star shots, when I wasn't in the hated rear turret. I had been wondering if I would be dropped from the crew as had our previous navigator, because of airsickness but I was reassured when Skipper was over-heard telling the training pilot officer in no uncertain terms that he could have demonstrated the Corkscrew quite well without throwing the aircraft around so wildly. As I found later, the Corkscrew would only be resorted to on ops in the event of an actual attack. But in the meantime our on-going training meant that I would have to endure airsickness during many more Corkscrews.

Before we could graduate we were required to take part in two exercises in enemy patrolled air space, designed to give us a relatively risk-free introduction to what is now termed 'being in harm's way'. The first, in mid-July, was to drop illustrated French language leaflets over Laval, in north-west France, to inform its citizens of the progress of the Allied armies since the Normandy landings six weeks earlier. We were naturally keyed up – a Wellington bomber from our own OTU had been lost a few weeks earlier in a similar exercise but ours was uneventful. Two nights later, we took part in what was called a diversion exercise. We were among a small number of training aircraft that flew within 15 miles of the Dutch coast to delude the enemy defences into thinking that we were the spearhead of an impending attack. The motive was to draw enemy fighters towards us and away from the main force which was on its way to a target much farther south. I kept watch through the astro-dome while Frank sat behind his four guns. We would of course be no match in a chance meeting with a Focke-Wulf 190 or a Junkers 88, with their formidable 20mm cannon, but this was a risk that the Air Ministry deemed worth taking. In the event, all we saw was some flak and searchlights on the Dutch coast before we turned for home.

Both Frank and I graduated with an 'average' assessment and after a few more days' leave, we were posted to a short gunnery course at Ingham near Lincoln, now known as the aircrew city, because it was the Mecca for hundreds of aircrew based in the flat Lincolnshire countryside that was so suitable for the long runways the heavily-laden bombers needed for take-off. It was now August and as I noted in my diary, 'ruddy earwigs keep crawling up the curved walls of our Nissen hut and dropping on us in bed.' Despite this diversion, we both graduated in category 'A' in the use of the camera gun and I still possess a twenty-second strip of film I took of a simulated attack, a reminder of uncomfortable sessions in the rear turret of a Wellington bomber on hot, sweaty summer afternoons, being see-sawed up and down and trying to concentrate on the incoming fighter while at the same time fighting down the urge to be sick. And of course, like other gunners so afflicted, I had to clean out the turret on landing. How I got an 'A' I'll never know.

While Frank and I were on the gunnery course, Skipper, Frank and Bert were at what was called Heavy Conversion Unit, at Sandtoft in Yorkshire. Here they began to familiarize themselves with a four-engined bomber, the Handley-Page Halifax, which had entered service in Bomber Command in 1941. Frank and I arrived at Sandtoft, as a Halifax made a crash landing. The starboard undercarriage had failed to lock and it slewed over on one wing. It was only later in the mess that we learned that the pilot was Skipper! The only casualty however was Bert, who injured his shoulder. Also in the aircraft was the final addition to our crew, our flight engineer, Stan. Like Freddy he was somewhat older than Mac, Bert, Frank and I; married but with no children. He had been a sewing machine mechanic in Civvy Street and was happy to monitor the gauges, dials and red winking lights that told him when all was well and when it wasn't! Stan was always neatly turned out – even after a gruelling ten hour trip he always looked well-groomed and tidy!

Over the next three weeks we did many cross-country exercises, mainly for the benefit of every member of the crew except for Frank and me. We had just one half hour of 'fighter affiliation' with a training pilot who did everything, it seemed to me, except loop the loop. I was predictably very sick. This Corkscrew manoeuvre would be my Achilles Heel I told myself miserably and reported sick next day. It never occurred to me to ask to be taken off flying duties; all I wanted was something to prevent myself from retching and retching until there was nothing left to bring up but bile. The Medical Officer gave me two capsules which I saved for the next ordeal. Before that however, our crew was given a few days' leave and on the night of 11 September 1944, I happily went to sleep in a familiar bedroom in our suburb south of London. Its residents knew that it was still in the front line but the flying bombs – 78 had exploded in our town, Beckenham, in the two months to the end of August – now seemed to be directed north of the Thames, giving Eden Way a welcome but short-lived respite. At about 6:30 next morning we heard a big explosion that shook the house and there was another one at about 9 o'clock. There had been rumours for some time that Hitler was about to launch his second Vengeance Weapon, possibly a rocket. The government decided to issue no immediate statement, to deprive Hitler of confirmation that any rockets were reaching their objective, London. There were two more big bumps two nights later and another one in the early hours of the following morning.

I returned to my unit that evening after four days of relaxation, reflecting how everyone back home had calmly continued to go about their daily business, bumps or no bumps. The war was going well. American troops in the south of France had just crossed the German frontier. At this rate, the war might be over by Christmas. Although I didn't give voice to my thoughts I wouldn't have been disappointed. I was too aware of the burden being carried by the folks back home to feel otherwise. Our final training unit was No. 1 Lancaster Finishing School at Hemswell, Lincolnshire. This was our introduction to the aircraft we would use on our operational tour, the start of which must surely now be just weeks away. Skipper practised landings and take-offs, known as 'circuits and bumps' and I wrote in my diary on 26 September, 'Skipper can certainly land Lancs beautifully.' I was obviously feeling very confident. But the next day our final exercise was the now dreaded 'fighter affiliation' with a training pilot who seemed to take a delight in doing every-thing but stand the Lancaster on its head. I later wrote in my diary. 'It was sheer torture.' I was as sick as I've ever been, despite the chlorotone tablets. We have must done 30 to 40 Corkscrews. At times I was suspended in air. I was too ill to go into the rear turret when my turn came.

I can't recall Skipper ever discussing with me my obvious inability to function during Corkscrews. Perhaps he took the view that, at this stage of the war, the chances of having to take evasive action in the event of a night fighter attack would be relatively small and the Corkscrew would probably be of short duration at night because the enemy fighter would, hopefully, zoom over our heads and disappear into the darkness. In the event, this was the case. But I, in my inexperience, didn't know that and all I could do was my best. Again, it never occurred to me to ask to be 'grounded'. Without realizing it, we had in four months bonded together as a fighting unit. We trusted each other to do the jobs we had been trained to do and we also knew a little about each others' jobs, so that if there were casualties on board, the Lancaster had a fighting chance to get back to base to fight another day. Apart from airsickness during Cork-screws, my training assessments had always been satisfactory to good and I was never aware of any misgivings among the rest of the crew about my overall performance in the air.

Next day our crew was posted to Wickenby and to 626 Squadron. The Station Commander was Group Captain Phillip Haynes, a stocky, broad-shouldered pre-war pilot, and the Squadron Commander was Wing Commander John Molesworth, a tall, rangy second tour pilot. Our Flight Commander was Flight Lieutenant Reginald Aldus. After about two weeks of cross country flights designed to familiarize ourselves with our respective tasks, we were at last included in a sequence of events that would become the very kernel of our existence for the foreseeable future. On the evening of the 13th we found our names on the battle order for 14 October. This was the culmination of two years of training that I had begun in September 1942, throughout which, the Royal Air Force had discreetly omitted any reference to the Geneva Convention, to which Britain was a signatory. It stipulated that civilians and their property were not to be regarded as military objectives. Being a reasonably intelligent young man who had had some experience of being on the receiving end of bombs, I knew that in the area bombing of Germany's industrial cities, civilians and their property could not possibly remain untouched, any more than had been the case in Britain's industrial cities in the *Blitz*. I can't recall if I had any misgivings.

We had an early night and were roused from our beds at 02:30 next morning by our Flight Commander. After breakfast of bacon and eggs, the standard meal before and after every operation, we trooped into the briefing room at 04:30 to join dozens of other crews. Although all pilots, navigators and bomb-aimers had already had a mini-briefing and knew the target, they were sworn to secrecy. The arrival of the Station Commander was the signal for all of us to scramble to our feet. 'Be seated, gentlemen.'

The Station Commander ordered an airman to uncover the route map on the wall. The red tape wended its way south-east in zigzag fashion and ended in the south-west corner of a big circle. 'Bloody Hell, not the Ruhr again!' grumbled the more experienced crews. Duisburg, Germany's greatest inland port was the target.

'OK chaps, simmer down', said the Adjutant sharply. Next up was the Intelligence Officer. This operation, he said, marked the resumption of the bombing offensive against Hitler's armament production after six months of concentration on transportation networks, supply bases and fuel depots in Northern France, under the direction of the Supreme Commander of Allied Forces in Europe, General Eisenhower. Operation *Hurricane*, as it was called in the Air Ministry directive that Bomber Command had received, was to 'apply within the shortest practical period the maximum effort possible, to demonstrate to the enemy the overwhelming superiority of the Allied Air Forces.'[1]

After the meteorological officer had indicated that weather conditions would be fair to good, brief reports came from the Bombing, Signals and Gunnery Leaders. Of special interest to Frank and I was the knowledge that we would be escorted by our fighter aircraft, based in France for the first time in four years since the liberation of that country just two months earlier.

Finally, 'Good luck, chaps', from the Station Commander and we dispersed, chattering as we made our way to the crew room to don our flying suits and collect our parachutes and then on to a crew bus to take us out to our aircraft. Both Wickenby squadrons, 12 and 626, were on this 'maximum effort' and the airfield was in top gear as dawn broke.

At Methwold bomb aimer Flight Lieutenant Dick Perry, whose crew on 218 Squadron had flown just one bombing raid on Germany, waited with some trepidation in the Briefing Room as they listened to the CO describing the trip to Duisburg.[2]

'Well gentlemen today will be a little different. You'll be part of a force of one thousand aircraft.' Then he added reassuringly, 'I know what you're thinking, but our operational research scientists have computed that, statistically, there should be no more than two aircraft colliding over the target area.' Dead silence? Which two? We were aware of the fact that raids with 500 aircraft were a regular occurrence but 1,000 bombers in the air at one time, impossible? Briefing over, we were driven out to our aircraft, settled ourselves in, Robbie started up, we trundled out and in due course, took off. Time was 7am and we had a full bomb load, eleven 1,000 pounders and four 500 pounders.

Peter Bone continues:

We were flying in 'Charlie Two' piloted by a 34 ops man, Flight Lieutenant Hicks, while our Skipper was doing the mandatory stint as 'second dickey' on a first op. We set course at 6:30 am, the grey slate roof and the three sturdy towers of the 800 years old Lincoln Cathedral seemingly wishing us Godspeed and a safe return as we left it behind in the morning mist. We were on our way, one of 519 Lancasters, 474 Halifaxes and 20 Mosquitoes carrying 3,574 tons of high explosive and 820 tons of incendiaries to Duisburg. It was a Saturday morning and as the Intelligence Officer remarked, it was market day. As the minutes passed, I saw more and more bombers joining the stream. It was an awesome sight. High above us I could see vapour trails behind little black dots: our fighter escort was on the job already.

Dick Perry again:

It was a beautiful day. We climbed to 18,000 feet to meet the bomber stream and away we went across the Channel headed for Belgium. Everything was uneventful until we reached the target area. I looked out the side window and as far as I could see there were aircraft, looking like a cloud of gnats. Then ahead of us, smudges of smoke among the gnats, slowly expanding into black blobs. To our left a pale blue smoke trail suddenly appeared, spiralling down from the cloud of gnats in front, somebody hit. It was time to get into the nose and prepare for action. Up ahead were the winding Rhine and the docks and the red flashes of ack-ack and about a dozen smoke trails, apparently an attempt to hide the area. Heavy flak and we were going right into the bursts. About this time, we received a call from 'Freehand' the Master Bomber who was somewhere below us. So taking him at his word, I lined us up with a bridge, which looked like a good target and released our string of bombs. (The photograph later showed a direct hit.) Looking out through the nose, when the ground wasn't obscured by flak bursts, I noted a great black ball of smoke rising up from the dock site which looked like an oil tank fire. The layout of the city was just as clear as a map as we turned and headed out of the target area and, looking back, underneath, I could see the concentric rings around the bomb blasts, the whole area around the docks was disappearing in smoke. We raced away, turned for home and when I clambered up into the cockpit again, there was nothing but a great pall of smoke behind us.

Peter Bone continues:

There was no opposition of any kind until we drew near to the target, where radar-controlled anti-aircraft fire became intense. I saw a bomber go down in flames and huge explosions in the sky at our height of 17,000 feet. We had heard that these 'scarecrows', as we called them, were shells timed to explode to simulate a bomber disintegrating. But we later learned that the explosions were in fact bombers blowing up before they had released their bombs. We dropped our bombs and quickly turned for home. The attack was still in progress. The sky was peppered with black smoke puffs, some still ringed with red, others disintegrating in the wind. Smoke trails, earthward bound, told their own tale. I looked down at a fiery cauldron slowly receding behind the rear turret. I knew that Duisburg was a vital Ruhr port that also produced steel, had extensive rail yards and coking, tar and benzyl plants. I also knew that, even as I gazed down, people were being blown to pieces and burnt beyond recognition and that among them were certain to be women and children.

On our return to base, we found that our Flight Commander and his crew were missing and in fact they never came back.[3] Whatever feelings we had about it were quickly doused by the news that the morning attack had not been as accurate as hoped. Bomber Harris was annoyed and therefore every crew would have to go back in the early hours of next morning and do the job properly. We did. At 01.30 we were over Duisburg again; our first night op.

Dick Perry's crew had landed back at Methwold at 2pm after map reading all the way across Belgium:

We were no sooner on the ground than we were told that we were going back again and that take-off time would be 22.15, just time for some lunch, a short nap and the briefing again. We joined the bomber stream over Reading and, once again, headed out over the Channel. The night's work was much grimmer. Now we were faced with searchlight creeping towards us. This was very different, flying into flashes and then black smoke puffs. Markers showered down and lay in the city like shimmering flower beds, while others were lost in the smoke. Flak of all kinds shattered the darkness. Duisburg and a great cylinder above it, was ablaze. This time we bombed on the markers. The city that I had seen below me on our last trip was now outlined in fire. Once again we turned and headed for home and looking back, as we crossed into Belgium, we could see the glow from the fires. This time we went in two waves, of which we were in the first. The second wave went in some two hours later. This was the greatest weight of bombs that had ever been dropped on one city, 4,500 tons and actually almost equalled the combined weight of all the bombs dropped on London. Our losses were, comparatively light, only twenty planes of a combined force of 1,000 were shot down, bombed on or collided, just 2%.[4]

Peter Bone recorded in his diary later:

'Impossible to keep up search over target. Whole sky lit up with flashes and flares. Lots of flak and searchlights – effective but few. Down below, Duisburg an inferno.' We had been part of another

1,005 bombers to attack one city twice in less than 24 hours. Altogether, 1,898 bombers had dropped nearly 9,000 tons of bombs on Duisburg, for a loss of 21 aircraft.[5] There must have been indescribable scenes of destruction and carnage down there in the streets as the firemen and civil defence workers did their best to cope with what must have seemed like Armageddon. But I don't recall dwelling on it. I soon learned to suppress such thoughts and to concentrate on the job I had to do – to keep my eyes peeled for up to ten hours for enemy fighter aircraft, closing anti-aircraft fire and other bombers that might be straying too close for comfort. In short, I and my fellow crew members learned to discipline ourselves so that all our energies and skills were channelled into getting to the target on time, bombing as accurately as possible and returning to base in one piece.[6]

Over Duisburg a Halifax was coned by searchlights after dropping its load. Flak came up, set an engine on fire and partially blinded the pilot, Flight Sergeant A K Cockerill RAAF. For a moment he lost control and the Halifax dived steeply. Then he regained partial consciousness and fought to save his aircraft and his crew. With the crew's help – the navigator was Flight Sergeant H R Day, another Australian – he pulled the Halifax out of its dive. Cockerill refused morphia. He knew that he alone could land the aircraft safely when, or if, it reached Britain. He refused, too, to leave the pilot's seat and when the crew tried to drag him out he fought until they had to let him stay. Then he piloted the Halifax on the instructions of the bomb aimer, who sat beside him on the journey home. The engineer put out the flames in the damaged engine and the bomber flew back, without further harm, through flares dropped about it by packs of fighters. At the wounded pilot's first attempt to land, the bomber overshot and skimmed a few feet above the runway. After a second circuit, Cockerill put the bomber down to a masterly landing and it came to rest with the pilot slumped over the controls. He had held on by sheer will power to the end of the ordeal. He was awarded the DSO.

During the six months that Peter Bone was flying on operations over Germany and its occupied territories, he was able to get home on leave every six weeks:

In retrospect I think that such a generous leave policy had been fully justified up to about *D-Day* but since the spring of 1944, Hitler's transportation networks, supply dumps and oil refineries in Northern France had been designated priority targets and by the time I began flying on ops, his war machine was beginning to show signs of slow strangulation. That meant that there were fewer night fighters in the air compared with just a year earlier. That meant that more aircrew were completing their tour of operations more or less intact. Because of this, the Air Ministry decided to extend a tour of operations from thirty to thirty-six, which didn't please us a bit. But the war ended before this could be implemented. However, the generous leave policy remained. You don't look a gift horse in the mouth and we didn't complain. But knowing that many men and women in the armed forces were unable to get home for months, even years if they were serving in Italy or Burma, I always felt uncomfortable when greeted by a neighbour with a surprised, 'What, you home AGAIN?' Before I could answer, the neighbour would sometimes add, in a low voice, because you never knew if a spy was hiding behind the hedge, 'Did you hear about the bomb just up the road? Terrible mess; terrible. The whole family too.'

Four years earlier, in the *Blitz* of 1940/1941, the Luftwaffe's attacks on British cities were relatively indiscriminate, as were Bomber Command's attacks on German cities, because neither side was used to night bombing and the RAF had not yet been given the electronic navigational and bombing aids that were needed for long hours in the air in total darkness. But by the time I joined my squadron in the fall of 1944, all operational bombers were equipped with a variety of these electronic aids. They were primitive and malfunctions had to be ironed out on the job. But whereas Hitler was by then pinning his hopes on pilotless missiles that were too experimental to be precise, Bomber Command could, on most nights send over Germany about 10,500 highly trained aircrew in about 1,500 heavy bombers equipped with the best electronic aids the scientists could provide. It wasn't the 4,000 bombers Harris was convinced that could defeat Germany on their own but it was nevertheless a formidable force. Its task was 'area bombing' because Harris, a realist, had always known that while precise bombing by day was perhaps feasible in good clear weather and with a strong fighter escort, it was not possible while the RAF had no long range fighters, and good clear weather, especially in winter, was a rarity. So Bomber Command would have to use the cover of darkness and be limited to area bombing. But that didn't mean dumping bombs on German cities willy-nilly. Each operation was meticulously planned by Harris' staff, almost to a split second.

This is what was entailed. It was commonplace during my tour of operations for a bomber stream of over a thousand 'heavies' to head for Germany in a loose gaggle about sixty miles long and two or three miles wide, feinting this way and that to keep the defences guessing and reaching heights of 16,000 to 23,000 feet. The attack was timed to ensure that every aircraft bombed within about twenty minutes, to overwhelm the defences. Such a concentration over the target posed not only the risk of collisions but also of being hit by bombs falling from aircraft above. Surprisingly, either occurrence was rare, although near misses were not uncommon. Crew alertness minimized the risk of collisions but falling bombs couldn't be avoided. They either missed you or they didn't. There was nothing we could do about it, so they were the least of our concerns.

There was always an aiming point, a factory complex or a city centre where railway yards or administrative buildings were known to be located. Every effort was made to avoid purely residential areas. Costly aircraft and bombs and highly-trained aircrew were never so plentiful that they were there just to destroy people's homes. Harris had no problem with following the political directive issued in January 1943 to 'further the progressive destruction of the German military, industrial and economic system and the under-mining of the morale of the German people to a point where their capacity for armed resistance is fatally weakened.' But I think it is fair to emphasize that Harris' policies and techniques were designed to minimise as much as humanly possible the civilian casualties that were inevitable in area bombing by night, which for four years, was the only way of taking the war to the German homeland. The key to the greatest possible accuracy in conditions that were far from conducive to accuracy, involved many factors, not least of which was Europe's notoriously bad weather, especially in winter. Like Britain, Germany didn't issue public weather forecasts for obvious reasons. The best evaluation of the weather over the proposed route was, from 1942 onwards, provided by a fast, high-flying Mosquito fighter-bomber that would fly the route shortly beforehand. To predict local weather is often difficult enough. To predict it over a round trip of up to ten hours and 1,200 miles could be no more than an educated guess. This is what Harris had to make every 24 hours for three years. It will never be known how many bombers were lost because of icing-up, dense fog over the bases on returning, or strong, unpredicted head winds which sent them falling unseen into the sea, out of fuel. There were bound to be miscalculations. To minimise errors, every bomber in the stream was required to transmit back to base the current wind speed and direction at specified intervals. An average was struck and rebroadcast to every bomber. These corrections made all the difference between bombing a factory turning out aircraft engines and unintentionally bombing a residential area five miles away. The transmissions were of course picked up by German civil defence services, enabling them to track the bombers' route more easily.

Like Britain, Germany was blacked out at night. To add to the permanent smoke haze over its industrial cities and the artificial smoke generators that could quickly be activated, predicted scattered cloud often turned out to be ten-tenths cloud over the target, especially in winter. By 1944 however, the electronic navigational and bombing aids enabled bomb aimers to achieve hits within 150 yards of the aiming point, in perfect conditions, which of course seldom presented themselves. A burst of flak under a wing, straying into the slipstream of another bomber, or a fighter attack could throw a bomb-aimer off his balance and that of his delicate bomb-sight, just as he pressed the release button. To give the bomb-aimer the steadiest possible platform, the pilot was required to fly straight and level for one minute, often through a concentrated box barrage of lethal anti-aircraft fire.

To guide pilots through this crucial period, which seemed endless, a small hand-picked force of the most highly skilled aircrew was formed in 1943. This 'Path Finder Force' preceded the main force to mark the aiming point with brightly coloured flares, either on the ground, or, if cloud obscured the target, attached to small parachutes, positioned so that when the main force bomb-aimers had them in their bomb-sights, the known trajectory of the bombs would carry them to the aiming point. As these 'sky-markers' naturally drifted in the wind, the Path Finders would follow up with different pre-arranged colours. The best-laid plans, however, can go awry and they 'often did. So a Master Bomber would circle the aiming point in a Mosquito at a very low level. His job was to watch where the bombs were falling and radio any needed corrections to the Main Force above him. He had particularly to look for what was called creep-back. Some inexperienced crews, especially those on their first op, sometimes lost their nerve and were tempted to jettison their bombs short of the aiming point and 'get the hell out of it' just as some Luftwaffe crews had done over the outskirts of British cities in the *Blitz*. To eradicate what we called 'wide bombing errors' each bomber carried a camera which was calibrated to take an infra-red photograph at the second the bombs exploded. These were examined by intelligence personnel within hours of the crews' return and woe betide any crew whose photograph was not of the designated aiming point. The penalty, besides incurring the displeasure of the Bombing Leader and the Squadron Commander, was to spend many tedious hours on the bombing range until the offending crew were deemed proficient. This is why Freddy stubbornly advised the Wing Commander over Essen that he would log the reason why our photo flash would probably record a wide bombing error.

I have mentioned that sometimes new crews would lose their nerve. As a rule, this was soon overcome as individual members gained confidence in their skills and ability to perform their tasks under fire. Occasionally, however, a crew would return to base with one or more members dead and badly injured after a horrific experience at the hands of night fighters, anti-aircraft fire and searchlights, during which a fire might have to be battled. A crew member might be so traumatized that he would refuse to fly again, for the very good reason that he knew he would probably be unable to function efficiently and thereby endanger the lives of the rest of the crew. If the Medical Officer thought he was malingering however, Air Ministry policy was harsh. He was labelled as having 'Lack of Moral Fibre'. A special parade was ordered, at which the sergeant or officer was ignominiously stripped of his wings in front of the whole squadron. He would then be posted from the base within the hour, to disappear swiftly from the memory of those who would carry on flying. Or so it was hoped. The policy was to deter aircrew from following his example. I can't recall anyone at Wickenby being labelled LMF while I was on ops but I suspect that those who were forced to watch the degradation of a fellow aircrew member probably muttered sympathetically to each other, 'There but for the grace of God, go I.'

Jack Stephens' first op in October was on Thursday the 5th when he was roused at 2am for a 'daylight' on Wilhelmshaven. He wrote in his diary:

Carried $10 \times 1,000$ SAPs $+ 4 \times$ J clusters. Mustang (fighter) escort. Take off delayed 2 hours after run up, got off at 5 to 8, rendezvoused at the Humber and flew in gaggle. A very wet early morning cleared up into a beautiful day with plenty of sunshine under which the Third and (we hope) last Reich looked very nice but a sheet of cloud covered the target and we had to bomb blind. George bragged about bombing a big farm house, which we hope and think he didn't get. We went out at 1,000 feet and bombed from 16,500 feet and then broke formation again, put the nose down and did between 200 and 270 mph all the way back. Stooged around as usual while the mob landed and shot up (flew very low over) a wood and Johnnie's girl friend's house at Lowdham. Then back for lunch. Then to the 'Horse and Jockey' for partridge and cider. One kite from 467 was lost out of the force.[7] There was no opposition at all except a couple of guns miles away.

His diary entries continued:

Friday 6th October: New crew took Dog to Bremen again at night. 'B' didn't return.

Saturday 7th October. Daylight (morning) on dykes near Flushing (WALCHEREN). Carried $14 \times 1,000$ lb SAP ½ hour delays. Dropped in 2 sticks from 5,000 feet in line astern. Weather quite good over the target and so were the flak gunners. There was only a little light and heavy flak but very accurate because of our line astern formation. Nothing hit us, quite, but we heard a couple burst and saw plenty of tracers whipping past. Aim was to flood the defences on the island

and so open up the way for supplies to Antwerp. Flew in 'F' as crew had USd (made unserviceable) 'D' the night before.

Wednesday 11th October. Rush daylight. Only 1½ hours notice before take-off. The usual step-down formation from the coast. Attacked heavy flak positions which had been missed by the flood from the last attack. Our particular target didn't shoot at us. Dropped 10 × 1,000lb and 4 × 500lb GPs. One 500 hung up so we jettisoned manually, double carrier and all. On return the weather was putrid, an excuse for cloud base about 1,000 feet, bags of rain and mist, a gale warning and hundreds of kites trying to get in. We were 45 minutes on the circuit, some were longer. Had lunch at 6 pm.

Thursday 12th October. Briefed for an hour. Night trip to Munich with incendiaries, via France, Italy and southern Switzerland – scrubbed.

Friday 13th. Lucky – the weather was duff.

Saturday 14th October. To BRUNSWICK via the south of France. 16 cans of 4lb incendiaries and a 1,000lb GP. Bombed the town, factories etc. Synchronised with big attacks on Duisberg, Cologne etc. Very quiet, no combat, negligible search lights but a bit of heavy flak bursting was above us. (Colin went without parachute harness and Taffy's wasn't clipped on). Very clear weather and visibility. Really set the place alight. W/T bombing winds screwy (winds advised by radio were wrong). Landed 05.45, 7¼ hours. Spare mid upper Gunner.

Sunday 15th October. Slept. Daylight scrubbed.

Monday 16th October. Rain.

Tuesday 17th October. Saw film of the raid on Brunswick. Acclaimed best aerial photography of the war. Showed attack from the first few incendiaries until streets, then the whole city was alight. Also some heavy flak bursts. The boys went to Walcheren again but we didn't get a seat.

Wednesday 18th October. Weather duff.

Thursday 19th October. Last time NUERNBERG was hit 94 kites were lost. This time 9 went [shot down], mainly from the Stuttgart raids and it took 350 fighters to do it. I saw the Wanganui [code name for aerial target indicators] go down on Stuttgart on our way to the target. We had our navigation lights on over France and so could see the stream concentration. Carried a spare navigator as Taffy was sick. Carried a 2,000lb and 11 J types with full tanks. Bombed at 17,500 at 20.55. There was a nice thick layer of cloud below us except over the target, so searchlights were ineffective and flak only moderate. We saw no fighters. On the way home the BBC played 'This is a Lovely Way to Spend an Evening.' To bed at 2 am.

Friday 20th October. It rained.

Saturday 21st October. Ops scrubbed at the last moment due to weather.

Sunday 22nd October. Daylight scrubbo.

Monday 23rd October. Rain and a daylight attack with 14 × 1,000 lbs at FLUSHING on guns which were shelling our troops on the other side of the Scheldt Estuary. H 16.00. The weather all the way was pretty terrible and we could just see the target from 6,000 feet and it's very unlikely that most of the boys hit it. The light flak was very accurate and intense, giving rise to the Mk II twitch (nervous symptoms). We lost two kites from the squadron, three from the station – to flak. We had Spitfire escort, but couldn't even see each other, let alone the escort. One kite was seen diving straight into the water and parachutes from another.

By now the fuel crisis in Germany had reached such proportions that only the *Experten* were sent against incoming raids.[8] *Nachtjagd* was rendered less effective by the Allied advance into the continent and the technical and tactical countermeasures employed and the German warning and inland plotting systems were thrown into confusion.[9] Low-level and high-level *Intruder* played no small part by causing the enemy to plot hostile aircraft over very wide areas as well as forcing him to broadcast frequent warnings of the presence of hostile aircraft to his own fighters.[10]

On 23 October, 112 Lancasters of 5 Group bombed battery positions at Flushing (Vlissingen) in the Scheldt estuary at Walcheren. From all around Waddington airfield came the sound of two hundred mighty Rolls Royce Merlin engines starting up and going through their warm-up procedures. About twenty-five Lancasters on 463 Squadron RAAF began snaking away from their dispersal points to line up at the runway, waiting to take off. Minutes later followed the aircraft on 467 Squadron. At 14.22 *P-Peter*, which had received the name *Piratical Pete*, reached the head of the queue and sat facing down the runway. Flying Officer John Dack DFC RAAF waited for the 'green'. This was the crew's 33rd trip and scheduled to be the last of their tour of operations. Bill Forbes the squadron commander had said at the end of briefing: 'You can lead the Squadron today Dack seeing that it's the last trip of your tour.' Dack continues:

The brakes were full on as I slowly pushed forward on the four throttles. The runway controller flashed a green Aldis lamp at me and I released the brakes. *Piratical Pete* gathered speed down the runway and took off, climbing away into the low cloud. Navigator Jimmy Maple knew his job well. All the crew knew we would be at the target at exactly 4,000 feet at exactly 16.00 hours. The gunners had a fairly easy time. Flying through cloud all the way meant not many fighters to worry about. Jock Easton, the wireless operator, had his work to do, listening out for messages and weather information and the radar screen to watch, the biggest problem being collisions with other Lancasters.

Jimmy McWilliam the bomb aimer was readying his bombsight and studying his bombing instructions ready for arrival at the target.

'Start descending to 4,000 feet, Skip,' came the voice of the navigator.

'OK Jim.'

'Ten minutes to target Skip.'

'Thanks Jim.'

'Target coming up in two minutes Skip.'

'OK Jim. We're almost down to 4,000 feet but I can't see the ground yet.'

According to the various reports from other pilots the cloud base varied from about 3,500 feet to 4,500 feet. Where we were it was about 3,900 feet and we were skipping through the bottom of the clouds without being able to see the ground. But they could see us in our black painted night bomber.

'Hello Skip, there's light flak coming very close. You'd better get weaving Laddie,' came the surprisingly urgent voice of Charlie Kirby, the rear gunner.

Before he had finished the sentence, Bob Coward the mid-upper gunner called 'We've been hit' and the aircraft was instantly on fire and full of thick, choking, burning yellow-brown smoke.

'Prepare to abandon aircraft,' I shouted, but nobody heard me; the intercom, along with many other things, having apparently been severely damaged. But they all knew they had to go. Jimmy McWilliam took the cover off the escape hatch and let it fall away from the aircraft, following it out. Lofty Lee the flight engineer went after him.

'I'm sorry June, I'm sorry June,' I remember saying before smoke and fumes overcame me. Although I remember Lofty had gone without giving me my parachute, his first duty before evacuating. The pilot's parachute pack was stowed in a rack behind the pilot's head and had to be hooked onto two large hooks on the front of the harness that the pilot wore. I must have found it myself somehow, or someone else found it for me, because the next thing I knew was being whacked under the chin by something that woke me out of my daze. I looked down and there was the water of the River Scheldt and I was in it. *Piratical Pete* hit the water only about 200 yards away and disappeared in the spray. As I hit the water the wind picked up the top half of my parachute, as it laid half-open on the sea. I was steering towards the land that looked about a mile or more away. The fickle wind, however, dropped in a few seconds and left me floundering. I hit the release button of the parachute harness and it and the 'chute floated away, but the waves kept going over my head. 'I don't think much of this Mae West,' I said to myself, having forgotten to pull the handle to inflate it. When I remembered to do so, my head stayed above the waves. The wind and tide, which fortunately was running in, were taking me towards a long narrow jetty, which had a lonely lamppost at the end with one electric light bulb in a goose-necked fitting at the top. The lamp was alight and in broad daylight. I couldn't understand why. I puzzled over that, despite my predicament. Why would a country at war leave an electric light burning on the end of a pier so close to the open North Sea in broad daylight?

After about half an hour I thought the raid must be nearly over. It was supposed to last half an hour, wasn't it? I suddenly thought of the shockproof, waterproof sportsman's watch my family had given me for my 21st birthday, just six days short of two years before. Wonder what time it is? I pulled back the left sleeve of my battle-dress to look, but there was no watch, just a large tear in my arm where the watch should have been. The tear was not so deep where the watchband would have been. This may have saved the artery being cut. That and the cold salt water may have prevented any excessive bleeding. I then remembered the whistle hanging on the lapel of my battle dress jacket. 'This is the time to use it,' I thought. 'This is what it's for, to blow and see if any of your mates are over the next wave.' So I put the whistle in my mouth to blow, only to discover that my bottom dentures had gone and the top ones were broken in half. That must have happened when the parachute strap whacked me under the chin as the parachute opened. It would seem that the parachute had been attached by only one hook instead of two. For some inexplicable reason I thought this was very funny and started to laugh and laughed myself into hysterical oblivion. The next thing I knew, some hours later, was a young blond German soldier saying, *Fur Sie der Krieg ist beendet.*

The room was large, old fashioned and dilapidated. It may once have been the best lounge room in the home of a well-to-do family.[11] The walls were about 13 or 14 feet high. Around the top of the walls was a large ornate cornice on which the remnants of a colourful past could still be seen. Around the bottom of the walls was a deep moulded timber skirting. On the wall to the left was an old fashioned fireplace with a marble mantle-shelf and a huge cast iron grate in which was a roaring fire. On the wall in front was a single door surrounded by wide moulded timber architraves. Between the door and my slowly awakening eyes was the foot-end of an old fashioned cast-iron bedstead. Sitting on a chair between the foot of my bed and the fireplace was a young blond in a strange green jacket. The blond, seeing me beginning to stir, handed me a cigarette with a comment that, even had I been in full command of my senses, I would not have understood. *Fur Sie der Krieg ist beendet.*

Consciousness was gradually increasing as the blond in the green costume went out the door, to return a minute or so later with a tall slim man in a black uniform, who handed me a small glass of cognac, which, although it increased my awareness, also increased my bewilderment. Particularly puzzling was the black uniform on which I began to notice different coloured ribbons and badges and epaulets with silver linings. It was the high fronted, narrow peaked cap, which also had a badge on the front that brought me to the realisation that all was not well. It was the uniform of a German officer. Then I realised the significance of the green uniform. He was a German soldier, a medical orderly and he was watching over me.

Fur Sie der Krieg ist beendet, said the German officer.

'For you the war is over,' he translated.

Hans Bannick saw an unconscious British airman floating in the River and that he and another man rowed out in a rubber boat and rescued the man.

'You were floating unconscious about a mile out in the middle of the river,' he continued, in a strangely familiar accent.

'My crew!

'My God!'

By now I am fully awake although, despite the roaring fire, still shaking and shivering with cold and shock. Note: After Hans and his mate carried me ashore I was taken away, still unconscious, by his senior officers and he knew no more of me. I had become a PoW; as had my bomb aimer and flight engineer. It is my belief, that Jim Maple must have found my parachute and hooked it onto my harness and somehow thrown me out of the escape hatch. This would have cost him his life. I do not know the truth or otherwise of that, of course, because I was unconscious. The other three members of the crew were most likely killed during the attack on the aircraft.[12]

This couldn't be happening. It's a dream. Geez, we were only doing a short trip, an hour there and an hour back. Nobby Blundell our Chiefy and his boys would be crook on me for not bringing back *Piratical Pete* our beloved Lancaster. We had a room booked at the 'Horse and Jockey' in Waddington village and the favourite of the boys on 467 and 463 Squadrons for the night's celebrations with our ground crew. No, this can't be happening ...

The German officer was still talking. 'Where do you come from in Australia?' he asked, seeing the 'Australia's' on the shoulders of my battle dress uniform.

'Melbourne,' I said, forgetting all about 'name rank and number only'.

'Oh,' he said, 'I know Melbourne well. I was an engineer and I served for two years installing the Lurgi Plant at Yallourn.'

As he talked on I realised through my daze that he knew Melbourne better than I did. No wonder his accent was familiar. How stupid.

Makes you wonder what war is all about. He's trying to shell the allied troops across the river, I'm trying to drop bombs on him, he shoots my aircraft down and says he's shot all my crew and yet he risks the life of his own men to save my life. 'What's it all about?' I thought, as I drifted back into unconsciousness ...[13]

On the night of 23/24 October Bomber Command despatched 1,055 aircraft to Essen to bomb the Krupps works. This was the heaviest raid so far on the already devastated German city and the number of aircraft – 561 Lancasters, 463 Halifaxes and 31 Mosquitoes – was also the greatest to any target since the war began. Altogether the force dropped 4,538 tons of bombs including 509 4,000 pounders on Essen. More than 90 per cent of the tonnage carried was high explosive because intelligence estimated that most of the city's housing and buildings had been destroyed in fire raids in 1943. Five Lancasters and three Halifaxes failed to return from the raid. None were claimed by *Nachtjagd*.

On the night of the 24/25th there was no Main Force activity. Sixty-seven Mosquito bombers visited Hannover and other cities while 25 Lancasters and nine Halifaxes again sowed mines in the Kattegat and off Oslo. Next day daylight raids were carried out on Essen and Homberg where sky-markers guided the heavies to their aiming points.

On the 26th it was Leverkusen, with Cologne and Walcheren two days later. At the early morning briefings on 28 October several German gun batteries were identified for attack by 358 aircraft of 1, 3, 4 and 8 Groups at Dishoek, Domberg, Oostkapelle, Westkapelle and seven others to the east and west of the harbour town of Flushing. At debriefing all crews reported weather good, clear visibility, target identified and bombed visually at between 7,000 and 8,000 feet. Results were described as 'excellent'. Lancaster *Y-Yoke* on 90 Squadron at Tuddenham piloted by Flying Officer Robert J C Higgins, which was shot down into the sea, was the only aircraft that failed to return. Four parachutes were seen to emerge from the aircraft. Two landed in the sea. The others were seen to land on the ground and tragically, they were straddled by the bombs. Only the Australian bomb aimer Flight Sergeant Francis Frederick Austerbury was found. His body was discovered on a beach near Rithem very close to Flushing. He was laid to rest in the Bergen-oop-Zoom war cemetery.

Jack Stephens had not flown for five days because Bomber Command was grounded by unfavourable weather conditions – or 'duff met', as he wrote in his diary, each entry followed by 'No war'. But when night raids resumed on Saturday 28/Sunday 29 October, 237 Lancasters and seven Mosquitoes of 5 Group were detailed to attack the U-boat pens at Bergen and he wrote:

> Night war on Bergen under a big, bright harvest moon. The visibility over the target was p-poor (bad); all we could see was a few flares, so most of us bought our bombs back. The target was a U-boat base and shipping facilities. On the way back we were struck by lightning which seemed to explode inside the kite from the nose to the T/E (trailing aerial) which was nearly ripped off. We got diverted to Hallibag drome (airfield with Halifax aircraft) called 'Holme' near the Humber, returning Sunday afternoon.

Walcheren was bombed again in daylight on the 29th and the 30th but Jack Stephens was not 'on' that night, nor the next. In his diary he just wrote: 'No seats'. And then, on Wednesday 1 November he was able to write in his diary: 'Tour brought down to 30 trips so we finish.' He applied for a commission. This entailed being interviewed by his Flight Commander 'Buck' Buckham DFC, the 'Wingco' (Wing Commander Bill Forbes) and 'TR9' (Group Captain Bonham-Carter because he wore a hearing aid and TR9 was a wireless set). Stephens was successful and he went on leave to London, to the ACF (Australian Comforts Fund) Club and he saw newsreels and a show called 'Sweeter and Lower' before finishing up with a short sojourn at Taffy's (one of his fellow crew) place in Merthyr Tydfil.

Bomber Command had rounded off October with raids on Cologne and Bottrop, and Cologne was revisited on the last night of the month by 493 aircraft in another *Oboe*-marked attack. Frank Aspden on 218 Squadron at Methwold recalls:

> Cologne was a target that will always be well remembered by our crew – we went there four times and on two occasions we had a very shaky experience, to put it mildly, yet the other two were quite easy. This first trip to Cologne was our fifth op and the first after six days leave, which had put us rather out of touch with things. It was amazing really what changes could occur in the air war, as seen through our eyes, in six days. Sometimes there would be a couple of crews missing, a tour raised or lowered, or a certain target would be hotter or easier than it was before, or the fighters, day or night, would be up in strength, or have disappeared. That was the trouble at that time – you could never be certain of the defences at any given place, except, say, places such as Hamburg, which could always cook up a hot reception. Anyway, the boys were always ready to

give the gen on the past six days as soon as the leave crew returned and if after hearing all the stories you decided things were better, you could think the first target was going to be easy and so on. When we returned from leave things were much the same, so we thought Cologne would be a normal target, where flak would be heavy, if the skies were clear and moderate to slight depending on the amount of cloud over the target. No one seemed particularly worried by the target at the briefing, in fact the shortness of the trip tended to make me at any rate, in a happy frame of mind. We took off and set course as usual via Reading, across the Channel and way across France – always the dreariest part of the trip I thought. It seems a morbid thought maybe, but if I had a few moments to spare I used to look at my watch then at H-hour and think, 'Mm, 50 minutes to go; I wonder if I shall still be sat here in an hour's time; if so, that'll be one more done!'

Then '5° east. "Carpet" on Reg, 6° east. Time to Window, Dick – 0610E.' Across the lines, 'watch out now gunners' – and then that last leg into the target. On this trip we were on time and were soon running up on the Target Indicators. Below us the searchlights were trying to get us through the broken cloud whilst the brilliant full moon illuminated the aircraft around us quite clearly. Odd bursts of flak came up, but soon the bombs were gone and we turned out of the target area, nose down, revs up, 240 on the clock and homeward bound again. What a feeling of achievement, of relief. I always felt as if I'd sneaked, into someone's garden, pinched some of his choice fruit and was climbing the fence out again when the owner discovered the theft. Could I escape before he saw me? Well, he didn't on this occasion, not on any other for that matter. Yes, it was a nice trip home that night under the full moon and in a couple of hours or so we were back at base and by twelve we were cycling back to bed in our billet amongst the lovely trees at Methwold. I remember standing outside the hut and admiring the beauty of the night, the silver moon, the millions of stars and the tree silhouetted against the night sky; then a Mosquito roared overhead and I thought again of Cologne and the hell that I had helped rain down on them only three hours before. It didn't seem possible.[14]

Dick Perry on 218 Squadron recalled:

We took off from Methwold, on our first Cologne raid, to bomb the marshalling yards. The weather was atrocious when we took off but we carried on to the target over 10/10ths cloud. It cleared before we reached the target. Our bomb load, for this, the 5th trip of our tour, was a 'cookie' and 14 cans of incendiaries. We bombed on sky markers. There was not too much flak but on the run in to the target we were amazed to see an aircraft come up, through the cloud, go completely through the bomber stream and climb to about 4,000 feet above us and begin circling around at high speed. It did not do anything and we last saw it travelling at high speed away from us in a Northerly direction. It was quite visible and you could see the glow from its tail pipe as it went past. We described what we had seen when we got back to base at 11.30 but got no comment from the debriefing officer. It must have been a Me 262.[15]

One Lancaster was shot down, another crash-landed in Belgium and Flight Lieutenant F Fish flying a Lancaster on 153 Squadron had a lucky escape, as he recalls:

On our run in to the target to bomb, we suddenly heeled over to starboard and thinking that it was flak under our port wing which had lifted us up, just straightened and continued. I noted in the log that we bombed at 21.08 and were holed in our starboard wing. The wireless operator (who was keeping a look-out in the astrodome over the target) now revealed that he had seen a 1,000lb bomb coming straight at us from above. When asked in no uncertain terms why he had not shouted a warning, he replied 'I was too paralysed to speak.' We eventually agreed that perhaps this was under-standable. When we examined the aircraft the following day, we discovered that by a miracle it had missed the starboard petrol tank by about three inches. Fortunately the bomb had not completed its arming cycle and did not explode. I suspect that we must have lost quite a few of our own aircraft in this way.

On the first and second days of November two daylight raids on the Meerbeck oil plant at Homberg were attempted. At Spilsby, Flying Officer A T 'Ack' Loveless, on his first operation as a Lancaster captain on 207 Squadron, pushed the red-tipped throttle levers through the gate and N-Nan's four Merlins responded. But then Nan took a violent swing to port, raced across the grass and crashed into Z–Zebra, a 429 'Bison' Squadron RCAF Halifax, which had landed at Spilsby after the operation to Cologne the night before. As well, Nan hit a Nissen hut before stopping. Most of Ack's crew leapt out of the Lancaster as the bomber burst into flames but the bomb aimer was trapped. Loveless and a station officer freed him just before Nan's fuel load exploded. Windows and most of the window frames of the briefing room were blown out. Ten bombers that were waiting were called to take off. The first three got away safely but as the fourth was half way down the runway Nan's bomb load exploded and showered the bomber with debris as it flew through the smoke. It got airborne and flew to the target as if nothing had happened, but operations were halted. Pilot Officer Frederick Patrick Platt, the Canadian flight engineer on *G-George*, another of the 'Bison' Squadron Halifaxes that had landed at Spilsby, witnessed the crash and ran to his aircraft with the intention of getting it clear of the inferno. He was helped by Spilsby's CTO and together they started one engine but this promptly spun *George* round and before they could rectify the situation there was an explosion and the nose of the Halifax was blown in. Both men were badly injured. Platt was rushed by ambulance to RAF Hospital Rauceby but he died on the way. Two other Halifaxes were also set on fire and were destroyed and *N-Nan* made it five aircraft lost in total. 'Ack' Loveless went on to complete his tour of operations.[16]

The first raid on Homberg by over 220 Lancasters and two Mosquitoes of 5 Group was relatively unsuccessful. The marking was scattered and only 159 of the Lancaster crews attempted to bomb. One of the Lancasters failed to return. The raids on Homberg were interspersed with a night attack on Oberhausen by 288 aircraft of 6 and 8 Groups but the target area was cloud-covered and the bombing was not concentrated. The second attack on the Meerbeck oil plant by 184 Lancasters of 3 Group using 'G-H' was successful with large fires and thick column of smoke being seen. Five Lancasters were lost.

On 2 November, 992 crews[17] were briefed for a heavy raid on Düsseldorf. One of the Lancaster crews on 550 Squadron that attended the briefing at North Killingholme at 13.45 hours was captained by Flight Lieutenant Joseph Phillip Morris, who learned that the 'Happy Valley' was the target that night and that they would be flying with Flight Lieutenant David Shaw, a Scot who was at the end of his tour. He had been a sergeant in the Home Guard before joining the RAF in September 1942. In his words, he 'traded in a broomstick for a Lancaster'! Morris' crew had only just returned from leave that same morning. Sergeant Johnnie Byrne the wireless-operator recalled:

We went out to dispersal and had our photographs taken outside our 'kite'. We incidentally were taking *F-Fox* on its 100th operational sortie; the aircraft's name being *Press-on-Regardless*. We taxied out to the runway just after 16.00 hours. The weather was exceptionally nice. Cloud about 9,000 feet. At last the moment had arrived. We turned into the main runway – a green was flashed from the ACP and with throttle pushed fully forward we raced into wind. I went into the astrodome and a group of fellow air crews and ground staff officers waved 'good luck' to us. I replied with a proud 'thumbs-up' and then realised: 'Would this be my last contact with England and home?' At this moment we seemed to have reached the end of the runway and we were not as yet 'airborne'. We were carrying a full HE bomb load and enough petrol for 8¼ hours in our tanks. But 'Jock' knew what he was doing. At the last moment, he pulled the 'stick' back. And the old Lancaster shot straight into the sky; at this moment, another photograph was taken.

I settled down to do the job in hand now and I was rather hard worked during the next five or more hours. Oxygen, heating, lighting, listening watch to base and Bomber Command, frequent checks at the three gauges on the main electrical hand were a few of my duties. We went out over Reading, Beachy Head on the South Coast, across the Channel and over now Liberated France. I again went into the astrodome and could see in the coming darkness numerous other 'heavies' on either side of us – in the main bomber stream. Several Lancs were very near us, missing colliding by what seemed feet. Navigation lights were showing too.

At long last Germany was only minutes' flying time away: I now felt frightened. I wondered just how I would react to the coming flak, searchlights, fighters, etc. But then at 19.27 hours, we were attacking the Ruhr. Searchlights were moderate and flak moderate. The target was now in view! A blazing inferno of many coloured lights. With flak bursting about 1,000 feet below and about 50 searchlights sweeping the skies in what seemed a useless attempt to cone our bombers. They didn't seem to have a clue.

I now remained in the astrodome on the lookout for fighters, but 'good-show' – 'no joy' in that respect.

Now the bombing run over Düsseldorf. I was almost shouting aloud, 'Cursing the Hun to do his damndest.' 'The filthy Hun'. How proud I was at that moment. I remembered Manchester. I alone had a four-year debt to pay. Our bomb aimer from London wouldn't have much sympathy either! 'Let the bastards die like the rats they are!'

The bomb aimer was giving his orders to his Captain 'Right a bit' – 'Steady' – 'Bombs-away'. The time was exactly 19.33½. The kite lifted a little, now relieved of its heavy missiles of destruction. Then Jock took a firm hold – the stick was pushed forward and we dived straight out of Düsseldorf and the target area. With flak, fighter flares, searchlights all over the sky. The target looked a wizard sight. The moon was fully visible, only a slight indication of cloud. On the ground far below I could just imagine the Hun confused and frightened to Hell as 851 heavy bombers blasted hell out of his heavily fortified town. Fires were blazing everywhere, smoke could be seen, HEs exploding, 'Really a wizard show'. Red and green TIs and many more … grotesque sights.

The trip home was uneventful. I received a station weather forecast and visibility report for Base. D/F. I was hellish hot and tired. We had been to the Continent and back in just under 6 hours!

At 21.56 hours we 'pancaked'. Interrogation and hot sweet coffee followed. We then retired to the mess for eggs, beans, chips, sausage. And later bed.

Flying Officer Elwyn D Fieldson DFC, pilot of Halifax *Clueless I* on 76 Squadron, recalls:

It was all pretty routine on the outward trip. Frequent turbulence from the wash of aircraft ahead gave a comforting reassurance that we were nicely in the stream, although only rarely was another aircraft sighted. We arrived over the target on time to find the city well ablaze and made our run. The call of 'Bombs gone!' from the bomb-aimer Flight Sergeant Gerry Tierney was immediately followed by 'Dive starboard', which I did. Another aircraft, perhaps a Halifax, was turning towards us not waiting for those critical two miles beyond the target. Then there was a God-awful thump on our rear end, which knocked us into a near vertical dive with the whole aircraft vibrating madly. A propeller had sliced through our fuselage, leaving the tail unit attached by the top half only. The gun rams were bent into hairpins and the tail surface was considerably damaged. Remarkably Flight Sergeant Jimmy 'Junior' Ross the rear gunner was not even scratched. After losing about 2,000 feet I seemed to be getting some control back, only the aircraft became increasingly tail heavy and even with full forward elevator trim I soon had to push hard on the stick. Pilot Officer Frank Newland the engineer surveyed the damage and tied the dinghy mooring rope and the escape rope across the gap to prevent further opening.

After a quick conference with Flight Sergeant Malcolm 'Mac' McLeod the navigator, we decided to try to follow the planned route as far as the French coast in order not to become easy prey for a fighter, then dodge across to Manston, which had a nice long runway. I had my elbows locked trying to hold the stick forward far enough to keep descending to the planned 8,000 feet but my arms were getting very tired and the crew took turns to stand alongside me and help push the controls forward. Thus we arrived at Manston, where I planned a flapless landing, as I did not think there was enough control left to cope with the flap extension. But it wasn't quite over yet. On final, up went the red Very lights. (We had no radio as the aerials had been carried away.) So I overshot and went round again ('staggered round' might be a better description) at about 500 feet coming in very fast at 160 mph, this time I was allowed to land, only to end ignominiously in the mud at the end of the runway. (The Halifax always had lousy brakes.) But at least the tail didn't break off. I had feared it might. Three days later we were back on ops.[18]

The next major night raid was on 4/5 November when Bochum and the Dortmund-Ems Canal were the objectives for the Main Force. Some 749 aircraft of 1, 4, 6 and 8 Groups attacked the centre of Bochum and more than 4,000 buildings were left in ruins or seriously damaged. Three Lancasters from the 174 dispatched by 5 Group failed to return from the raid on the Dortmund-Ems Canal and 23 Halifaxes and five Lancasters were missing from the raid on Bochum, where 346 *Groupe Guyenne* Free French Squadron alone lost five of its 16 Halifaxes. Most of the night's bomber losses were due to *Nachtjagd* fighters. Over 60 Mosquitoes flew Bomber Support operations and five 100 Group crews were credited with the destruction of eight German aircraft.

On 6/7 November when 235 Lancasters and seven Mosquitoes of 5 Group again attempted to cut the Mittelland Canal at Gravenhorst, crews were confronted with a cold front of exceptional violence and ice quickly froze on windscreens. Only 31 Lancasters bombed before the Master Bomber abandoned the raid due to low cloud. Ten Lancasters failed to return. Three of these were shot down west of the Rhine in just 16 minutes by *Leutnant* Otto Fries and his *Bordfunker Feldwebel* Alfred Staffa of 2./NJG1 flying a He 219.[19] Of 128 Lancasters of 3 Group that raided Koblenz, two failed to return. A Mosquito B.XX on 128 Squadron failed to return from Gelsenkirchen and a RCM Fortress and two Mosquito Intruders were lost.

On Sunday morning, 12 November, in the third attack made on the *Tirpitz* in Tromsö Fjord, Norway by Bomber Command, Lancasters with 'Tallboy' bombs at last sent the 45,000 ton battleship to the bottom.[20] The weather was clear and there was no smokescreen. The *Tirpitz* was first sighted when the attacking force of 30 Lancasters of 9 and 617 Squadrons led by Wing Commander Willy Tait DSO*** DFC* was about 20 miles away. She was a black shape clearly seen against the clear waters of the fjord, surrounded by the snow-covered hills, which were glowing pink in the low Arctic sun. A plume of smoke rose slowly from the big ship's funnel. When the force was about ten miles away the peaceful scene changed suddenly; the ship opened fire with her main armament and billows of orange-brown smoke, shot through by the flashes of the guns, hid her for a moment and then drifted away. One 12,000 pounder apparently hit the *Tirpitz* amidships, another in the bows and a third towards the stern and there were also two very near misses which must themselves have done serious underwater damage.

Probably the last of the Lancaster crews to see the *Tirpitz* after the attack were the tour expired crew of a 463 Squadron RAAF movie-Lancaster captained by Flight Lieutenant Bruce Buckham DFC RAAF. This crew plus two BCFU cameramen and 26-year-old Guy Byams of the BBC and W E West of Associated Press had flown on the first raid.[21] Now the crew of six Australians and one Englishman and two BCFU cameramen saw the first wave go in and drop their bombs, getting some near misses and the direct hit amidships. After this only the forward guns continued firing. Then the second wave went in and the Australians saw hits on the stern, amidships and finally on the bows. All the ship's guns stopped firing but the ground defences were still throwing up a screen of light and heavy flak. Heavy black smoke hung over the vessel as the movie-Lancaster went down and circled it close in. Bruce Buckham recalled:

We flew over it, around it, all about it and still it sat there with dignity under a huge mushroom of smoke which plumed up a few thousand feet in the air. There were fires and more explosions on board; a huge gaping hole existed on the port side where a section had been blown out. We had now been flying close around *Tirpitz* for 30 minutes or so and decided to call it a day, so we headed out towards the mouth of the fjord. Just then Flying Officer Eric Giersch the rear gunner called out, 'I think she is turning over.' I turned back to port to have a look and sure enough she was, so back we went again. This time we flew in at 50 feet and watched with baited breath as *Tirpitz* heeled over to port, ever so slowly and gracefully. We could see German sailors swimming, diving, jumping and by the time she was over to 85° and subsiding slowly into the water of Tromsö Fjord, there must have been the best part of 60 men on her side as we skimmed over for the last pass. That was the final glimpse we had as we flew out of the fjord and over the North Sea. After a 14-hour flight we landed back at Waddington where the interrogation was conducted by AVM Sir Ralph Cochrane. When asked how it went, my one remark was, 'Well we won't have to go back after this one; *Tirpitz* is finished.'[22]

On the afternoon of 16 November, 1,188 aircraft of Bomber Command bombed Düren, Heinsburg and Jülich, where a high concentration of troops including the *Hermann Goering* Division had been reported. Over 1,200 American bombers made attacks on targets in the same area, all with the aim of cutting communications behind the German lines so that the American 1st and 9th Armies could advance in the area between Aachen and the Rhine. All three towns were virtually destroyed and four Lancasters were lost but the American advance was slow and costly.

The bombing offensive against German cities and oil targets continued unabated with raids in November on Homberg, Wanne-Eickel, Harburg and Dortmund among others and the Mittelland Canal again on the 21st/22nd. This time the canal banks were successfully breached near Gravenhorst. Lancasters flying as low as 4,000 feet also breached the Dortmund-Ems Canal near Ladbergen. Then on the night of 26/27 November 270 Lancasters and eight Mosquitoes of 5 Group went to Munich. Bomber Command claimed that this was 'an accurate raid' in good visibility 'with much fresh damage'. Two Lancasters crashed in England just after take-off and one Lancaster crashed in France on the way home. A raid by over 350 Lancasters and ten Mosquitoes of 1 and 8 Groups on Freiburg, a minor railway centre, followed on 27/28 November. Some 1,900 tons of bombs were dropped on the town in the space of 25 minutes and over 2,000 houses were destroyed, more than 2,000 people were killed and over 4,000 were injured. Freiburg was not an industrial town and had not been bombed before but it was believed that many German troops were billeted in the town and that these could threaten American and French units advancing in the Vosges, only 35 miles to the west. One Lancaster failed to return. One Mosquito was missing from the raid by 290 aircraft of 1, 6 and 8 Groups on Neuss on the western edge of the Ruhr. The central and eastern districts were heavily bombed and many fires started.

Bomber Command went back to Neuss the following night, when Essen also was targeted by another force of 316 aircraft. This time 150 Lancasters of 1 and 3 Groups carried out a mainly 'G-H' attack at Neuss. All aircraft returned safely from the raid on Neuss. A Halifax was attacked in the target area at Essen and crash-landed in the Pas-de-Calais, and a second Halifax, which was hit by bombs from another aircraft over Essen, was abandoned over Belgium. A third Halifax which ran low on fuel returned and force landed in Yorkshire. Next day, 29 November, over 300 Main Force aircraft took off for Dortmund but bad weather interfered with the operation and the bombing was scattered. Six Lancasters, including one that was involved in a mid-air collision with another Lancaster, were lost. Just two men survived from the six aircraft lost. On the 30th, Bomber Command dispatched two forces, to a coking plant at Bottrop and a benzyl plant at Osterfeld. All 60 Lancasters of 3 Group returned safely from Bottrop. Two Lancasters were shot down by flak on the operation to Osterfeld. An attack on Duisburg on the last night of the month was hampered by cloud cover and three Halifaxes, including two that were involved in a mid-air collision, were lost.

When on 2/3 December, 504 bombers were dispatched to Hagen and 66 Mosquitoes to Giessen the operations were supported by 44 RCM sorties and 62 Mosquito patrols of 100 Group. A Halifax and a Lancaster were lost when they crashed in France. *Nachtjäger* could claim only one Wellington north of Baltrum and a Stirling, one of ten on Resistance operations this night. Two nights' later there was a spoof on Dortmund while 892 heavies set out for Karlsruhe, Heilbronn, Hagen and Hamm in the north and south of the Ruhr. The Spoof Force of 112 aircraft of 100 Group went straight into 'Happy Valley' supported by PFF marking, and not less than 90–100 German night fighters were sent to the spoof. They waited in the area for about 15 minutes for the attack to start. However, they found nothing but high intruders and they were too late for their deployment against the heavies. Losses to the Main Force were

15 aircraft. A handful of *Nachtjäger* engaged the bomber stream on their run-in to the target at Heilbronn and shot down 12 Lancasters. 100 Group Mosquito night-fighters equipped with AI shot down five of the fighters and probably destroyed another.

On 5/6 December, when Bomber Command sent 497 aircraft to Soest, 53 Mosquitoes to Ludwigshafen, 32 to Nürnburg and four to Duisburg, only two Halifaxes were lost. The raid on Soest was successful with most of the bombing occurring in the northern part of the town where the railway installations were situated. About 1,000 houses and over 50 other buildings were completely flattened and over 280 Germans and foreign workers were killed.

On the night following, 6/7 December, Bomber Command were given three targets. Over 470 Lancaster and a dozen Mosquito crews were told that their target was Leuna near Merseburg, just west of Leipzig. It would be Bomber Command's first major raid on an oil plant in Eastern Germany. Another 453 aircraft were briefed for the first major raid on Osnabrück since August 1942. Their target was the railway yards. Over 250 Lancasters and 10 Mosquitoes of 5 Group were given the town centre and railway yards at Giessen as their objectives. Flight Lieutenant Joe Morris and crew on 550 Squadron at North Killingholme were 'on' that night but Sergeant Johnnie Byrne, the wireless operator, would have to miss the trip with his crew to Leuna as he had an interview with the station commander about his commission. It would have been his 11th op. Byrne's place was taken by Sergeant Bill Roberts, who was making his first operation over Germany. There was considerable cloud at Leuna but much damage was caused to the synthetic oil plant for five Lancasters lost. Severe damage was caused to Giessen, eight Lancasters going missing in action. Next morning whilst again waiting to see the station commander Johnnie Byrne read from a teleprinter that his crew were reported missing from the operation. Byrne wrote: 'I came on a useless errand but quite possibly my life was saved by a mere chance.' They had crashed at Dolzig. All were dead.

At Osnabrück the railway yards were only slightly damaged but four factories including the *Teuto-Metallwerke* munitions factory were hit and over 200 houses were destroyed. Seven Halifaxes and one Lancaster failed to return. One of the Halifaxes that were lost was *J-Johnny* on 429 'Bison' Squadron RCAF at Leeming. The pilot, Flying Officer James Millar Prentice RCAF, Pilot Officer Bill Barty the mid-upper gunner and Lieutenant F M McRoberts USAAF and three others on the crew had been rescued after ditching off the coast of France returning from Boulogne on 17 September when their Halifax had been hit by flak, which damaged both starboard engines. Another Halifax crew had witnessed the ditching that day and remained overhead until an ASR Walrus, escorted by two Spitfires, arrived to pick them up. The Walrus was eventually met by a High Speed Launch, which took the crew into Newhaven. This time there was no such luck. All eight on the crew, six of whom were Canadian, were lost without trace. Flight Lieutenant Harold Douglas O'Neil RCAF was on his first op; the rest were about two-thirds of the way through their tours.[23]

On Monday 11 December, Lancasters of 8 Group and 3 Group carried out daylight raids on the Urft Dam and the railway yards and the benzol plant at Osterfeld. These raids appeared successful and just two aircraft were lost. Flight Lieutenant Harry Warwick who flew as 'second dickey' with another crew to Osterfeld 'to see what it was like over there' impressed with his enthusiasm and he could hardly wait to lead his own crew on an operation. Warwick, just under six feet tall, well-built and charismatic, had been brought up from the age of two by his mother in Westminster, London after the death of his father from influenza during the 1918 epidemic. He had been a Metropolitan policeman before joining up in August 1941. Ivor Turley the rear-gunner from Birmingham was glad to see him safely back. He wrote:

For a few hours we had been headless full of foreboding, morose, irritable, deep in thought and prayer, willing him back to us. A whole day, it seemed, of sickness and worry. What if he didn't come back was a question I asked myself many, many times. We'd watched his aeroplane take off that cold, crisp morning: it was a short daylight op. As I watched, hands in pockets, fingers firmly crossed, I'd wished that I was there with him. If he was going I wanted to go too. At last he'd gone. The crew were out watching also: Tom, Joe and 'Mac'. As his kite disappeared we turned, looked at each other and read the anguish in each other's faces. Suddenly we were all alone: we turned and slowly walked away.

We had joined the Squadron only a few days earlier; men, boys, young, brash and well-disciplined in flight. Harry Warwick had seen to that! We felt as If we were the best crew in the business. No one could shoot straighter or faster than 'Mac' and I. Mac Thompson was the mid-upper gunner. No one could bomb more accurately than Bill Perry, from Charlton Kings near Cheltenham who had played Rugby for Gloucestershire: Alec Stott, an Oxford under-graduate from Plymouth, could navigate through a rice pudding. He would be the Skipper's best man at his wedding the following January. Tom Waring from Sheffield could engineer our flying back on a tube of lighter fuel. Joe Naisbitt, our wireless op from Liverpool, well! We never really found out what he listened to! Our Skipper could fly anything, anywhere, anytime!

He was back! The station was alive again! There were bods everywhere: I had never experienced anything like it. It was as if we had all died when the squadron took off. We talked quietly, almost in whispers: the station brooded. Somehow we had found our way to the airfield before their ETA and we had quietly waited for the first one back. Suddenly they were back the sky full of airplanes thundering onto the circuits on our own and neighbouring airfields, the air full of wonderful engine noise. We could talk loud again: the place vibrated, airplanes landed.

'Skipper's back!' shouted Mac. 'I've just seen his kite!'

The crew buses raced around the peri-track to pick up returning crews. We dodged returning crew buses and bods and ran to the briefing room. Yes, there was the Skipper back safe and sound, a broad smile on his face as he came towards us.

'Hello boys,' he said, 'it's a piece of cake.'

Notes

1. According to the directive issued to Sir Arthur Harris, *Hurricane's* purpose was, 'In order to demonstrate to the enemy in Germany generally the overwhelming superiority of the Allied Air Forces in this theatre ... the intention is to apply within the shortest practical period the maximum effort of the RAF Bomber Command and the US 8th Bomber Command against objectives in the densely populated Ruhr.'

2. Escorted by RAF fighters, just over 1,000 Lancasters, Halifaxes and Mosquitoes were detailed to raid the city while 1,251 American bombers escorted by 749 fighters hit targets in the Cologne area. At Duisburg 957 RAF heavies dropped 3,574 tons of high explosive and 820 tons of incendiaries for the loss of 13 Lancasters and a Halifax to flak. American casualties were just five bombers and one fighter.

3. F/L Reginald Major Aldus was killed.

4. *218 Gold Coast Squadron Assoc Newsletter No.43* October 2006.

5. That night, which was fine and cloudless, 1,005 RAF heavies attacked Duisburg for the second time in 24 hours in two waves and dropped 4,040 tons of high explosive and 500 tons of incendiaries and losing five Lancasters and two Halifaxes. Bomber Support and forces on minor operations had played their part with 141 training aircraft flying a diversionary feint towards Hamburg and turning back before reaching Heligoland, and 46 Mosquitoes raiding Hamburg, Berlin, Mannheim and Düsseldorf while 132 aircraft of 100 Group flew RCM, *Serrate* and *Intruder* sorties. One Halifax of the diversionary force was lost. Five Lancasters were lost. One fell victim to *Leutnant* Arnold Döring, an experienced 27-year-old fighter pilot of 7./NJG2 at Volkel aerodrome in Holland flying the Ju 88G-6. It was his 20th aerial victory. In summer 1943 Döring had completed 348 operational sorties as a bomber pilot in KG53 and KG55, seeing action during the Battles of France and Britain and in the Russian campaign, where he destroyed 10 aircraft in the air (inc. three 4-engined TB-3 bombers over Stalingrad one night) flying a He 111 fitted with extra machine-guns. He claimed a further 8 a/c destroyed as a *Wild Boar* pilot in JG 300 and 3 more night victories in NJG2 and NJG3. Despite the enormous effort involved in Operation *Hurricane* that same night

RAF Bomber Command was even able to dispatch 233 Lancasters and seven Mosquitoes of 5 Group to bomb Brunswick.

6. *A Square Peg* by E P Bone (November 2006).

7. Sgt E F Vevers on 463 Squadron crashed in the North Sea.

8. They flew 866 sorties, resulting in just 56 victories (or 0.5% of 10,000 Bomber Command sorties). *Nachtjagd* ranks were further depleted by 54 aircraft and crews (or 6.2%) during October. November saw 959 night-fighter sorties dispatched, crews returning with claims for 87 kills (or 0.9% of Bomber Command's night raids).

9. Even in broad daylight, Bomber Command was able to operate in relative safety. During October–December 1944, 15 out of 20 raids on the Ruhr were in daylight. 100 Group's RCM bombers caused further confusion and disruption by its faint raids and jamming of the *Luftwaffe's* radio traffic and radar and often prevented German night fighters from reaching the bomber streams at all. 100 Group Mosquitoes, which had claimed 257 German aircraft (mainly night-fighters) destroyed by 1945, hunted down the *Nachtjagd* crews and complimented the offensive by 2nd TAF, ADGB and 8 Group over the continent.

10. On 7/8 October, in riposte to the enemy R/T communications used in its *Zahme Sau* operations, Lancasters on 101 Squadron, fitted with *Airborne Cigar* (ABC) carried out jamming of the enemy R/T frequencies. These Lancasters also carried a specially trained German-speaking operator. The order 'All butterflies go home' was broadcast on the German night-fighter frequency and many pilots returned to their airfields! The most outstanding *Window* success of the month was perhaps on 14/15th when 1,013 heavies went to Duisburg and 200 to Brunswick. It was anticipated that the Duisburg raid, by low approach, radar silence and shallow penetration, would get through with little trouble but that the Brunswick force might be strongly opposed. A *Window* Force was therefore routed to break off from the Brunswick route and strike at Mannheim. This had success beyond all expectations, for the Brunswick attack was almost ignored because the Mannheim area was anticipated as the main target. Just one bomber from the Brunswick force was lost. October also saw the introduction of *Dina*; the jammer used against FuG 220 *Lichtenstein* SN-2. *Dina* was installed in the *Jostle*-fitted Fortresses on 214 Squadron. This was frequently used in the *Window* force, as were *Jostle*, H_2S and *Carpet*, thereby more effectively giving the simulation of a bombing force. A further realistic effect, also born in October, was created through the co-operation of PFF, which, on several occasions *Oboe*-marked and bombed the 'Spoof' target. (The *Window* Force itself had not yet arrived at the bomb-carrying stage.) The noise of *Oboe*, which had until that time always preceded real attacks only, was thought to give still more confusion to the German controller.

11. It may have been the sick bay in the Britannia Hotel, which was then the German Headquarters.

12. W/O Jim Maple RAAF, F/Sgt Alexander Easton, Bob Coward and F/Sgt Charles Frederick Kirby were all dead. W/O J R M McWilliam RAAF and Sgt H E Lee survived and were taken into captivity.

13. *P-Peter* was one of four Lancasters lost on the raid.

14. *218 Gold Coast Squadron Assoc Newsletter No.52* November 2008.

15. *218 Gold Coast Squadron Assoc Newsletter No.42* August 2006 and *No.58* April 2010.

16. See *Chased By The Sun*.

17. 561 Lancasters, 400 Halifaxes and 31 Mosquitoes supported by 37 RCM sorties and 51 Mosquito fighter patrols.

18. More than 5,000 houses were destroyed or badly damaged in the northern half of Düsseldorf, plus 7 industrial premises destroyed and 18 seriously damaged. This was Bomber Command's last major raid on the city. Eleven Halifaxes and 8 Lancasters FTR, 4 of these a/c crashing behind Allied lines in France and Belgium. 92 crewmembers were lost, 28 becoming PoWs. 5 men evaded and 6 were hospitalised, 1 dying later from wounds received.

19. Fries and his *Bordfunker Feldwebel* Fred Staffa had become a very experienced night-fighting team. They were credited with 10 confirmed night kills August 1943–April 1944, plus 2 unconfirmed *Abschüsse* in daylight, a B-17 on 17 August and a P-47 on 14 October 1943. On 9 July 1944 they had been posted to 2./NJG1 at Venlo airfield.

20. On 15 September the attack, by 28 Lancasters of 9 and 617 Squadrons, 20 of which were carrying *Tallboys* and 6 or 7 others, 12 × 500lb *Johnny Walker* oscillating mines, caused considerable damage to the battleship. Subsequent PR revealed that although badly damaged, the *Tirpitz* was still afloat (albeit beyond practical repair, although this was not known at the time). The Norwegian resistance stated that the ship left for Tromsö Fjord, where it was to be used as a heavy artillery battery. On 29 October, 37 Lancasters of 9 and 617 Squadrons took off from Lossiemouth and attacked the *Tirpitz* in Tromsö Fjord. Thirty-two Lancasters dropped *Tallboys* on estimated position of the capital ship. No direct hits were scored but a near-miss by the stern caused considerable damage, distorting the propeller shaft and rudder, which flooded the bilges over a 100 foot length of the ship's port side. It meant that the *Tirpitz* was no longer able to steam under her own power. By the time that the attack was over various decoded Ultra code-cipher intercepts revealed that the *Tirpitz* was no longer seaworthy but the War Cabinet decided that the battleship must be sunk.

21. Byams was killed on board B-17G *The Rose of York* in the 306th Bomb Group, 8th Air Force over Berlin on a daylight raid on 3 February 1945. In the early years of the war Byams saw action with the RNVR and Combined Operations but was wounded and invalided out. He joined the BBC War Reporting Unit in April 1944. Two months later he parachuted into Normandy with British paratroopers on D-Day and his reports made him a household name. A listener wrote after his death: 'All looked forward to hearing his enthusiastic and youthful voice in the 9 o'clock news.'

22. At least two *Tallboys* hit the ship, which capsized to remain bottom upwards. The crew of the *Tirpitz* had been reduced from a complement of 2,000 to about 1,600, most of whom were engine room personnel, after the second attack. Around 900 men were killed, drowned or suffocated, having been trapped on board in watertight compartments. Only 87 sailors were recovered from the ship by cutting through the double bottom from the outside. One Lancaster, on 9 Squadron, was severely damaged by flak and landed safely in Sweden with its crew unhurt.

23. Chorley. During December *Nachtjagd* flew 1,070 sorties, which resulted in 66 victories or 0.7 per cent of all Bomber Command night bomber sorties. Despite the declining effectiveness of *Nachtjagd* during late 1944, an all-time record of 2,216 aircraft destroyed was claimed that year. *Luftflotte Reich* had 905 operational night-fighter aircraft on 17 November but losses from air combat, ground attacks and accidents rose steeply and 114 aircraft were destroyed during November–December 1944.

CHAPTER 2

Down In The Drink

Dig asked for his can. A few moments later it was passed forward and I tipped out its contents watching the urine freeze into smears of ice as it touched the sides of the 'Window' chute.

We were about thirty miles from the target when Dig said, 'What do you make of these specks ahead, Mike?'

I climbed into the front turret. In the blue distance it seemed that a cluster of midges were darting erratically up and down; then one fell, leaving a thin spiral of smoke in its wake. 'It looks like a dog-fight' I said and the words as they passed my lips sounded strange, an echo of schoolboy magazines and stories of aerial combat.

'My oath,' said Dig. 'Where's our fighter cover? ... This is supposed to be a virgin target.'

'Looks more like a whore to me', Paul's voice piped through.

The Eighth Passenger by Miles Tripp

'Wakey-wakey!'

It's 07.20, 12 December 1944.

Ivor Turley, accepting his fate, now uncertain, now nervous – what to do now? Oh yes: get dressed! Long aircrew Johns, thick vest, ordinary socks, pullover over-vest, short tie, (stupid order – got to wear the tie!) Blow that: I'd die with my tie off! It won't be seen under my polo sweater, anyway. No, wars are wars; must wear the tie! Electric suit over this lot: zip up front and legs, put on battle-dress trousers, polo sweater: movements slowing as everything felt tight. Oh, God, it'll be bloody cold up there! More panic of all the stupid!!! – I'd forgotten to wash: I'd shaved the night before. Rubbed my chin. No stubble. Was it growing? An oxygen mask and a stubbly chin didn't go well together. Oh well a wipe round would have to do.

'Getting your feet off the deck then, Warwick's crew? It's time you got airborne!' It was Banton's lot. We ate bacon and eggs in silence,

39

each in thought. Other bods were chattering and laughing but we were the 'new boys'.

After breakfast twelve crews assembled for briefing for the operation that afternoon. What was it really like? Suddenly it seemed I was confident as we made our way to the briefing room. The clamp shut of air-gunners in their heavy fur lined boots, the muffled chatter of other bods as in groups we converged on the briefing room door. Through the door into the locker-room, past the SP on the inner door and I saw the well-lit room full of men in stages of aircrew dress and the long tables with navigators' bags on. The navigators were briefed an hour before us; there was a flurry of activity, navigation maps everywhere: Navigators drawing lines, flight engineers working on charts, pilots gazing at maps. God, What confusion! We joined the rest of our crew at a long table and sat down. Harry was there, smiling as usual. The focus of attention was the stage at the far end of the long hut. A large map of Germany was the backcloth. From a red-knobbed pin in England, which represented our airfield, ran red tape to other pins on, over the top end, out down the bottom end and back to base.

The briefing began with a roll-call for Skipper's aircraft. I was absorbed, excited and unafraid: realising this was the point of no turning back. It was to be a 'G-H' attack by 140 Lancasters covered by a fighter escort of RAF Mustangs. The target was the Ruhrstahl steelworks at Witten, a railway town on the Ruhr River at the far end of 'Happy Valley'. Frankly, we'd never heard of Witten! The Bombing and Intelligence officer told us that this was a virgin target. Reconnaissance had shown it as a very busy target and it was time it went out of production. The aiming points were to be the large coke ovens. We were given the bomb jettison areas for hang-ups or recall. The Met-men gave us the weather conditions: clouds to avoid, icing up, how to get out of it, where to expect it. Temperature 35/40 below freezing. That's blooming cold, I thought. Visibility 3 miles: cloud cover 4/5 tenths, thickening to 5/8 tenths in the south and over base at 4,000 feet.

The briefing was over: a babble of voices broke out. We stood up, happier now: we knew at last. I felt part of it. All gone was the uncertainty, I had a job to do – I was one of the boys at last At least I had survived my first briefing We moved from the briefing-room, drew our parachutes and from our lockers took the rest of our flying clothing: Sidcott outer, electric gloves, leather gauntlets, helmet. Sitting on low benches we put on our clothing, stuffing things in our pockets: handkerchief in right-hand Sidcott pocket. Escape pack in back pocket – no, that would be uncomfortable. That can go in my left-hand pocket. Wakey-Wakey pills? Yes, put those in a twist of paper and put them in the little square breast pocket of my Sidcott.

Mae West over the lot; the straps tight. I didn't want that floating off on the remote chance of my having to use it.

Check every detail of dress: Plenty of clothing? Yes. Mae West okay? Yes. Wakey-Wakey tablets? Yes. Fluorescent marker block in Mae West? Yes. Floating lamp in Mae West? Yes. CO_2 bottle and lever on Mae West? Bottle unbroken? Yes. Escape kit? Yes. Sweets? Yes. All okay? Good; we are ready to ...! Oh, no, no!! The long brown lead from my electric suit was still inside my trousers and I was wearing them!! Off with 'chute harness, off with Mae West, off with Sidcott: off with ... Oh, what a clot am I. At last, with electric suit lead hanging out and with the socket and lead stuffed into my Sidcott pocket, I was ready to go.

As I sat in the crew bus I realised it was daylight. Take-off was at 10.30. It was now 09.15. How long ago it seemed that I had woken up: so much had happened. My mind was numb – I was afraid again. The briefing, the excitement, the handing-in of all identity in case we were shot down – dog-tags only was the rule – the cheerful WAAFs handing out hot tea with briefing, the dreaded checking, the helping; all served to fill the mind that suddenly we're leaving it all behind – and you can't help feeling it's for good. And I thought; what if I do get the chop? I looked at others in the crew bus as it moved onto the peri-track. Had they the same thoughts? We stopped. The driver called 'B-Baker' and a few bods moved with their kit and jumped out. We moved and stopped again. 'C-Charlie' was the call; that was us. Mac, Tom, Joe and I gathered our kit and jumped out. The crew bus moved on, gears changing, leaving us standing on the grass.

We looked and there she was: C-Charlie. Silent, bomb bay doors open, ready to take us on board. She looked proud, majestic, determined and very useful. Tears stung my eyes: was this to be no return? Was she to be my coffin? Was I going to let her lay, a twisted, broken wreck in some German field? Oh, no, not me! This was my airplane. She was a Lancaster. At last the crew were assembled round the airplane. I had taken off a lot of my flying clothing in order to move more easily on my pre-flight checks of gun and turret. It was good to be busy. Harry had checked the tyres, flaps and wings: in fact I'm sure he's checked everything. We were all very serious now: guns working okay, breech blocks were free. Tanks full of ammo. And yes: three ball, two armour-piercing, one tracer-repeated; ammunition free in its fuselage ducts. Servo mechanism free, oxygen point okay, emergency lighter push-button okay, cocking toggle in right-hand holster, turret locked, hand mechanism okay, sight, ring and bead okay and so on and so on. Everything, yes everything had to function properly. Outside once again for a final breather.

'Okay chaps' said Harry; 'Time to go.'

We started to board again. Mac knelt on the ground and kissed it. Slapping the ground affectionately he exclaimed: 'Ta-ta love, shan't be long. Don't forget to be here when I come back!' He got up. We grabbed him, pushed him up the ladder into the kite and bundled his flying clothes after him. Flying helmet and gloves on at last, I turned and gave the thumbs-up to Mac before he finally wormed his way into his mid-upper turret. One by one the engines started: the airplane started to shake and shudder as she roared into life. I closed and secured the rear door, plugging in to a nearby intercom point and reported to the Skipper: 'Okay, Skip, rear door closed and locked!' Unplugging the intercom I made my way rather laboriously to my turret. Greatly hampered by my flying clothing it proved to be quite an effort to crawl through the gap made by the tail-plane spar and the fuselage. After some contortions I got into my turret and sat, limp and exhausted, gasping for breath and wondering is it worth it? I unlocked the turret and put my hand on the controls, applied pressure to the grips and the turret came to life. I swung the turret round, depressing and raising the guns, making sure that rotation was free. I plugged in my intercom and heated suit. Check, check, check: everything in order, sit as comfortable as possible, I'm ready to go. Groping with my right hand I suddenly realised I'd forgotten my thermos flask of hot tea! Oh Lord and was I thirsty already!

We started to move off. I felt the tail end swing as the Skipper lined the kite up with the exit from the dispersal pan. Slowly power was applied, the slipstream sending bits of paper and leaves dancing away over the grass. We moved off dispersal and onto perimeter track. The ground crew boys gave us the thumbs-up as we passed. For the moment their work was finished; for them just the long wait until we returned and then to start all over again repairing, checking and re-checking the tired engines.

We moved faster now, the roar of the engines fluctuating as power was applied on take-off to control our speed. The tail wheel jolted over ruts and holes in the peri-track: the rear turret shook and rattled – and me with it. The briefing room came into view and with it crowds of bods watching each kite as it rolled by. They gave the V-sign to us all. The Skipper and flight engineer had finished their verbal check prior to take-off: it had gone something like this:

'Pumps on, two tanks full, pitch fully fine' and other type patter which, as a gunner, I could not fully understand, but it went on at every take-off, training or otherwise. I heard the engines of the kite in front of us roar with extra power as it received the green light and with that peculiar throb start to trundle down the runway. Our turn next: we moved forward into position, the tail swinging around as the Skipper lined up with the runway. Tom's voice came over the intercom: 'Okay Harry. There's the green!'

'Okay,' replied Harry. 'Hold tight boys; here we GO!'

My rear turret was facing port: guns elevated, sliding door behind me open. I was ready to roll out backwards if anything went wrong. The engines filled with power, we moved forward: I had loosed the turret controls and was holding hard onto the side stays. Faster we rolled, the engines roared, the caravan passed and started to recede into the distance. I felt the tail rise and quiver: I was at least airborne. We were half-way down the runway – or it seemed so to me and we were still on it. I could feel the vibration of the wheels. Harry's voice came over the intercom:

'Okay, Tom; full power on!'

The note of the engines changed to a loud and more high-pitched roar. Now we were really travelling the seconds seemed like minutes, the length of the runway looked longer and longer – it seemed we wouldn't make it. We seemed to lift a little, the wheel vibration stopped. I felt the kite sway and the side of the runway slid slowly under us as we drifted slightly to port. We were airborne! Below, seemingly, just a split second after we left the deck, the end of the runway flashed by underneath and started to recede below and away. Hedges and fields moved beneath us, slower now and further below.

'Undercarriage up,' was the next order. 'Flaps up, revs 2650.' I felt the airplane drop a little as the flaps came up. The roar of the engine died a little as the revs were reduced. 'Revs 2300!' Once more the engines quietened: our movement was smoother now. Just then we hit the slipstream of another plane: I felt the bump. The airplane shook and we side-slipped I clutched madly at the turret stays and held tight. No, I wasn't afraid – MUCH!

All this time we circled, catching up slowly with our formation leader, I rotated my turret left to right, right to left, slowly and deliberately, searching for aircraft which weren't ours. The rule was: 'start looking from take-off and don't stop.'

'Hello Skip: There's our leader on the port out to bow,' called up Mac, breaking into a brooding intercom silence.

'Okay Mac, I see them. I'll get a bit closer and make sure. It's *Q-Queenie* we are supposed to follow,' replied the Skipper.

'Yes, it's them all right I can see *W-Willie*'s letter. He's the other follower and he's closing pretty tight.' I heard the click as Mac switched off his intercom.

'We should be setting course now, Skip,' Alec's voice broke over the intercom.

'We're just starting to turn now,' replied Harry.

The monotony of flight was beginning to set in. My legs were already stiff with cramp. How I wanted to stretch them. My flying clothing fell tight. No wonder I felt cramp, but with waves of excitement surging within me I had little time to dwell on my own discomfort.

'Five minutes to go and we turn onto the first leg.' Alec's words over the intercom startled me. For the last twenty minutes not a word had been spoken.

'Okay Alec.' replied the Skipper. 'Hello rear-gunner: how does the stream look now?' continued Harry.

'Pretty good, Skip' I replied. 'A couple of kites have turned back, but everything okay.'

Looking down I could see we were flying parallel with the coast. We turned to port and below us was the town of Clacton-on-Sea. The noise of the engines changed as we started to climb.

'Put the revs up, Tom' said Harry. 'We're starting to climb. Hallo Alec: what's our altitude on this leg?'

'Ten thousand feet or above cloud' replied Alec. He meant that if cloud base was below ten thousand feet we should climb through and above the cloud.

'Okay boys; stand by to take oxygen – oxygen on, Tom.'

'Okay, Harry, oxygen going on,' replied Tom. He was in charge of the tap that supplied oxygen.

I watched the needle of the oxygen meet between my legs swing to 'on'. I connected my oxygen mask to bayonet tube on the meter, held the mask to my cheek and waited for the puff of oxygen to tell me everything was okay. This was the part I disliked: I wouldn't be taking this thing off for three or four hours I hated the smell of rubber and the peculiar smell of the oxygen assailed my nostrils. I breathed deeply, sucking oxygen into my lungs: securing my mask I managed some degree of comfort.

The lower cloud grew thicker as we continued to climb: formation in the stream behind had loosened, for it only takes a split second to collide in cloud. Clouds swirled past my turret, moisture condensed on my Perspex and I watched the rivulets of moisture run in parallel lines across my side-panels. With a swirl the clouds thickened and my vision was reduced to a few feet. The clouds formed two cylindrical hollow tubes behind as the vortex of current from our wing-tips rolled them. It was as though we were boring two holes in a solid mass and I was looking along two perfect cylinders.

I gripped the turret controls tighter. I was straining to see further into the cloud. The moment of collision was here. Suddenly my heart leapt into my mouth and my hand to my mike-switch. I guessed, looked again: yes, there it was another Lanc. Damn close too. The blurred outline was slowly defining itself It was getting nearer: a rainbow halo shrouded it lay to port and slightly down. It was suddenly keeping perfect formation with us: what shall I do? If we moved we could collide with another airplane, if we stayed still this one would collide with us. It suddenly moved too close. I clicked on my mike-switch and then we were breaking cloud. The other Lanc wavered and disappeared. I breathed deep, clicked off my mike-switch. I was sweating – and then I cursed. It had been our own shadow on the inside of the clouds! We started culling the upper layer of cloud, leaving long furrows from our slipstream. It was getting colder and the slipstream was whipping it through the open front of my turret, making my cheeks smart and my eyes water. I pulled my muffler closer around my throat and pulled my goggles down over my eyes. By squeezing further back in my turret I found I could escape some of the draught I closed my eyes: they felt tired and the glare from the white cloud was intense. My goggles steamed up, but when I raised them the slipstream hit my eyes again. I shivered, the cold running sharply up and down my spine: my flesh crawled with the intense cold. I switched on my electric suit and felt the warmth percolating through my underwear. It wasn't really warm, but it took the bite from the cold away: it felt better. I turned my attention to my guns, cocking them to see if they were okay. I then realised I should have had them cocked and ready as soon as we'd got airborne. I looked at my fire and safety mechanisms: they were all on 'Safe'. Frantically I switched them to 'Fire'. I cursed and cursed. I had been sitting all this time in a gun-turret with four machine-guns that between them could not have fired a cork, let alone a bullet. A fine ruddy gunner I was turning out to be! Alec's voice came over the intercom.

'We should be well over the sea now Skip. Can you see it?'

'No, I can't Alec. It's pretty well ten-tenths cloud. The leader should be opening his bomb bays doors now.'

This was a signal to Bill to get into his bomb bay and check his equipment He reported 'all okay'.

'Leader is opening his bomb doors now!' exclaimed Harry.

'Okay bomb doors open' came Bill's quiet voice.

'Bomb doors open' replied Harry.

After a couple of minutes Bill's voice came over the intercom. 'Okay Skip, bombs selected and fused. Everything Okay; Bomb doors closed.'

'Bomb doors closed' replied Harry. 'Hello rear-gunner: you okay back there?'

'I switched my mike on. 'Everything Okay Skipper; guns checked and ready to go.'

'You okay, Mac?' asked Harry.

'Yes, bang on Skipper. Everything okay, guns checked on.'

'Good show', replied Harry. 'It won't be long now and don't forget if there are any fighters over there, I shall expect you to chalk one up. We didn't see any yesterday and from what I hear they prefer to attack the Yanks. Keep your eyes open everybody. Don't forget, gunners: shoot first and we'll be all right.'

With that he switched off. It had been quite a babble of conversation for our crew. I was gelling sore with cramp: I wriggled about in my flying suit to ease the cramps. I first sat on one cheek of my backside and then the other: after a while I achieved some degree of comfort. The monotony of flight seemed to have set in over the whole stream. One could feel the soreness of other gunners and sense an air of quiet and bored resignation.

'Hello Skip, nav' here. We should be crossing the coast in about five minutes. Dunkirk will be on our starboard side.'

'Okay Alec,' replied Harry.

France at last. I searched the clouds below for a break to get a glimpse of the French coast, but no luck. I tried counting the minutes, trying to estimate the time when we would be actually crossing the French coast, for at this point on we could expect flak. Alec saved me the trouble of further search: 'Hello, Skip: nav' here. We are crossing the coast'. Pause. 'NOW! That's as near as I can get without a visual check.'

I looked down the length of the stream and noted a kink as aircrafts skirted around something. I searched and saw the cause of the movement. Just to starboard and approximately 1,000 feet above the stream, hung eight ominous black puffs of smoke. They hung motionless and I watched as they bloomed slowly into large black mushrooms. Then I saw another cluster of eight: this time they looked white, the sun rays glinting off them: they were large and spent. How pretty they looked, hanging there in the clear air like ragged balloons. This then was flak!

'Hello Skipper. Flak on the starboard quarter up at the rear of the stream' I reported. 'The stream weaving a little, but there doesn't seem to be much of it.' We were in the second of three airplanes and our squadron had the honour of leading the stream into the attack. The comforting thought was that we would be first in and first away.

'Okay, Tom: S Gear,' came Harry's voice.

'Okay, Skipper: S Gear.' replied Tom.

The engine changed suddenly I felt a shudder course through the aircraft as S Gear went in. The engine roar now took on a higher, more strained note. I could feel the pull as the aircraft continued to climb even higher. We were nearing our bombing height of 20,000 feet.

'Hello, Skip,' the nav's calm voice now came over the intercom. 'We are approximately at the fighter rendezvous. You should see them any minute now.'

'Okay, Alec,' replied Harry. 'Well, boys, our guardians should be on hand soon, I expect. On this tour we'll be glad we've got a fighter escort from time to time.'

I searched the skies in detail but couldn't see any fighters. My operating of the turret controls was now fully automatic: port to starboard, starboard to port. What monotony! Search, search and search again. Monotony, yes: but our lives depended on it. The numbness of my limbs became more intense: the cramp was spreading, especially my knees, which were now so painful I could almost hear them, screaming for relief. The cramp was maddening – I yearned to stand up and run. The structure of the turret seemed to stand out in detail: spars, guns, sights, buttons and switches. I was just a pair of eyes enclosed in this cramped space. In front and past the gun-sight clear vision: open space where the Perspex had been cut away. No armour: this had also been removed to give clearer vision downwards. I wanted to squeeze out, jump onto the cloud layer below and just walk. By leaning over my ammunition feed mechanism and with my head nearly out of the turret, I found that I could straighten my legs and get as near as I could to a bent forward standing position. I felt the numbness leaving my knees and legs as blood started to course through the veins. Freed now from the strangulation of my flying clothes, by alternately sitting and straightening my legs while bent forward, I got the blood circulation going. Oh, what relief at last!

I pushed my head further out of the turret I could feel the slipstream rushing by. I realised that I could virtually look straight down. With relief I sat down. Within two minutes the numbness was back: I gave up. The stream had lengthened considerably, the rear formations now small dots in my line of vision. Occasionally the dots would become distorted as heat and slipstream from our engines cut across my vision. Vapour trails whipped intermittently from the wing-tips of some of the following airplanes. I watched for a while as the trails broke from wing-tips and fell back, snaking and twisting into the stream.

'Okay Alec,' replied Harry, 'I think I can see the line now. Looks like a bit of artillery barrage down there.'

It was very cold: I could feel a draught hitting my knees and the cold was getting through my flying clothes. As I leaned forward the icy blast coming from my clear vision panel hit my forehead and eyes. My forehead soon became icily numb. Pushing my gauntleted fingers under my flying helmet, I pulled the front of my balaclava helmet down so that only my eyes were uncovered. I could no longer feel any warmth from the elements in my electric suit chills were coursing up my spine and I shivered. I thought my electric suit had packed up: I switched the power off. Within seconds I felt the icy cold reach every part of me. I was stiffening. Hurriedly I switched my electric suit back on. They weren't kidding when they said it was cold at 20,000ft!

'Hello, Mac,' I called. 'Have you seen anything of our escort yet?'

'No, not a sausage' came the mid-upper gunner's reply. 'I saw some fighters a few minutes back, but they were too far away to identify.' Harry's voice crackled over the intercom: 'Don't worry, boys, they're there all right, probably sitting high up astern of us. They get a better view that way there's probably a bunch of Spits sitting in full view right now watching over us.'

'Hello Skip. *Window* should be going out now,' Alec's voice came over the intercom.

'Okay Alec. Ready, Tom? Two bundles every minute' said Harry. As I looked astern I could see the glint of silver as other aircraft started discharging *Window*. A stream of *Window* started appearing from under our tail and trailed for a moment behind us. Tom had discharged his first bundle: a piece of brown paper went after it as Tom pushed that out as well. Soon the sky was full of glinting pieces of silver foil: the air seemed to shimmer in the distance as the sun caught the *Window* as it tossed and spun in millions of small pieces. We were laying our protective shield to jam radar and prevent spot detection. It was small comfort as we were in front. No *Window* floated passed us and the leading aircraft could generally be picked up on a radar screen. I searched and searched, the glare of the sun on the clouds hit me – I was tired of searching. I lowered my anti-glare goggles. They immediately steamed up. My vision was cut and they were bloody useless. I lifted them and decided to check my oxygen valve to make sure it wasn't freezing up. The rubber inlet dial was kicking as I breathed in. Raising my hand to my oxygen mask valve, I felt a click as I broke off an icicle two inches long. Squeezing my oxygen tube along its length I broke off the ice forming inside. Taking a deep breath I whipped off my mask, disconnected the tube from its coupling, removed ice from the valve, shook it and put my mask back on, making sure the coupling was home. I could breathe again I checked the guns, sliding the breech blocks backwards and forward an inch: they were okay. Depressing the guns and finding clear space, I fired a short burst into the clouds to clear the barrels. The ring and bead sight was switched on and the spare bolts were still in their holders. Yes, everything still okay. Feeling for my cocking toggle I pulled it out a little further from its leather holster. It was by my right knee. I'd have to snatch for it pretty quickly if I had a gun jam in combat, although I doubted whether I would have bothered or even noticed a stoppage in combat. I checked the ammunition and the feed mechanism: a misaligned bullet could cause trouble. Yes, everything was still in order and I hoped it would remain so.

'Hello Skip.' It was Alec's voice. 'We'll be turning onto the bombing run soon. It'll be a long leg in as we're bombing on course and then turning directly over the target. However, the leader has the gen, so just follow him. I'll check as we go.'

'Okay navigator,' Harry replied. 'I'll stick to the leader. How long have we got to the target after this turn?'

'About twenty minutes,' replied Alec. 'We're a little to port of track, but otherwise okay, Skipper.'

'Are you okay back there rear-gunner?' said Harry.

'Okay, Skipper,' I replied. 'All checked and ready.'

'You okay, Mac?' asked Harry.

'Yep, bang on' said Mac. 'I still can't see our fighters, though: I'm beginning to wonder if they are there.'

'Don't worry, Mac: they're there all right' said Harry.

Somehow I sympathised with Mac: I hadn't seen the fighter escort either I'm not sure who saw them first and I'm not sure why I didn't seem them sooner, but a sixth sense suddenly made me swing my turret hard to port. I stared, tense and shocked at the whirling column of small airplanes flying on our port beam, behind them a tall column of white cloud. 'Hey Mac,' I shouted, 'Do you see them? To port. Fighters?'

There was a pause as though Mac was swinging his turret round to look for the first time at this whirling melee of fighters. 'Yeah, I can see them' was Mac's reply. 'Too far away to identify: 109s and Mustangs look very much alike at a distance.'

'Hello Skip,' I called. 'Fighters on the port beam level. We can't identify them yet, but from the way they're flying they look like ...!' My whole being screwed up: my heart seemed to thump and then stop. I caught my breath and fear swelled within me, for at this point a brown plummet of smoke snaked down the swirling column. As it fell my scalp prickled and my body felt icy within. Oh, God: this is it. 'Mac, I think they're enemy fighters!' I called out.

'Yes, they are and not a ruddy Spit or Mustang in sight. That smoke plummet is a signal to attack and they're leaving now! Here the bastards come!'

'Hello Skip, they're enemy fighters' I called. 'Stand by for combat; intercoms on.'

'Okay, boys,' replied Harry in a calm voice. 'It looks as though we're going to fight this one out. Watch them closely: they may try to pick us off as leaders. I'm closing on our leader now; he may need our fire power.'

The signal lights in the turret flashed as Harry called up Joe, our wireless operator.

'Hello Skipper, WOP here' came Joe's sleepy voice. 'Everything okay?'

'It is as yet,' replied Harry. 'We're being intercepted by fighters, so stay on the intercom. We may have to act quickly if things go against us.'

'Okay, Harry,' replied Joe. 'I'll be listening.'

Joe switched off his mike and then all hell broke loose. Lancasters began to weave. It was all happening so fast now and to port and below a Lanc was corkscrewing as a fighter bore in to attack. I saw the lines made by the Me 109's tracers; the Lanc dived and then started to pull out. A tongue of flame sprang from the port wing. The 109 was still firing, it seemed that suddenly all was slow motion. Bits started to fall off, flames spread and smoke thickened. She did not return the 109's fire: she ducked forward; a pall of smoke engulfed her and with a slow spiral she fell earthwards. With an effort I diverted my eyes from the spectacle. I was numb with feeling that it was my turn next. More smoke, more flame. Another Lanc was trailing brown smoke from an engine. She was flying lower and lower. Lancasters were everywhere. A parachute floated here, fighters were racing in, diving, whirling and climbing. My mind was going. I couldn't think fast enough. Tears were stinging my eyes; which way to turn! Another twisting, turning airplane: I was trying to scan every piece of the sky at once, trying to watch every fighter. Which one was going to single us out? Where would the attack come from? The icy finger was really running up and down my spine. A fighter reared up and broke off its attack on a Lanc close by. The sound of heavy breathing smote my ears: all the crews had their mikes on. Suddenly, Whoosh! Wham! Our airplane rose the noise of an explosion deafened me. The cold hand of panic clutched at my heart I heard the sound of metal clattering along the fuselage and tail. I felt a blow on the back of the turret: a Me 109 lined up on our port quarter and started to hare in to attack.

As the German attack opened, every bomber in the vicinity fired off a red Very cartridge, signalling their own fighters. The Mustangs came down at full bore and two of them joined in this particular melee but one was shot down immediately. About 40 Me 109 had circled above and slightly to port of the Lancasters and about 20 of them dived down and attacked from 300 yards astern. Leslie Harlow, piloting *H-Harry*, was leading a vic of three with Flying Officer Ronald Martin Herapath RAAF on 195 Squadron in the box in *C-Charlie*. Harlow and his engineer observed dog fights on the port bow level. George Gardiner, Harlow's mid-upper gunner, spotted and identified three Messerschmitt 109s in formation standing off on a parallel course at about a thousand yards range. The fighters wasted no time but immediately flipped over and developed a perfect curve-of-pursuit attack, picking one bomber apiece and leaving Herapath, who put his nose down and dived straight out of the box. *C-Charlie* was pounced on below, shot up and was seen disappearing through the clouds leaving a great trail of smoke. Herapath and five of crew were killed and only one man survived to be taken prisoner. When the

Messerschmitts had closed to 600 yards Leslie Harlow heard Sergeant Dick Moseley his rear gunner giving the word to go and corkscrewed to port violently. Moseley, born in Barry, South Wales and brought up in the Forest of Dean was 18, pleasant, likeable and a strong character with a dry sense of humour, reliable with a cool head in emergency, dependable and proud of his Welsh nationality. Moseley only got 60 rounds away when a hydraulic leak stopped his guns firing but he kept briefing the rest of the crew on what was happening and what to do about it. Gardiner let the enemy have it and shot the enemy down despite one of his two guns having a stoppage, which he was able to clear immediately.

Q-Queenie, the Lancaster on the starboard side piloted by Flight Sergeant Robert Edward Roberts RAAF, was hit by flak. Rowland Mason, the rear gunner on *J-Jig* flown by Flight Lieutenant John B O'Brien, whose crew were on their 18th trip, noticed that the Lancaster was flying with its 'followers' slightly higher and behind on their port quarter:

> Suddenly there was a terrific explosion and *Q-Queenie* disappeared in one big bang. It was a case of 'first you see them and then you don't.' All the crew were friends of ours. They were gone to glory. They never knew what hit them. It must have been a direct hit in the bomb bay. It was one big melee, aircraft being slung about all over the sky, the bombers endeavouring to reach their target and drop their bomb load and at the same time taking evasive action where possible from the enemy fighters. I saw two Lancasters shot down by fighters, one of which was attacked by a 109 who sat on his tail as it spiralled down still firing. I recall saying at the time 'Doing a corkscrew wouldn't shake off that guy. One Me 109 who I think must have made an attack on our aircraft whizzed past my turret so close that I thought if I had reached out I could have touched him. I don't know who was the most surprised. I know that I was because he crossed from the port side and down – can't remember being scared but on reflection I couldn't have been otherwise.[1]

The other 'follower' was holed in the No. 1 port side tank but he stuck gamely to Harlow through the complicated movements of the corkscrew, his guns blazing away splendidly and he registered strikes on both a 109 and a twin-engined Messerschmitt fighter, which broke off the action and disappeared through cloud, being claimed as destroyed although proof in such cases was hard to establish. Harlow did not have time to close his bomb doors. The Lancaster took it without a murmur although the increased drag, particularly on the first dive of the corkscrew must have been very great. As they straightened up with the fighters beaten off, they could see aircraft in their own vicinity trying to get back into position in time to bomb. They finished their run as well as they could. Gussie Gordon's navigation gear was all over the inside of the aircraft and his 'Gee' charts had disappeared entirely, probably sucked through the floor of the bomb bay.

As the 109 came racing in on Harry Warwick's Lancaster he said in a calm voice: 'It's okay, boys. I've got her and we're under control.'

Ivor Turley's turret seemed slow and sluggish as he turned and sighted to meet the attack:

My foot felt a hole in the bottom of the turret metal grating on metal. I subconsciously realised we were flying in flak. My sights lined up. I had him: the air felt thin. Crump! Whoosh! Wham! Another explosion. The airplane jumped, shook, shuddered: I could hear metal tearing. I dimly realised we were trailing smoke from our port wing: a black circle started from the outside of my vision. It was closing in. The Me 109 was still in my sights. Its spinner looked enormous. The blackness closed further. I was looking through a hole. 'Fire, fire, fire the bloody guns!' I was screaming to myself. Cracks appeared across my vision: a flash of Perspex pieces and cold air hit me. A piercing pain in my chest; no strength in my arms. I saw the yellow belly of the 109 as he pulled up in my sights. I struggled. 'My oxygen's gone' I said over the intercom.

Just after bombs away C- *Charlie*'s crew switched on the new VHF to hear Frank Blenkin just behind them saying 'there's quite a lot of fluid coming out of your aeroplane Harry.'

Ivor Turley came to, sitting on the Elsan closet, which was situated forward of the tail-plane spars:

My oxygen pipe was plugged in: a pair of knees was in front of me. A dark figure holding an oxygen bottle was in front of me: a tube from the oxygen bottle was connected to his mask. I gave a thumbs-up and waved the body away. I was all right. The body showed me my intercom plug and signalled me to plug into a lead hanging in the fuselage. Giving me thumbs-up, he turned and struggled his way forward. It was Joe. I plugged into the intercom and reported to the Skipper. 'Hello Skipper, rear-gunner here. I'm okay now. Joe is going back.'

'Good show' replied Harry, 'we'll soon have you home.'

'How are we doing and where are we?' I asked.

'We've bombed the target and we're on our way home' replied Harry. 'The starboard inner has been hit and we've got holes in the wing. We're trailing fuel but don't worry, we're under control.'

Harry sounded as calm as ever. I was sure he was enjoying every minute I took stock of my surroundings. The fuselage was torn and I could see the petrol gushing along the trailing edge of our port wing. Turning, I looked towards and beyond my turret. We were leaving a trail of vapour. I got up and tried to crawl back to my turret, stretching the oxygen pipe as far as it would go. I couldn't reach the turret, quite: but I could see it was useless: no bottom to it, no Perspex; jagged chunks of fuselage curled in from the tail unit. Oil was everywhere from the broken servo pipes. I crawled backwards and sat once more on the Elsan closet. I was useless and felt it, sitting there looking through the flak holes. Just morbid curiosity – a bloody useless gunner!

'How are we doing Tom?' Harry's voice came over the intercom.

'We're losing fuel fast,' replied Tom. 'We won't make it if we follow the stream.'

'Okay Tom,' said Harry. 'Alec, plot us the straightest course to base, will you? Give me a heading: we're leaving the main stream.'

'I've already got it,' replied Alec.

I felt the airplane turning and through a flak hole I saw the rest of the stream flying further to port as we left them. We would soon be on our own and at the mercy of any fighter who cared to jump us, or any ack-ack gunner who cared to lay his sights with care.

'How's the petrol Tom?' asked Harry. 'Have we got enough?'

'Yes' replied Tom, 'I've worked out that we can make it to Woodbridge on three at the present rate.'

I quickly looked out of a hole on the port side. Looking forward at the wing I saw that the port outer engine was stopped and prop feathered. We were flying on three engines.

'Okay boys, don't worry; we'll make it,' said Harry. 'We've got enough petrol and she's flying okay. Stay on intercom though.'

'Hello Skipper, we've got company on the starboard beam – a fighter.'

My heart jumped as Mac's voice hit the intercom. A fighter and me helpless: this must be it. 'It's one of ours. It's okay,' said Mac.

I looked out of a hole in the starboard side and saw a Mustang [flown by Flight Sergeant Wright from Andrews Field] jinking to form up with us on our starboard beam. He moved in close, tucking his wing in behind ours and slightly below. I could see the pilot looking at us: he gave us a thumbs-up signal and moved out slightly to take up a steady formation position on our starboard beam.

'Yes, we've got company, boys,' said Harry. 'He'll look after us now.'

I felt relief flood through me: the sight of a Mustang fighter sitting close to us was glorious. At least I fell that the danger from fighter attack had diminished: things were looking up – the situation wasn't half so bad now. A sudden vibration shook the airplane: an engine coughed and missed a beat. I felt us dip to port.

'Port inner's going' said Harry. 'I'm feathering now.'

Suddenly all the noise seemed to be on the starboard side as Harry cut the port inner engine. The notes from the starboard engine became higher as revs were increased. The airplane twisted to starboard as Harry lowered the starboard wing. I saw the alien tail wires move as Harry corrected the tail position. Fortunately, although they ran down the length of the fuselage and disappeared into the tail section by the Elsan. They had not been hit. I quickly ran my eyes along the cables and pulleys: they seemed okay. A flak hole was just above a pulley on the fuselage. An inch lower and the pulley would have been smashed and the wires severed.

'Okay boys, I've got her okay' said Harry. 'We're flying and losing height a little: we're 14,000 feet now. How's the petrol Tom?'

'I'm not sure' said Tom. 'We're getting very low though: I'll have to work it out again – we seem to be losing much faster.'

'Hello Alec: are we still on course for Woodbridge? We're losing height and the air speed is dropping. I'll have to keep the nose down a little to maintain flying speed. What rate of descent can I have on this course? I'm going straight in at Woodbridge: no circuit,' said Harry.

'Twelve thousand feet now, Alec' said Harry.

I looked down. The cloud-tops were very close. It was still ten tenths cover: they were coming up to meet us, so it seemed.

'Where are we now, Alec?' said Harry.

'Somewhere over the Zuider Zee in Holland' was the reply.

'Sorry Skip, we won't make it,' said Tom suddenly over the intercom. The tempo quickened.

What now? I thought. I listened hard, oblivious to everything except the shaking and shuddering of the airplane and the voices on the intercom. My thoughts and concentration were on the situation at hand: my nerves were taut, but I was now quite calm. Things were happening fast. I had nothing to do. I could just sit and concentrate on what was going on up front. There was heavy breathing on the intercom – Harry, I presumed, struggling to keep the airplane flying.

'Ten thousand feet now Alec: 130 knots' said Harry.

'We won't make it Harry' came Alec's low, calm voice. 'We're too low unless you can glide us in most of the way, or stay at this height for a bit.'

Splutter! Roar! Splutter! The airplane dipped and then pulled up as power was suddenly lost and restored.

'The starboard inner's going' said Harry. There was a sudden increase in engine noise and just as suddenly it was cut by half.

'Starboard inner engine's severed' said Harry.

'We've lost too much petrol anyway' said Tom. 'She's packed up. I'm on wing-tanks to starboard: we're losing them. I can't balance the tanks.'

'Okay Tom' said Harry. 'I'll try and hold her on the starboard outer, but we're losing height fast.'

The revs on the starboard outer increased: the engines screamed. The airplane shuddered and yawed.

'Okay boys, do we bail out or stay with the airplane?' asked Harry. 'We're over the Zuider Zee but with a bit of luck we can get to the North Sea and ditch her.'

Without hesitation we all reported to stay with Harry and the airplane I didn't much fancy a drop into the Zuider Zee anyway I now more than ever wanted to stay with OUR airplane and MY crew.

'Okay boys' said Harry, 'let's see how far we can go. We're at 9,000 feet and just entering the cloud. Joe, send out emergency signals: give us our position, Alec.'

'Okay Harry,' said Joe, 'signal going out.'

Alec gave Harry our position as somewhere over the Zuider Zee. If we maintained our present course we would be over the sea in fifteen minutes – but close to the Dutch Coast.

'We're at 8,000 feet,' called Harry.

Suddenly there was a change in engine note. It went very low, coughed and stopped. The nose of the airplane dropped, slipstream and wind screamed. I sat and watched: I felt the airplane dip as we lost height. I felt the negative 'G' lifting me from my seat on the Elsan closet. I gripped the rim of the seat: THIS WAS IT! I was paralysed. To go in from this height we hadn't a chance. There were no thoughts of either past or future, only a gaze up the fuselage, past the well of the mid-upper's turret, past the first compartment, through the cabin to the half noon. I could just see the cockpit window: not a sign of other bods, no movements, just numbness. Suddenly, with a cough and a roar, the starboard outer engine picked up and I felt a little surge as the airplane yawed. I thought: God, at this height he must be joking, but he wanted us in position so that he could concentrate on flying the plane. 'I'll call out our altitude as we go down. Stay on intercom and don't worry, we'll be okay.' Harry, I was now sure, was enjoying it. My confidence soared for a moment: I felt happy that it was Harry at the controls.

I disconnected my oxygen pipe and intercom plug and moved forward to help Mac who was sliding down from his turret. Bill, our bomb aimer, was squeezing through a fuselage doorway and I saw him getting onto the bunk, his ditching position. Mac jettisoned the overhead escape hatch and we lay down on the floor that formed the top of the bomb bay. Mac on the left of me, our feet placed firmly on the flapjack funnel to stop us sliding forward, knees slightly flexed. I plugged into the intercom point hanging next to me: Mac did not have an intercom point on his side and was to rely on me and my signals. I put my left around his shoulder and gave him a squeeze: looking at each other we smiled. I lifted the ear-flap of his helmet and yelled above the noise into his ear. 'I'll give you a squeeze as we're about to hit. I'll show height on my fingers. Can you hear me?'

Mac raised his hand and gave thumbs-up. I clipped my mask to my face, switched it on my mike and reported. 'Rear and mid-upper gunner's in position Skipper and good luck.' The crew reported in turn and then all that could be heard on the Intercom was the sound of fast heavy breathing. I lay there with Mac, listening to the roar of our one engine seeing the fuselage twitch as we rolled and yawed and the Skipper corrected. There were no other thoughts except what if I broke a leg or arm on impact? Would it hurt much?

'Four thousand feet' called Harry. I signalled 'four' to Mac and just as I did this the engine coughed and went dead. The nose tilted forward: just as suddenly the engine roared into life. We straightened up: the airplane twisted and yawed. 'Three thousand feet' said Harry.

I signalled 'three' to Mac. This time the engine kept roaring. A few seconds after it cut again, only to roar into life as we dipped forward. It seemed to me that somewhere petrol was swilling into the carburettor pipes when we dipped forward sufficiently to cause the engine to pick up as long as the prop turned it over. I lay perfectly calm now, listening and waiting for what was now inevitable.'

'Can't see a bloody thing yet' came Harry's voice. We're still in cloud.

Once more the engine cut and the nose dipped. I waited for it to roar into life again. It didn't. The wind started to howl. 'Two thousand feet' shouted Harry. 'One thousand feet'. God, we're going in fast, I thought. Sweat broke on my skin: Mac was looking at me with a frown and puzzled look on his face. I signalled 'one'. Mac looked at me as though to say 'what happened to two'? I looked at him, gently held him closer and shook my head, listening hard. I felt Mac start to tense his body: he too probably realised we were going to hit fast and hard.

Suddenly, with a cough and roar, the engine started again: the airplane swung, the nose pulled up and the tail went down a little. 'I see it' shouted Harry. 'Four hundred feet. Stand by for impact.'

I squeezed Mac's shoulder hard and we braced each other. I squeezed harder several times, quickly turning my head to Mac I tried with my right hand to grab the side of the fuselage – and then 'WHAM"'! The inside of the airplane then blurred with vibration: I wasn't conscious of it stopping or slewing around – just a sudden surge of water from Lord knows where and suddenly I was on my feet. Mac was already up: a wave of water poured through the escape hatch, which had been open above our heads in the roof

though the Belgian port of Antwerp had been occupied by the British Second Army on
September 1944, it could not be used while the mouth of the River Scheldt, on which it lay, was
minated by the German-held island of Walcheren. After a number of attacks on enemy artillery
tteries there, Bomber Command dispatched 252 Lancasters, led by seven *Oboe* Mosquitoes, on a
ylight operation on 3 October to breach the island's protective dykes at Westkapelle. (*IWM*)

Halifax III of 6 Group over the oil plant at Wanne-Eickel in the Ruhr on 12 October 1944. Only
e aircraft failed to return from this operation, but three more were written off in crashes in Britain
their return. (*IWM*)

On 21 October, seventy-five Lancasters of 3 Group carried out a daylight attack on a German coast battery at Flushing on the Dutch Island of Walcheren. Bombing was very accurate and one Lancaster failed to return.

Halifax II Z5-E LL599 on 462 Squadron at Driffield, which on 23 October 1944 collided with Lancaster III LM691 on 625 Squadron on the return from the operation on Essen. Both aircraft exploded. Flying Officer Frank Edward Neider RAAF and five crew died, and only Flight Sergeant J Grace RAAF managed to bail out, landing safely behind Allied lines. Squadron Leader C W C Hamilton, the pilot of the Lancaster, was the only one to survive on his aircraft and he too landed safely behind Allied lines.

Lancaster III PB509 OJ-C, a 'G-H' leader with horse and chariot nose art begins to roll from its dispersal at Methwold early in 1945.

On 16 November 1944 in support of a US Army offensive, 1,880 RAF Bomber Command 'heavies' attacked the supposedly fortified towns of Duren (pictured), Jülich and Heinsburg, ahead of the advance.

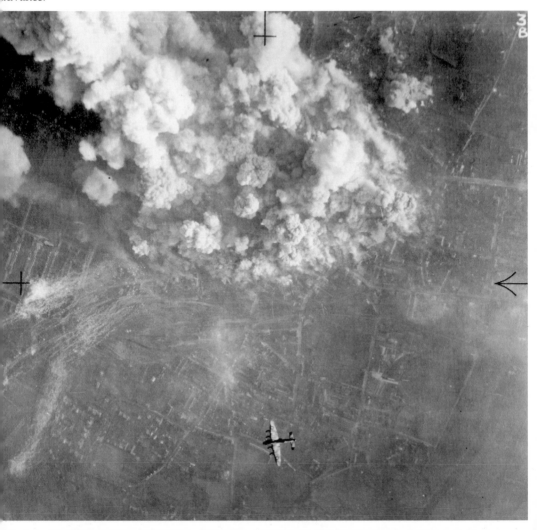

Duren from 10,000 feet on 16 November 1944.

The marshalling yards at Rheydt from 20,000 feet on 27 December 1944. Some 200 Lancasters and eleven Mosquitoes of 1, 3, 5 and 8 Groups attacked the yards for the loss of one Lancaster, and one Mosquito that crashed behind the Allied lines in Holland.

Left) Leutnant Gustav Mohr, a *Wild Boar* Bf 109 pilot, claimed five night *Abschüsse* serving with 2./NJG 1 from 1 September to December 1944. Whilst shooting down his fifth victim (a Lancaster) on 12/13 December 1944 he was injured by return fire and was forced to bail out of his Bf 109G-6, which effectively ended his career in the *Nachtjagd*. (*Steve Hall via John Foreman*)

Right) Flight Sergeant George Thompson, the 24-year-old Scottish wireless operator on the crew of Flying Officer Harry Denton RNZAF on 9 Squadron, was awarded the VC for his bravery on the raid on the Dortmund-Ems Canal at Ladbergen on New Year's Day 1945.

Halifax III MZ335 KN-A on 77 Squadron suffered an engine failure on take-off from Full Sutton for Ludwigshafen at 15:04 hours on 2 January 1945 and Flight Sergeant D W Muggeridge bellied-in beyond the airfield perimeter. All the crew scrambled to safety but the aircraft was declared a write-off. (*IWM*)

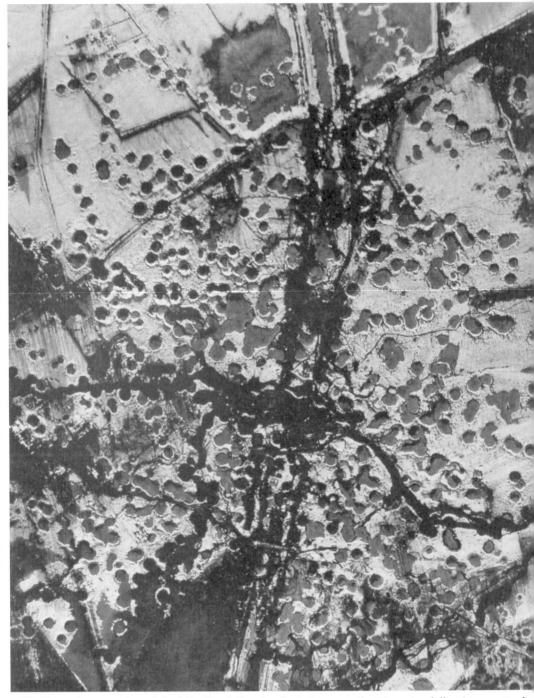

The Gravenhorst section of the Mittelland Canal, where it crosses the River Aa, following an attack by 152 Lancasters and five Mosquitoes of 5 Group on the night of 1/2 January 1945, which pitted half a mile of banks with bomb craters and successfully breached some parts of the waterway. No aircraft were lost. (*IWM*)

…e ground crew of Lancaster III ND458 *Able Mabel* of 100 Squadron who had serviced the aircraft …ce arrival on the squadron congratulate Canadian pilot Flight Lieutenant John 'Jack' D Playford …c RCAF, who flew the aircraft on twenty-six ops including its 100th on 1 February 1945. Sergeant … Hearn, who was from West Wickham, shakes hands with Playford, while Corporal R T Withey …m Henley and LACs J E Robinson from Solihull, J Hales from Tottenham, and J Cowls from …nzance, look on. *Able Mabel*, which has 119 ops on the bomb log, was destined to complete …4 ops, the 127th and last operational raid being 25 April to Berchtesgaden. *Able Mabel* also flew an …odus trip on 27 April and six *Manna* sorties. Another aircraft, ND644 HW-N *N-Nan*, completed …2 sorties on the squadron before it was lost on 16/17 March 1945.

…ancaster I R5868 *S-Sugar* …n 467 Squadron RAAF at an American base on 8 February 1945. The Göring quotation, 'NO ENEMY PLANE WILL FLY OVER THE REICH …ERRITORY' was added …y LAC Willoughby, one of the engine fitters, around the time that *Sugar* had completed eighty-eight ops. (*USAF*)

Halifax III MZ465 MH-Y on 51 Squadron flown by Flying Officer A L Wilson, which was involved in a mid-air collision with LL590/L on 347 (French) Squadron over Saarbrücken on 13/14 January 1945. Wilson's navigator, Flight Sergeant T S H Whitehouse and bomb aimer Flight Sergeant David Hauber, who were in the nose at the time of the impact, were killed. Nine feet of the nose section was destroyed but Wilson flew back with only three instruments working and landed at Ford.

Lancaster I (Special) PD119 YZ-J on 617 Squadron, one of thirty-three aircraft modified in February 1945 to carry the 22,000lb 'Grand Slam' deep-penetration bomb. Mk I Specials were flown without wireless operators and had their front and mid-upper turrets removed. The first operational drop of a 'Grand Slam' was on 14 March when fourteen Lancasters carrying 'Tallboys' and one with a 'Grand Slam' destroyed the Bielefeld railway viaduct which carried the main line from Hamm to Hannover. (*IWM*).

Pölitz from 14,000 feet on 8/9 February 1945 when 475 Lancasters and seven Mosquitoes of 1, 5 and 8 Groups attacked it in two waves, the first being marked and carried out entirely by the 5 Group method and the second being marked by the Pathfinders of 8 Group. Twelve Lancasters were lost; one of which went down in Sweden. (*via 'Pat' Patfield*)

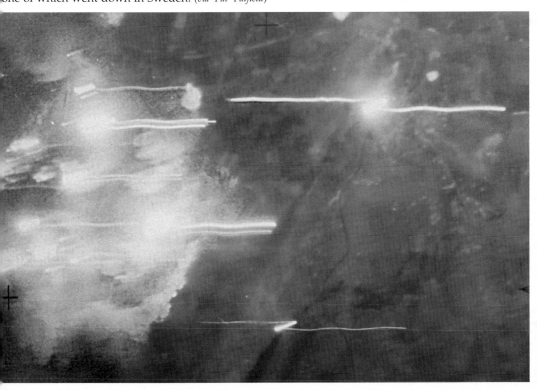

Engine fitters working on Lancaster I HK593 JN-X on 75 Squadron RNZAF at Mepal, Cambridgeshire on 9 February 1945. (*IWM*)

The raid on Dresden in progress on the night of 13/14 February 1945. The city was devastated by 796 Lancasters, and by 311 bombers of the 8th Air Force the following day. (*IWM*)

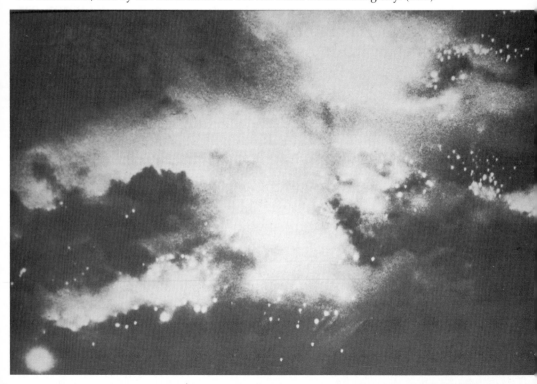

Fires in Dresden on the night of 13/14 February 1945.

A victim of the bombing.

TIs going down over Pforzheim on the night of 23/24 February 1945 when 367 Lancasters and thirteen Mosquitoes of 1, 6, and 8 Groups, and a Film Unit Lancaster, carried out the first and only area-bombing raid of the war on this target. Ten Lancasters were lost and two more crashed in France. The marking and bombing, from only 8,000 feet, were particularly accurate and 1,825 tons bombs were dropped in 22 minutes. More than 17,000 people died.

Free French Halifax crew on 347 'Tunisie' Squadron at Elvington, Yorkshire in March 1945. (*IWM*)

2,000lb bomb with the Cross of Lorraine and 'Pour Hitler' chalked on the side being loaded into a
7 Squadron Halifax at Elvington. (*IWM*)

lifaxes on 1664 HCU in a hangar at Dishforth in March 1945. (*IWM*)

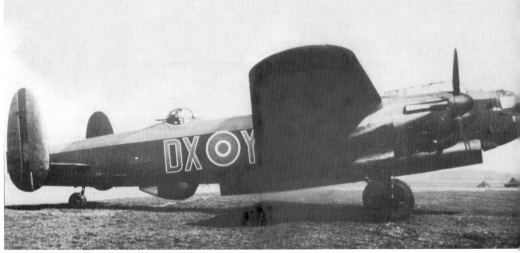

Lancaster I RA530 DX-Y *Y-Yorker* on 57 Squadron with the squadron's identification stripes of a black vertical bar on a red background. *Yorker* hit a house at Stickney after take-off from East Kirkby at 23.45 hours on 20 March 1945 on the operation on Bohlen. Flying Officer Charles Alan Cobern RAAF and two of his crew were killed; a third man died of his injuries on 1 April. The two other crew members were injured.

Sergeant J Nicholson, mid-upper gunner, Flight Sergeant Jack Bold, bomb aimer and Sergeant M McCutcheon, rear gunner boarding Lancaster III PA995 BQ-V *The Vulture Strikes!* of 550 Squadron at North Killingholme for its 100th operation on the night of 5/6 March 1945, when the target was Chemnitz. The aircraft was piloted by Pilot Officer George E Blackler, who flew *The Vulture Strikes* on twenty-seven raids, plus one abort and one recall, out of his tour of 37 ops, and returned safely. Blackler then became tour-expired, going to 1656 CU. PA995 was lost on its next sortie, a raid on Dessau on 7/8 March, when Flying Officer Cyril John Jones RCAF and crew failed to return. Jones and two Canadian crewmen, John Buckmaster and Leslie Harvey, were killed. The four other crew were taken prisoner. (*IWM*)

Halifax LV937/MH-E *Expensive Babe* on 51 Squadron which recorded its 100th op on the Osnabrück raid on 25 March 1945. Group Captain B D Sellick DFC, the station commander at Snaith, was there to greet the crew on their return. They were Flight Lieutenant R Kemp, pilot; Flight Sergeant A C Townsend, navigator; Flight Sergeant J D Silberberg, air bomber; Warrant Officer R J Williams, wireless operator; Sergeant E S Hawkins, flight engineer; Flight Sergeant R T Jackson, air gunner; and Flight Sergeant F Thwaites, air gunner. Townsend and Silberberg were Australians and Hawkins a New Zealander. LV937 had started out with 578 Squadron in March 1944, with which it served for only a month. The swastika symbol is for a Ju88 claim.

Lancasters bracketed by heavy flak on 10 March 1945 when 155 Lancasters of 3 Group carried out a G-H attack on the oil refinery at Scolven/Buer. No aircraft were lost. *('Spud' Taylor)*

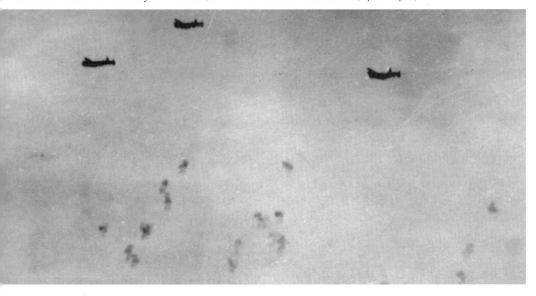

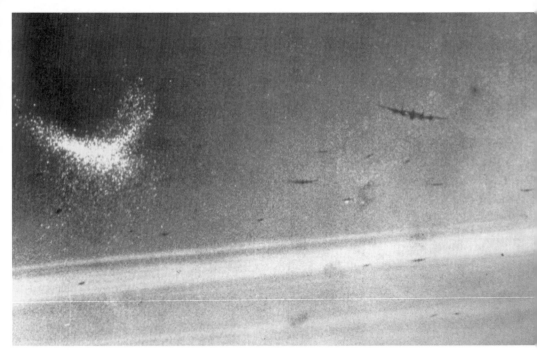

In the largest daylight raid of the war, on 11 March 1945, a cloud of 'Window' goes down over Essen to disrupt gun-laying radar as Bomber Command launched the 28th and last main force raid on the doomed city. The 1,079 aircraft from all groups was the second largest total ever sent out by Bomber Command to a single target. Only three Lancasters were lost. As a complete undercast veiled Essen, *Oboe* marking was used. Extensive cloud can be seen in this photograph. More raids were made on Essen than on any other city in Germany, laying waste an estimated 50 per cent of this major site of Ruhr industry. *(IWM)*

Flight Sergeant J P Jackson and his crew survived when Lancaster JB228 on 1668 HCU crashed on landing at Fiskerton on 10 March 1945.

of the fuselage. Mac moved to the emergency dinghy release cord housed along the top right-hand side of the fuselage. It was housed in a long tube with convenient gaps like the communication cord on a train. Mac pulled: the cord came easy. Hand over hand he pulled until his hand held the broken end of cord. He waved it at me. 'It's broken' he said. 'Must have been the impact.'

I was now conscious of the up and down movement of the floor. We were still floating – but for how long? I glanced back and to my horror saw that the aircraft had broken in two just aft of the bomb bay. The tail-plane and my turret were beginning to float away. Must get out quickly now, I thought: this lot will go down any minute. Sea water sprayed and slopped around our feet. Mac was signalling quickly to use the escape hatch. I pushed him up through it as he swung himself up: I pulled myself up. Mac was kneeling on top of the fuselage: he grabbed my arm and shoulder and pulled them as I squeezed and struggled through the hatch. My bulky flying clothing didn't make it easy.

At last I was on top of the fuselage. Harry was just pulling clear through the escape hatch which had been over his head. For a moment he sat on the edge on top of the cockpit canopy with his back to us. He looked round as he pulled his legs clear he was grinning at us.

'Well boys, we made it,' he shouted to us. A look of triumph was on his face. For a brief moment I felt that all was over and then just as quickly I felt that now we had to survive.

The next phase was just starting. Harry slid down onto the starboard wing and joined Alec, Tom and Joe, who were already there. I must admit I very vaguely remember others getting out: I remember Bill popping up and struggling out of his escape hatch with a yellow parcel, but everything had happened so quickly – much faster than one could read and write.

'Where's the bloody dinghy?' shouted Mac from the top of the fuselage.

Joe looked up from the wing where he was standing. 'Still in the hatch' he shouted, pointing to the dinghy panel in the wing. 'Nothing's worked' he explained.

We all slithered down onto the wing. It's queer, but I was not conscious of any pitching or tossing or of bods holding onto each other. I don't remember an engine or cowl; only us bods standing on the starboard wing looking at the dinghy panel and the line of reddish-brown tape sealing the panel all around. At the top right corner a Perspex panel showed, with water occasionally swilling across its face. There were several automatic dinghy release systems on the airplane, including the manual one which Mac had used, none of which had worked. We were down in the drink all right, but no dinghy. Joe was the first to move: standing over the panel he hammered the Perspex panel with the heel of his flying boot. After several blows it smashed. Alec was already kneeling. He had the least flying clothing on and as soon as the panel broke he thrust his arm into the hole. In a few seconds there was a bang and a hiss: the dinghy exploded violently as it inflated. A wave broke over the leading edge of the wing and washed the dinghy and Alec off the wing. The sea rapidly swept the dinghy and Alec away from the wing and towards the broken tail section, which was still floating about six feet away and to the rear of the fuselage, the gap spanned by chains of ammunition which was feeding along the ducts from panniers in the main fuselage. The weight was causing the belts of ammunition to sag in the middle.

Suddenly I saw Alec's head rise in the water and hit the bottom of the tail-plane fuselage: he was still holding the dinghy. Without hesitation I jumped into the icy water: I pushed to swim as best I could towards Alec. I had the most clothing on and was a good swimmer: those few yards in the icy water taxed my strength to the limit. I reached the dinghy and then tried to swim with it towards the rest of the crew standing on the wing. It was useless: the sea water was in my mouth: my Mae West kept me afloat, but my flying clothing was getting waterlogged. I kicked off my flying boots and immediately felt the icy water round my feet and legs. I suddenly became afraid that the dinghy would swing round the tail-plane and be washed away. It should have been secured by a green ratline so that it couldn't wash away, but I could not find it. In an ideal situation it should have been floating with its tether and we should have left the airplane to step into an already inflated dinghy, keeping reasonably dry in the process 'Come on' I yelled, 'you'll have to swim for it.'

The boys jumped in and with much thrashing of turbulent water made their way towards the dinghy. As they were swimming I made my way round the tossing dinghy to try and find the rope ladder hanging from the side. I found it, but my flying clothing was so heavy and waterlogged and I felt so weary that I couldn't use it. My legs and feet were numb: I couldn't feel them anyway. I turned the dinghy and let the rope ladder face the rest of the boys as they splashed and converged on the dinghy. I held onto the ratline round the dinghy to keep afloat. GOD, I was cold and numb!

I screwed my face and pressed it to the wall of the dinghy: anything to stop the icy spray and sea hitting me. I could feel the bobbing up and down: it was quite violent now. I felt myself being pulled up by many hands: the rest of the crew in the dinghy were helping to heave me up. I kicked up and felt myself being pulled over the rounded edge of the dinghy. I had a fleeting vision of wet knees and legs: the side of the dinghy pressed into my tummy as I rocked over the side. Someone was sitting on my head and my face plunged into the water washing around in the bottom of the dinghy. I felt someone pulling the seat of my pants, struggling to pull me aboard – I wasn't moving. In a flash I realised what had happened. Putting my hands across my face and then pushing hard on the dinghy bottom, I managed to turn my head and lift it. 'Push me back!' I screamed. 'I'm stuck: Push me back!'

Fortunately, above the noise of the sea and wind, they heard me and pushed me back into the water. The inflation lever on my Mae West had slid under the dinghy ratline and I'd been hooked to the outside of the dinghy. The offending lever had disengaged as I slid back and this time, with an almighty jump and pull, I landed flop into the fluorescent-stained water in the dinghy.

The boys were already hauling in the ration boxes and etceteras, which were tied by cords to various parts around the dinghy. For the first time we noticed Alec's hand as he was trying to wrap a sodden handkerchief round his finger. There was blood everywhere.

'What have you done, Alec?' asked Harry.

'Oh, it's nothing' said Alec. 'I cut my finger getting the dinghy out. It's nothing to worry about.'

The dinghy was tethered all right: the ratline I'd looked for had fouled the wreckage under the tail-plane and the dinghy was tethered close to the tail unit. No wonder I couldn't find it or swim with the dinghy back to the wing! Using the special curved knife Joe, who was nearest the tail, severed the cord. As Joe was doing this we undid the hand-panels from the ration tin and proceeded to paddle like fury away from the broken fuselage. At first we didn't make much headway but slowly we moved away from the floating wreckage. When we were about 20 to 30 yards away we stopped paddling. This was the time to take stock of our position and bandage Alec's finger.

Bill the air bomber was on my left side, Alec was on my right, with Mac, Joe, Tom and Harry sitting round in that order. Our feet were all together in the middle. Ration boxes and cords swirled in the water round our feet and formed a fine old tangle. Harry was opening the ration packet and was pulling out the first aid box. I had found the tins of various pistol cartridges and stuffed some down the bosom of my Mae West to keep them dry. Alec was removing the handkerchief from his finger. Yes, it was only a cut: it looked as though he had torn half his finger off. It was typical of Alec: only a cut!'

'Good Lord, Alec!' Harry exclaimed. 'That doesn't look so good.'

'Oh, it'll be all right: just put a bandage on it,' said Alec.

A large lump of flesh and skin fell from the in-turned finger and hung by a thread from the tip. Hurriedly Alec replaced the piece: he didn't intend leaving any part of himself behind. Leaning across Harry bound up the finger with a bandage he had produced: not a word was spoken and all was silent except for the noise of the sea as we all watched Harry roll the bandage clumsily around Alec's finger.

I became aware of an engine sound in the air. Our escort had found us and was now circling low beneath the cloud base. Our faithful escort, still there: I wondered what his thoughts were. I looked round at Bill: he was lower in the dinghy than the rest of us, his shoulders and head were against the wall of the dinghy, he looked ill and blue with cold. He wasn't wearing his flying helmet; neither was I for that matter. I had discarded it when I had removed my parachute harness. Removing the woollen scarf from around my neck I found it reasonably dry. I wrapped it around Bill's head, muffling his ears and throat: his teeth chattering rapidly, he looked a picture of misery.

Looking at the sea once more I noticed that we had floated further from the airplane. The swell seemed to be getting heavier, tossing the dinghy up and down mercilessly. The icy spray showered over us, stinging my face and eyes. The water in the bottom of the dinghy was increasing in volume and getting deeper. Harry spoke. 'Well, boys, this is it: thank God we're all alive. We could be much worse off than we are now: the first stage is past: we'd better take stock of ourselves and our position Have you any idea where we are, Alec?'

With his good hand Alec fumbled inside his Mae West and produced a sodden and crumpled map. Trust Alec to rescue his precious map, I thought. Good old Alec! 'Well, Harry' he said, 'I took a bearing when you gave us the order to take up ditching positions. I estimated then that we were off the Dutch coast, probably some ten miles. Taking that position as definite and working approximately, I'd say we are between 20 to 40 miles off the Dutch coast and in line with The Hague. In all possibility, we are about half way between England and Holland. My watch has stopped – I imagine with the shock of hitting the drink. If that was the case we ditched at 15.20 exactly. If you like I'll work from that and the time of my last bearing and get you a more definite position.'

'No, that doesn't matter' replied Harry. 'There isn't much that we can do if we know. Joe, was the wireless working?'

'I was sending our position from just aft of the target' replied Joe. 'Right up to your order to take ditching stations. I can't tell whether the messages were picked up or not. In any case, when we were down to one engine the set wouldn't be getting any juice except from the batteries and I may not have been able to transmit a signal with any degree of strength.'

'Okay' said Harry. 'In any case our faithful escort up there should be able to let them know we're okay and give our position.'

We all looked up: our escort was still circling. Mac grabbed a paddle and waved it and I did likewise and then we were all waving. It was quite some comfort to know that someone was watching us. 'We'd better bale some of this water out,' said Harry. I took the first aid tin, emptied its contents and started to bale. 'While we're at it we'll put the weather apron up. We may not get picked up tonight it'll give us some protection. It'll be damn cold tonight and we may not be in very good condition in the morning. They'll have a job finding us if this mist and low cloud persist. It'll lessen our chances of being picked up' went on Harry.

We unpacked the weather apron: this was a large band of rubber, yellow in colour and at intervals round its edges were leather tongues. These were threaded into corresponding buckets on the outside of the dinghy until it was fitted on the whole circumference. By pulling the top edge of the canopy over our heads and towards the centre of the dinghy a continuous canopy round the dinghy was formed It gave good protection and kept the wind and the spray off us. During this operation Bill was violently sick, spitting and gurgling: seasickness was adding to his discomfort. How long now before we all succumbed to it? I hoped that I would be a good sailor for I'd heard some pretty awful tales of a desire for a quick death when it hit you.

Having fixed the canopy I started to bale once more, throwing the water back over the canopy which I had pulled round my shoulders. I had to do something to stop me thinking and brooding. Coldness had me in its grip: my soaked underclothes felt unpleasantly clammy, my legs and feet were both numb and painful, I was shivering and my teeth started to chatter. I clamped my jaws hard together: I stopped baling – there wasn't much water left in the dinghy. Harry and Alec were looking round, searching. Harry had the Very pistol in his hand, ready to fire if he saw any sign of a boat. I looked round and saw, some way off, that the main fuselage of the airplane was still floating. The tail unit had gone down, taking with it my turret and a few possessions I had been forced to leave behind.

Sickness began to squirm in my stomach: Bill was still being sick, but there was nothing there for him to get rid of – unless his stomach came loose! Within a minute of feeling sick I was leaning over the side, weather apron down. Try as I may I couldn't fight it down. I was thankful to get rid of the fluorescent sea-water I had swallowed. I imagined my stomach was bright yellow with the dye! Once I'd got rid of it I thought that would be the end, but no, I'd had it: for me, during the moments of retching when nothing came up, death couldn't come quick enough. It wasn't long before I felt that I had a knot in every inch of my intestine.

Suddenly a now familiar sound started to fade: it was our escort. We looked up and saw him circle low through the thickening mist: he turned and came straight for us, waggling his wings. He was over us very low and then he was away, the note of his engine fading. He had said farewell, his petrol must have been very low, he had to leave us – and as the noise of his engine died I realised that within half an hour or so he would be home and warm. Good luck Mustang, I thought and thanks a lot. I could feel a sting in my eyes as I gazed at the wall of mist. We were now really on our own.

'Well boys, I'm going to fire the pistol to test it!' exclaimed Harry suddenly. 'If there is anyone looking for us they will see the flare. Our guardian has left us; the petrol must be very low: I hope he makes his base okay. If he does, they'll at least know at home that we're all right and alive and kicking.' Raising the pistol he fired and we all saw the flaming red ball of the distress signal curve into the mist banks. Its glow enveloped us; we watched the ball of fire descend slowly, finally to fizzle out. A trail of smoke marked its passage.

My thoughts took me to base. The rest of the squadron, or most of them were probably back by now, giving all their gen to the Interrogation Officers: we'd be in the news, for quite a few had seen us in trouble. I could imagine the excitement as they discussed the fighters, the flak combats and of course us who hadn't made it back. I looked once more towards our drifting airplane: it was much closer now. We were drifting together again. I saw the fuselage begin to tip a little and as the swell tossed the airplane around I could see the underside of the starboard wing. Too bad we had to lose her – she'd stood up well to the thrashing. It seemed hardly fair that, having got this far, she'd got to end up at the bottom of the drink.

I stared for a while at the now empty sea. I felt a great sorrow, as though I had lost my best friend. Above the noise of the waves and wind, a noise percolated which was different. My mind focussed slowly: I listened – we all suddenly listened to the sound of an airplane flying low. Quickly now Harry loaded the pistol, raised it in the air and fired. No word had been spoken: the red ball of fire curved into the air: once more we were in its ruddy glow, its brilliance all around us. The glow faded as the flare died. The smoky trail lingered a while then slowly dispersed. The noise of the engine grew louder, the vague shape of an airplane loomed through the mist, heading straight for us. It was barely 200 feet up: I recognised it as a Walrus seaplane. We all waved as it turned and circled overhead. An Aldis lamp flashed from the cabin. I thought that we'd be picked up there and then: I looked at the surging, swelling sea and my hopes receded. The flying boat could never land in this sea. Joe was already watching the winking light, his head turning as the Walrus circled. 'He says: position noted and transmitted to Air Sea Rescue' said Joe.

'Good show!' exclaimed Harry. 'They're all getting organised now, but nevertheless it may take some time for a boat to reach us. Even then they'll have to search around: we're bound to drift quite a distance and if night closes in before we're picked up it will make things very awkward for them.'

The Walrus flew away from us, turned and flew straight for us. A small black object fell from the Walrus and plunged into the sea. A few seconds later smoke was seen to billow up from the sea: brown smoke began to drift lazily across the turbulent water – it was a smoke-float. From this they would determine our drift and give the Air-sea Rescue a more definite line to search. Our hopes soared: I felt good and relieved. We now stood an excellent chance of being picked up. It couldn't be long now: the Walrus continued to circle.

I was feeling miserable again: the sickness didn't help any. The horrible retching every few minutes was twisting my intestine into more painful knots. Each time the pain became more intense and persisted longer. I thought of food and decided that I would never eat again. Oddly enough, although a fairly heavy smoker, the thought and desire for a smoke did not at any time occur to me. The hope of rescue was the only thought in my mind. The sound of the Walrus engine fading made me lift my head and look from under the canopy. I searched the cloudy sky: the Walrus had gone. The mist was closing in; the clouds seemed only a couple of hundred feet above our heads. We were alone again and the feeling of depression and eeriness seemed to be everywhere – the only relief being the bright yellow colour of our dinghy.

Alec was keeping watch, the canopy pulled around his shoulders so that only his head was protruding. He looked across at me. 'Okay Ivor?' he asked.

'Sure I'm okay,' I replied. 'We've lost our guardian I notice.'

'Yes but we'll be okay' said Alec.

'The ASR launches are probably on their way to us now' chimed in Harry, whose head had just popped from under the canopy. 'I'll search now for a bit Alec' he continued. 'We'd better not stay exposed too long: we'll probably need our strength for the night.'

The light was fading, the clouds became blacker, the atmosphere oppressive. I felt lonely and forgotten. Gone was the sound of a guardian engine, everywhere now the dull, dismal, grey monotony of sea and cloud. As the light dimmed so did my hopes of being rescued. We were in another world now a world of mystery, fear and strong, unearthly emotions. Over us hung the shadow of death.

Were we destined to become flotsam, tossed here and there on this great expanse of sea, mercilessly, along the highways and byways of the sea? Somehow I wasn't afraid any more: there was no panic or collapse at these thoughts I accepted the position we were in: the scales were poised and the final measure was in the lap of the Gods.

I could feel my legs stiffening with the cold. I moved them about as best I could and started to slap my knees to restore circulation. The retching started again and I felt even more miserable. Not a word was spoken, everyone was deep in thought I had lost all conception of time. There was no longer any measure; everything seemed at a standstill. The monotonous slapping and surging of the sea became even more oppressive: the grey curtain of mist seemed to enfold tighter and tighter about us. Waiting, waiting: would they ever find us? They were probably searching now, but in this weather it would be like looking for a needle in a haystack. I felt tired. My head lolled forward. I wanted to sleep, but somehow I could not. I was getting a headache and this was adding to my discomfort.

A sharp click broke the monotony. It was Harry loading a cartridge into the Very pistol. I pulled the canopy off my head and looked enquiringly at Harry. He was looking around out to sea. 'We'd better let off another flare' he said. 'If there's anyone around they'll want to know our position. They'll have to get cracking, though: it's getting darker.'

'Wouldn't it be better to fire the cartridges in pairs with a half-minute interval?' I said. 'You know one to attract attention and the next for a positive fix. The rescuers may only see the first out of the corner of their eye.'

'That's a good idea' said Harry. 'We'll try it for a while, but we'll have to go easy on the cartridges later on. We'll fire them in pairs until it gets really dark, Then, if we're not picked up, we'll fire one every hour through the night. Let's hope it's a fine day tomorrow.'

With that Harry raised the pistol again and fired. By now heads had appeared above the canopy – anything to break the monotony. Harry re-loaded, counted the seconds and fired again. The lights from the flares died and once more the grey of the mist surrounded us. We all looked round for an answering signal but there was none. One by one heads slowly ducked back beneath the canopy.

'Hey Harry' called Alec suddenly. 'I think I've seen a light.'

'Where, Alec? asked Harry.

'Hold on a minute' said Alec. 'We're in a trough. I've lost it.'

'Yes, there it is Skip,' cried Alec. 'It's a mast light, I'm sure.'

I heard the hammer of the pistol click, the accompanying explosion: the glare of the signal showed red on the canopy. The departing flare hissed and then all was blackness once more. This time it seemed impenetrable No one spoke: I could almost hear my heart thumping.

As the blackness cleared a little I could see that, except Bill who was lying still like a dead man, we were all craning and gazing in one direction.

'I see it, Alec,' exclaimed Harry suddenly. 'It's a ship all right! I could see the navigation lights.'

We rose on another swell and we saw the vague outline of a rapidly approaching ship. Another cartridge fired and we were once more bathed in its ruddy glow. The vessel took shape and we could now see some of the crew lining its side. She looked very big and as she drew nearer seemed to tower above us. We could hear orders being shouted: To me she looked like a destroyer: it was the Navy! We waved and cheered madly. 'Now, boys,' said Harry. 'Let's not make a fuss. Act like gentlemen and lets show the Navy how calm we are and don't forget: women and children first.'

The Skipper of this boat knew his job, for he brought his boat alongside us with about two feet to spare. His fine job was thwarted by a swell which suddenly picked us up and washed us 15 feet away off the ship's port beam. Someone threw a rope: it missed us by about six feet. Another rope snaked out and missed us again. 'Come on, you can't throw straight!' A tall black figure was pushing through the group of men. 'Give me the bloody rope!'

It was the Skipper of the boat. He uncoiled a rope and threw it to land straight across the dinghy: we grabbed it. The boat's Skipper was still shouting something about putting the lot in the dinghy and ended by shouting: 'Get 'em aboard! They've been there long enough!'

I grabbed the bulky ration box and threw it overboard. 'Don't do that, you bloody fool' shouted the Navy Skipper. 'You'll need that if we can't get you aboard tonight.'

Brother, did I feel foolish! He was right: I lugged the ration pack back into the dinghy and, for good measure, sat on it. The Skipper of the boat must have realised the difficulty for after a few minutes of struggling we were still in the dinghy. Although we were alongside the swell which must have risen to 12 feet was tossing us up and down the side of the boat. One minute we'd be level with the deck and the next knocking the keel. The position looked serious; the rope could not be tied to the deck, as we would be tipped out when the sea fell from beneath us, if the rope slipped from the hands holding it we would be washed away again. The position suddenly seemed hopeless again: minutes passed and no progress. As we rose level with the deck outstretched hands tried to grab us: we in turn hadn't the strength to grab and pull.

One of the seamen jumped into the dinghy and tried to bundle Tom onto the deck as we rose level, but it was hopeless. The tossing of the dinghy threw them off balance: it was impossible to stand. All we could do was crouch and try springing at the deck. It was hopeless for, as we tried to jump, the dinghy would fall away. It wouldn't be long before one of us missed and was washed away.

'Get that deck ladder, quickly!' shouted the Navy Skipper. 'We'll try that.'

A short stumpy ladder was produced and was being clipped to the side of the boat deck.

'Now' called the Navy Skipper, 'when you wash level with the ladder get a foot on a rung and let the dinghy drop from under you. We'll do the rest.'

Tom stood up first and as the dinghy rose level with the ladder he clambered onto it and helping hands did the rest. He was on board and being hustled below decks. The wind was now shrieking through the ship's spars: the icy spray whipped us violently with what appeared to be renewed vigour. The dinghy was now filling fast with water as we waited and took our turn. Joe was next: timing was perfect. He stepped aboard as the dinghy fell away: Bill, Mac, Alec next with each swell to the deck ladder. Everyone got aboard. 'Okay Ivor, after you' said Harry. We rose to meet the ladder: I stood up quickly with upraised hands and put my foot on a rung. I was poised on the ladder, the weight of my sodden clothing pulling me back. Hands grabbed me and with a kick I was on my hands and knees on the sea-washed deck. I was hurried below and there were the rest of the boys in the process of stripping off. Towels and hot cocoa were quickly produced. I stripped with great effort, helped by willing seamen. Rubbed down and dry at last, I could feel warmth at last starting to penetrate my flesh. A large mug of hot, steaming cocoa was put gently into my hand: I drank deeply of this nectar.

'Cigarette pal?' A packet of 'Senior Service' was offered. I lit up, inhaled deeply. I was on top of the world!

The boat picking us up was just returning from a patrol and had seen our signal by accident. It took us into Felixstowe, where we were all medically examined. The Mustang that had escorted us had given our position, but we had drifted some distance. The Walrus airplane had given our position but, due to some mix-up, ASR had searched the wrong area and due to heavy seas and bad visibility had given up on us. On phoning the squadron to let them know we were safe, Harry broke the news that Smithy wanted us to pick up a Lanc which had been repaired and fly it back to base. We told him what he could do with his airplane – via Harry, of course!

Apart from the navigator's fingers their only damage was ruined clothing. Each Mae West contained a fluorescent block intended to colour the sea yellow to help identification. As the water had got at them they all looked like Chinamen. They were given survivors' leave immediately. Harry Warwick was later awarded a Distinguished Flying Cross. At Chedburgh the dinghy sea switches on 218 Squadron's Lancasters were tested. None worked.

Altogether, eight Lancasters including three on 195 Squadron, plus *E-Easy,* which crash-landed at Grimbergen in Belgium, were lost. The steelworks were not hit and bombs fell all over the town, destroying 126 houses and five industrial premises and 398 people were killed or missing and 345 injured.

Weeks afterwards the British Army captured the *Hauptmann* of the German *Gruppe* that attacked the Lancasters. When Intelligence questioned him he said that his formation had been waiting to intercept the Americans when they saw the stream of bombers. He knew it was British because of its ragged nature. Even towards the end of the daylight attacks the Lancasters never approached the perfection of American formation flying. He thought that the Lancasters that corkscrewed were out of control and left them alone after the initial dive. Probably he wished to conserve ammunition as much as possible for the next target. This failure of pursuit is rather surprising for one would have expected a fighter pilot, particularly, to have appreciated such an evasive manoeuvre. The *Hauptmann* confirmed Leslie Harlow's gunner's kill. [2]

It was back to night raids on 12/13 December when 540 aircraft attacked Essen. Six Lancasters were missing in action. At Binbrook Jan Birch waited anxiously for the telephone to ring. After the death of her fiancée Colin in a training accident at Lichfield in November a year earlier, she had married another Australian, Flying Officer Brian Clapham Reid DFC who was a navigator on 460 Squadron RAAF. He would always phone her when he returned from an op but this particular night there was no call. She 'waited and waited'. Squadron Leader James Clark DFC AFC MiD RAAF and all of his Lancaster crew lay dead at Berghausen. Jan Birch continues:

> The whole place emptied. I sat down, looked at my watch and thought, 'I'll wait a few more moments' but there was no call and suddenly I felt cold and empty. You then talk yourself into 'don't be stupid. It's just a small thing that's happened. He couldn't ring.' As I got outside WAAF Section Officer Moneypenny, a funny character but very warm-hearted and very kind to me said, 'Oh Jan, would you cycle over to the MO? He wants to see you.' Doc Rogers said 'Jan, I've got to prepare you for something – Brian and the crew didn't return.' I felt cold inside. I couldn't cry; I couldn't do anything. I think I said, 'Oh but it isn't possible. It couldn't happen twice.' Afterwards I realised that none of those friends of mine could face telling me. They had been a part of that marriage. I felt so sorry for them. I cycled off the station and down a lane, got off my bike and ran into the woods. In a way, surrounded by beauty and solitude;

it wasn't sad at all. Amongst all the grass and under the trees were wood anemones, which were just like a cloud of white delicate things, blowing in the wind. I felt, 'Well it isn't all in vain. Whatever's happened, whatever has gone wrong, life does go on.' Brian would have felt like that. Colin too would have felt like that. The other boys I knew would feel that. It was a sudden solution to all my problems but it remained with me as a comfort.

When the 13th day of December broke it was under a very heavy frost and towards mid-morning thick fog enveloped stations in Norfolk and operations were scrubbed very early. That night 52 Lancasters and seven Mosquitoes of 5 Group flew to Norway to attack the German cruiser *Köln* but by the time they reached Oslo Fiord, the ship had sailed, so instead other ships were bombed. On 15/16 December 327 Lancasters and Mosquitoes of 1, 6 and 8 Groups raided the northern part of Ludwigshafen and the small town of Oppau where two important chemical factories, the vast BASF (Badische Anilin-und-Soda-Fabrik) and A G Farben Industrie were situated, at the point where the Neckar and Rhine rivers meet. It had been identified even during the First World War as a prime target for bombing and was a main source of explosive manufacture and production centre for poison gas in both world wars. In 1915 Canadian troops were some of the first to experience its effects at Pickelhem Ridge, Ypres. During WWI Bayer had a close association with other German chemical companies, including BASF and Hoechst. This relationship led to the 1925 merger of these companies, as well as AGFA and others, to form IG Farben Trust. Their *Zyklon B* became the cause of death for about six million men, women and children in concentration camps in World War Two.[3]

Johnnie Byrne on 550 Squadron at North Killingholme who had been absent when his crew had been lost a few nights' earlier, was 'very pleased' to be going on another op with another crew. The young wireless operator wrote:

I know now that I have really something to fly and fight for. No matter how long or dangerous the trip. My heart, body and soul are striving for one supreme purpose. That purpose being to avenge my crew. I am the only member of that gallant team left: I will not fail in my duty. My life is given now to my job. I must and will have German blood.

Notes

1. *218 Gold Coast Squadron Newsletter No. 32* February 2005.
2. *218 Gold Coast Squadron Association Newsletter No. 14* edited by Margery Griffiths.

3. Nigel Parker, writing in *218 Gold Coast Squadron Association Newsletter No. 58*. Auschwitz, the largest mass extermination factory in human history, was a 100% subsidiary of IG Farben. On 14 April 1941 in Ludwigshafen Otto Armbrust the IG Farben board member responsible for the Auschwitz project stated: 'Our new friendship with the SS is a blessing. We have determined all measures integrating the concentration camps to benefit our company.' Thousands of prisoners died during human experiments, drug and vaccine testing. Before long-time Bayer employee and SS Auschwitz Doctor Helmut Vetter was executed for administering fatal infections, he wrote: 'I have thrown myself into my work wholeheartedly. Especially as I have the opportunity to test our new preparations. I feel like I am in paradise.' The Nuremburg Tribunal convicted 24 IG Farben board members and executives on the basis of mass murder, slavery and other crimes. Most of them had been released by 1951 and continued to consult with German corporations. The Nuremburg Tribunal dissolved the IG Farben into Bayer, Hoechst and BASF, each company now 20 times as large as IG Farben in 1944. For almost three decades after WWII, BASF, Bayer and Hoechst (Aventis) filled its highest position, chairman of the board, with former members of the *Nazi* regime.

CHAPTER 3

Out For Blood

BBC extensively heard and believed by Germany.

Russian situation accurately known. Full realisation of implications of Russian victory. Internal revolution not yet likely due to food supplies from occupied territories. Considerable food rail traffic between Dusseldorf and Valenciennes which is collecting centre. Heavy bombing considered likely to speed up end of war. To date, not heavy enough. Present casualty rate on E. Front should settle Germany in six months. Have good anti-nazi contact in Germany. Maybe I'll be seeing you. Keep bombing these bastards to Hell.

Secret message inside a photograph typed on tracing paper received from Wing Commander Douglas Bader while a prisoner in *Offizierlager IVC* Colditz Castle

'Imagine my pleasure as we approached the target area,' wrote Johnnie Byrne on 550 Squadron:

The cloud had disappeared somewhat. And one could clearly see the fires burning on the deck. The red and green sky markers were now high over Ludwigshafen. Tremendous flashes filled the sky all round us. Searchlight beams pin-pointed the darkness and tried in vain to cone our 'beautiful' bombers. But we pressed onwards. Flak was moderate but barrage stuff. I went into the astrodome to look for enemy fighters. I was now counting the seconds as we came on to our actual bombing-run. 'Left – Left – Right – Steady – Steady – Bombs gone.' A sigh of relief. The a/c, now rid of its bomb-load, lifted skyward with an annoying jerk. My feelings at that moment would be very hard for me to explain. I cursed the Hun and inwardly wept for my crew. I was with another crew, new to me. But 19,500 feet over this German city I called the Jerry so much shit!! I sincerely hoped our bombs would smash his wicked filthy skull clean open: I had no mercy; my heart was cold now; I was only out for revenge!

The raid was very successful with 450 HE bombs and many incendiaries falling on the premises of I G Farbenindustrie. The plant ceased production of synthetic oil completely 'until further notice'. One Lancaster was lost.

Two nights later 96 aircraft of 100 Group supported operations when Ülm received 1,449 tons of bombs during a 25-minute raid by 317 Lancasters and 13 Mosquitoes of Nos. 1 and 8 Groups. Munich and Duisburg were also hit. Two *Tame Boars* each destroyed a Lancaster over Ülm. One square kilometre of the city was completely engulfed by fire and 29 industrial premises including the Magirius-Deutz and Kassbohrer large lorry factories were badly damaged. This was Bomber Command's first and only raid on the old city. A third Lancaster was lost after it collided and crashed at Laon in the Aisne. Eight Halifaxes were lost on Duisburg, which was the destination for 523 aircraft. Two of the missing aircraft were involved in a collision over the Ardennes. Losses rose to ten when a Halifax was wrecked on landing at Manston and another crashed at Alne in Yorkshire killing all eight crew.

Bomber Command claimed 'severe and widespread damage' in the old centre of Munich and at railway targets, which were attacked by 280 Lancasters and eight Mosquitoes of 5 Group. Eight Lancasters, including one which crashed and exploded at Worthing, Sussex killing all the crew, were lost on the Munich attack. One was a 467 Squadron RAAF aircraft flown by Flying Officer T R Evans RAAF, who had pushed on to Munich although one engine was failing and the rear turret had become unserviceable soon after leaving England. The bomber barely cleared the Alps but reached the target and the bombing run was begun. Suddenly there came further trouble. The starboard fin and rudder were almost entirely torn away by flak, 12 feet of the starboard main-plane was ripped off, the failing engine cut out completely and the bomber went into a spin, completing an orbit in the midst of the rest of the bomber stream. The navigator, Flying Officer D K Robson RAAF said later that Evans regained control by sheer strength at 7,000 feet and ordered parachutes on. Evans was struggling hard at the controls and the whole aircraft was vibrating horribly. The Lancaster had been flying two hours away from Munich and was down to 3,000 feet when it became completely uncontrollable and again went into a spiral dive. Evans ordered 'abandon aircraft,' but the bomber was down to 1,500 feet in the vicinity of Châlons-Sur-Marne. Evans' flying boot caught in the forward escape hatch of his spiralling Lancaster. He pulled the ripcord of his parachute in a final, desperate effort to get clear and was dragged out to safety. So violent was the tug that three panels of silk were ripped from the parachute but it held sufficiently to carry him. The bomber followed the parachuting crew down and almost hit them in its passage. It struck the ground with a great explosion when the crew were still about 200 feet up. Evans was slightly injured in the leg as the result of his ordeal but no one else was hurt. The crew were assisted by the French and soon they were back on their squadron in Britain. Evans was awarded a DFC two months later.

On 18/19 December, 308 bombers attacked Danzig (Gdynia) on the Baltic coast and caused damage to shipping, installations and housing in the port area. Münster and Nürnburg were also bombed, by 56 Mosquitoes, and 14 Lancasters of 5 Group dropped mines in Danzig Bay. In the Gotenhafen and Danzig areas three crews of I./NJG5 claimed all four Lancasters that failed to return from the Main Force raid on Danzig. Forty-eight aircraft of 100 Group supported the operation and Mosquitoes of 2nd TAF and FIU (Fighter Interception Unit) intruded over the continent.

On 21 December, 100 Lancasters of 3 Group again attempted to bomb the railway yards at Trier in two waves. Cloud covered the target and crews were unable to observe results but a large column of smoke eventually appeared and the second wave caused heavy casualties. All aircraft returned safely. That night a total of 475 heavies attacked the Köln-Nippes marshalling yards, which were being used to serve the German offensive in the Ardennes, railway areas at Bonn and the hydro-genation plant at Pölitz near Stettin, while four Lancasters of 5 Group flew a diversionary raid to Schneidemuhl. Thick cloud at Cologne and Bonn prevented accurate raids and photo reconnaissance revealed that only a few bombs fell on the yards at Nippes and none on the railway area at Bonn. No aircraft were lost on these raids. Sixteen Lancasters of 617 Squadron each carrying a 'Tallboy' formed part of an all 5 Group force of 207 Lancasters that attacked Pölitz. The Dam Busters were not happy about the choice of target or that it was at maximum range and the weather was bad. At some stations the fog was so thick that aircraft could not be seen taking off. Post-raid reconnaissance showed that the power-station chimneys had collapsed and that other parts of the plant were damaged[1] but overall the bombing results were not impressive. Of the eleven 'Tallboys' dropped, it was thought that at least three had fallen in the target area, probably to the north of the plant. It was considered afterwards that Wing Commander John Woodroffe the Master Bomber had assessed the markers as being closer to the target than they were, so leading much of the attack astray.[2] Four Lancasters were lost, two of them crashing in Norway killing everyone on board. Five more crashed in fog from Wick to Lincolnshire attempting to land back at their bases.

On 22/23 December, 166 Lancasters and two Mosquitoes attacked Koblenz without loss while 106 aircraft including 90 Halifaxes of 4 Group raided the Bingen marshalling yards on the Rhine 30 miles south-west of Frankfurt. Two Halifaxes and one Lancaster were lost on the Bingen raid and a Halifax crashed landing back at Melbourne while a Lancaster crash-landed at Downham Market. One of the Halifaxes shot down was X-X-Ray on 578 Squadron at Burn, southwest of Selby, which was piloted by Flying Officer G S Watson. Flight Lieutenant Neville E G Donmall the navigator recalls:

X-X-Ray was airborne at 16.11 hours, climbing to 18,000 feet on a cold sleeting December evening. We cleared cloud at 17,000 feet and set course for Southampton. Leaving our coast behind we were soon over Eastern France where the cloud started to break. Fifty miles from the target there was only 5/10ths cloud. Our flight to Bingen was fairly uneventful, with moderate flak in places. There was also some flak over the target. All markers went down on time and the main force was assembled over the marshalling yards within seven minutes. On the run in we could see the Rhine and the target and our bombs went down directly on the aiming point. After bombing the target we turned south for about ten miles and then set course for home. Over Bad Kreuznach after a few minutes on the new heading of 280° our gunners reported there was a Ju 88 on our tail. The enemy fighter-bomber and our rear and mid-upper turrets opened fire together. Both gunners reported hits on the Ju 88, which dived away beneath us. They also reported minor damage to our own tail-plane and fuselage. About two minutes later the mid-upper gunner called out that another Ju 88 was attacking from beneath us. Returning fire, our aircraft shuddered as more hits were registered on our starboard wing. Flames appeared near the petrol tank and our pilot ordered the crew to bail out. All crew positions acknowledged the call. Lifting my seat, I clipped on my parachute and released the emergency escape hatch beneath my feet. Positioning myself on the edge of the escape exit, I bailed out at 17,000 feet. I recollect counting up to three and pulling the ripcord but remembered nothing more until I found myself swinging beneath the parachute, with my jaw hurting and feeling a little sick. I must have been in the prone position when the chest-type chute deployed, for it had hit my chin and nearly knocked me out. I started to look for the ground but couldn't see it, due either to cloud or fog. The next second I clouted it with a hell of a wallop, once again hitting my chin, this time by my knee. Luckily I'd landed in a foot or so of snow, which some-what reduced the full impact of my landing. Shaking my head and gathering up my chute, I got my compass out and set off at a run towards what I hoped was Luxembourg. I knew how imperative it was for me to clear the area before the Germans found me.[3]

On 23 December a high pressure front pushed through enough moisture from the skies over the Ardennes after four days of fog, snow and freezing rain and 153 Lancasters of 3 Group attempted to bomb the railway yards at Trier through cloud. Another 27 Lancasters and three Mosquitoes carried out an attack on the Cologne/Gremburg railway marshalling yards to disrupt enemy reinforcements for the Battle of the Bulge. The force attacking Cologne was split into three formations, each led by an *Oboe*-equipped Lancaster with an *Oboe* Mosquito as reserve leader. Squadron Leader Robert A M Palmer DFC* on 109 Squadron and his crew at Little Staughton led the first formation in *V-Victor*; an *Oboe*-equipped Lancaster borrowed from 582 Squadron on the station. Palmer, who was 24 years old and had been promoted to squadron leader at age 23, had completed 110 sorties at this time having been on bombing operations since January 1941. He took part in the first Thousand Bomber raid on Cologne in 1942 and he was one of the first pilots to drop a 4,000lb bomb on Germany. It was known that he could be relied upon to press home his attack whatever the opposition and to bomb with great accuracy. He was always selected, therefore to take part in special operations against vital targets. The crew was short of a mid-upper gunner and Bill Lanning, a flight engineer who had never flown in the mid upper turret before, volunteered for the job in hand. It was very foggy when he boarded the Lancaster and the red warning light on the church spire at the end of the runway could hardly be seen. Everyone must have thought that the operation would be scrubbed but they received the order to board *V-Victor* and take off. Lanning clambered up into the mid-upper turret and the Lancaster taxied slowly off the dispersal point to the main runway. Just before the engines built up power and the brakes were released Lanning felt a tug on his trouser leg. He looked down to see Palmer beckoning him down. The door was open and Flying Officer William Dalgarno in full kit was climbing in. At the last minute Lanning was being replaced. He protested but to no avail. He climbed down and stood by the caravan as *V-Victor* took off.

The raid went very badly. During the outward flight *H-Harry* and *F-Freddie* on 35 Squadron collided over the French coast killing everyone on board the two Lancasters. *Major* Anton 'Toni' Hackl and his FW 190A-8 'Dora' fighters of II./JG26, which had duelled and fought P-51 Mustangs near the Ardennes, received word of an unescorted heavy bomber formation near Cologne. Hackl led five aircraft in that direction. At the target Palmer and *V-Victor* came under intense AA fire. Smoke billowed from *V-Victor* and then JG26 attacked the bomber. Two engines were knocked out and a tail fin destroyed but Palmer carried on and completed the bombing run. The Lancaster then went over on the port side and went down. Warrant Officer Russell Yeulett, the Canadian tail gunner, frantically tried to get his jammed turret doors open. He was tempted to give up and he said to himself, 'Relax, let yourself go unconscious; it'll soon be over.' Then *V-Victor* split in two, throwing out the mid-upper gunner who had replaced Lanning at the last minute. Dalgarno was not wearing his parachute. Yeulett's turret was blown off the fuselage, the back was open and the slipstream yanked him out and after his parachute opened, he drifted down into a back garden in Cologne. He was the only survivor. Palmer's Lancaster was followed down by four more Lancasters on 582 Squadron, one of which was abandoned over Belgium. A Mosquito XVI on 169 Squadron also was lost with its crew. Hackl successfully filed victory claims for the leading Lancaster and the Mosquito to add to one for a Mustang destroyed earlier that day. *Oberleutnant* Waldemar 'Waldi' Radener's claim for two Lancasters destroyed and one each by three more pilots was confirmed. Nothing other than sheer determination had kept Palmer on the bombing run and he carried out his duty in textbook fashion. In April 1945 the award of a posthumous Victoria Cross was made to Squadron Leader Robert Anthony Maurice Palmer.

Bill Lanning was lying in his bed many hours later when the Military Police put the lights on and asked where Russ [Lieutenant George Russell DFC] and Bert [Flight Sergeant Bert Nundy, the signals operator], two of the boys who had gone with Palmer, slept. Lanning watched them pack Flight and their kit and take it away. Later, in the mess, he started to cry.[4]

No aircraft were lost to German action on the night of 23/24 December when 52 Mosquitoes of the LNSF bombed rail yards at Limburg in Germany and another 40 attacked Siegburg.[5] On Christmas Eve German airfields were attacked by day by mostly Halifaxes and that night 104 Lancasters of 3 Group bombed Hangelar airfield near Bonn, losing one aircraft, while another 97 Lancasters and five Mosquitoes of 1 and 8 Groups attacked the marshalling yards at Cologne/Nippes. Mosquito squadrons in 100 Group and 2nd TAF celebrated the festive season in style. Thirteen German aircraft were shot down, five of them by four crews of 100 Group and eight by seven crews of 2nd TAF, which dispatched 139 Mosquitoes to targets in southwest Germany. The nights following were much quieter with no Main Force operations on Christmas night because of bad weather. On Boxing Day the weather at last improved and allowed Bomber Command to dispatch 294 aircraft against German troop positions near St-Vith. Two Halifaxes failed to return. Next day 200 Lancasters and 11 Mosquitoes attacked the railway yards at Rheydt for the loss of one Lancaster and a Mosquito on 109 Squadron, which crashed behind the Allied lines in Holland. That night over 320 aircraft attacked the marshalling yards at Opladen, some 3.5 hours after an earlier raid by Mosquitoes. Two Lancasters failed to return.

Next day 167 Lancasters of 3 Group attacked the Cologne/Gremberg marshalling yards. Bombing was accurate and no aircraft were lost. Walford Jones, flight engineer on Flight Lieutenant Joe Eyles' crew on 218 Squadron recalls:

This was our first operational flight, the journey there and back taking 5 hours 30 minutes. The flak around the city was pretty thick and as this was our first experience of it, caused a tense few minutes when we had to fly a steady course on our run into the target. But as soon as Pete shouted 'Bombs away', a fact we all detected by the aircraft lifting as they were released, Joe Eyles put the nose down to gain maximum speed and took evasive action to clear the target area as swiftly as possible. We were very pleased to see the coast of Holland on our way home as Jerry fighters were very unlikely to attack in strength this far from Germany, but we had to be vigilant all the way to base, as a single aircraft had been known to pick off home going bombers sometimes even on the approach to their home base, so it was with great elation that we touched down at Chedburgh without any mishap after our first operation flight.

At around this time Air Vice Marshal Cochrane, AOC 5 Group, told Wing Commander Willy Tait that he had done enough. Tait, whose four DSOs and two DFCs were a record, was posted to Headquarters, 100 Group. Wing Commander 'Johnny' Fauquier DSO** DFC took command of 617 Squadron. Cochrane told Fauquier that he had to see that 617 'was kept up to the mark and stayed as good as ever.' The tough, thick-set Canadian would get his crews out of bed in the frosty mornings for PT and when it snowed he made them shovel snow off the runways. When there was no flying he would give them lectures instead. While Fauquier settled in Squadron Leader 'Jock' Calder led 16 Lancasters of 617 Squadron in the afternoon of 29 December to bomb the *E-boat* pens at Waalhaven near Rotterdam. The clear winter skies made marking unnecessary and with no enemy fighters to concern them, 617 flew without any escort. There was only light flak over the pens so the Lancasters flew over at heights of between 16,000 and 18,000 feet to drop their 'Tallboys'. One bomb undershot the target by 200 yards and another was to the west but the rest hit the target.

Peter Bone was also flying on 29 December:

'Hell's bells', yelled Skipper. 'Mac, get us outta here!'
    It was in the early evening of 29 December 1944, we were flying in *'Jig 2'*, a Lancaster bomber on 626 Squadron at Wickenby just northeast of Lincoln, which is about a hundred miles north of London. Our last 'op' had been on 17 December but there'd been the customary Christmas lull in the bomber offensive against German industrial cities and now we were on our way to destroy an oil refinery at Scholven/Buer on the outskirts of the Ruhr, the heartland of Hitler's armament production. At least, we thought we were. The trouble was, we'd strayed off course due to an undetected malfunction of one of our electronic navigational aids and were flying over the outskirts of Cologne, 20 miles to the southwest and we were all alone. The first intimation that anything was wrong came suddenly, when anti-aircraft shells began to burst all around us. I can still see the port

wing dissecting a hideous ball of black smoke tinged with wicked orange flame and I can still smell the cordite. I was the mid-upper gunner and from my perspex turret set in the roof of the fuselage I saw other shells bursting all around us. But, with the roar of our engines in my ears, it was like watching with the sound turned off. I'd become used to being scared but this was different. This was real fear and there was nothing I could do. The next few seconds would be in the hands of our pilot. It was our twelfth op – eighteen more to go.

Skipper thrust the huge bomber, still heavily laden with fuel and about six tons of bombs, into a steep dive to port in an attempt to escape the lethal stream of shells coming up at us from radar-controlled anti-aircraft batteries 20,000 feet below us. 'Start *"Window-ing"* Fred' he snapped tersely. But we were not over the target, which we hadn't anticipated reaching for several minutes. We were well and truly caught with our pants down. Fred was our bomb-aimer and was busily preparing his bomb-sight for the run-up to the target. But it was now his job to tear open dozens of brown paper packages stacked in the fuselage and thrust hundreds of the silver strips down the flare chute. The effect was immediate. The shells ceased to be so terrifyingly close and then stopped coming altogether. Skipper was able to fly straight and level again.

Mac was our navigator and now his calm, unruffled voice came over the intercom. 'Steer 030 Skipper', he said, adding, 'estimated time of arrival over Gelsenkirchen, 19.06'.

'OK Mac'.

We settled down on to the new course and within seconds the intercom snapped on again, as I knew it would.

'OK Frank?'

'OK Skip'.

'OK Pete?'

'OK Skip'.

'Good show.'

Frank and I, as rear and mid-upper gunners respectively, were the only members of our seven-man crew whom Skipper couldn't see during a flight that could last up to ten hours and those few words, every half hour or so, were one of the many reasons why we all held Skipper – on the ground he was Squadron Leader Richard Lane – in such high regard.

We were a few minutes getting to the target and now we were no longer alone but one of 324 Lancasters and 24 Mosquito night fighters. We bombed and turned thankfully for home.

We were tucking into bacon and eggs in the mess by 22.00 that night. Half an hour later I was sitting on my bed in the Nissen hut I shared with thirteen other young men and writing in my diary,

'I didn't like that trip'. Next day we found that a larger sliver of flak had entered the starboard side of *'Jig 2'*, crossed the crew passage-way between Bert our wireless operator and the navigator, cut through the leads of the H_2S and exited through the port side to embed itself in the port inner engine, fortunately without putting it out of action. It was by sheer chance that we'd got away with only minimal damage and no injury to any crew member. But if there hadn't been solid cloud beneath us, we would have been immediately coned by numerous searchlights from which there was almost never any escape, because their powerful beams effectively blinded the bomber's crew. A night fighter could then close in for the kill. Although there was a full moon in a clear sky at our height, the searchlights were unable to penetrate the thick clouds beneath us and perhaps it was bad weather beneath them that prevented a night fighter from taking off. Perhaps the *Luftwaffe* fighter we saw as we approached the target, going in the direction from which we had come, was looking for us. The official report of the operation, made after the war, with the help of German records, stated that the oil refinery was badly hit, together with severe damage to coal-mine buildings and other industrial property. Four Lancasters were lost. It could so easily have been five.

Nachtjagd it seemed was powerless to stop the inexorable advance west-wards but the Luftwaffe made one last futile attempt to try to halt the allies. Since 20 December 1944 many *Jagdgruppen* had been transferred to airfields in the west for Operation *Bodenplatte,* when approximately 850 Luftwaffe fighters took off at 07.45 hours on Sunday morning 1 January to attack 27 airfields in northern France, Belgium and southern Holland. The four-hour operation succeeded in destroying about 100 Allied aircraft but it cost the *Luftwaffe* 300 aircraft, most of which were shot down by Allied anti-aircraft guns deployed primarily against the V-1s and by 'friendly' flak.

New Year's Eve had been very cold with sleet showers, and tempera-tures had plummeted to well below freezing and the air was still frosty, very cold and very dark early on New Year's Day when 152 Lancasters and five Mosquitoes of 5 Group began taking off just before dawn for the operation on the Dortmund-Ems Canal at Ladbergen, which the Germans had once more repaired. Bombing would be carried out from just 9,000 feet so crews were under no illusions about the nature of the operation but it was the weather that caused the first casualties.

At Bardney only two Lancasters had taken off when there was a huge explosion in the distance. *U-Uncle*, with Flying Officer Harry Denton RNZAF, a 25-year-old farmer from New Zealand at the controls, got airborne. Sergeant Ernest 'Ernie' John Potts, the 30-year-old mid-upper gunner from Newport, Monmouth was the daddy of the crew and the only married man. Both he and Sergeant Haydn Price, short and thick-set with a slow, friendly smile, the other Welsh gunner, loved singing and the intercom was often alive with Welsh melodies. Ernie Potts' wife Gwen had given birth to their only daughter two months earlier. Ernie Potts had been exempt from war service because of his work as an agricultural engineer, until he chose to volunteer. Like Flight Sergeant George Thompson, the 24-year-old Scottish wireless operator from Glencraig, he had begun on ground duties and then applied for a transfer to air crew. The son of a Kinross ploughman, Thompson had left school at 14 to become a grocer's assistant before becoming a wireless operator in 1944 and he was flying only his fifth operation. Ted Kneebone the navigator, who was from Manchester, promised that on their next leave they would all go to Potts' home in Newport to wet the baby's head.[6]

After Denton had taken off it was the turn of 22-year-old Flying Officer Clifford Sinclair Newton, an American from Rosewood near Detroit, Michigan and the crew of *R-Robert*. Newton pushed the four red-tipped throttle handles forward and the Sergeant Colin Booth, the flight engineer, held them in their stops as the pilot released the brakes, but shortly after getting airborne the engines cut out and the Lancaster smashed into a field near the base. Newton and five crew members died in the flash of fire. Two of the dead were in their thirties and were the only married members of the crew. Pilot Officer 'Paddy' Flynn RCAF the bomb aimer, who was thrown clear, was the only survivor. Cliff Newton and two young Canadian air gunners were later buried at Stonefall Cemetery at Harrogate in the centre of England. At first it was thought that the crashed aircraft had come from Woodhall Spa seven miles away and take offs at Bardney continued unabated. Next away was *A-Able* flown by Pilot Officer J W Buckley RAAF, which when barely off the ground also lost power from all four engines, probably caused by droplets of water in the petrol tanks. The Lancaster hurtled across the airfield and crashed. Amazingly, one broken leg was the sum total of the injuries sustained by the crew.

At the target *D-Dog* was shot down and the pilot, Flying Officer Peter William Reaks, and three of his crew including Sergeant Tom Scott, who was 19 and from Selkirk, were killed. On board *U-Uncle* Harry Denton's bomb aimer, Flying Officer Ron Goebel, crouched at his bomb sight in the bombing compartment calling instructions to Denton on the intercom. At last the crew felt a slight bump as the first thousand-pounder left the bomb bay, followed in quick succession by 11 more as the rest of the stick, spaced 12 yards apart, fell away. Denton pushed forward hard on the control column, correcting the tendency to climb as the load changed. The bombs hit their mark. Half a mile of banks were pitted with bomb craters and some parts were breached. In a moment Goebel would have completed his check and would give the signal 'Bombs gone' and Kneebone, back at the navigation table, working out the course to steer for home, waited like Denton for the signal from Goebel but it never came. *U-Uncle* was hit by a salvo of two 88mm shells and the Lancaster was set on fire. The first shell blew a gaping hole five or six feet square in the floor of the fuselage, just forward of the mid-upper turret and set fire to the whole rear section of the Lancaster. The front cockpit filled instantly with smoke, the rear fuselage was a sea of flames. Then a second hit from heavy flak shattered the nose compartment, set fire to an engine and blew large holes in the pilot's canopy. Denton pitched forward unconscious and the Lancaster dived out of control. Gale force air blasted through the shattered nose and canopy, dispersing the smoke in the cockpit and blowing out the flames in the fuselage. Denton too was blasted back into consciousness by the icy wind and he gradually regained control of *U-Uncle*, though the Lancaster had lost several thousand feet.

Potts was trapped in his blazing mid upper turret and Price too was trapped in the burning rear turret. George Thompson was not wearing gloves, which would have impeded his operation of the Morse key. He was not wearing a parachute either but when the smoke and dust cleared he made his way aft and managed to rescue both gunners from their burning turrets but he suffered severe burns in doing so. Goebel came up from the bombing compartment carrying shreds of his parachute. Another parachute in the fuselage was on fire. With at least two of the crew unable to bail out it was no use Denton giving the order to jump. Goebel, standing next to Denton on the look-out, pointed to a rash of anti-aircraft fire on the star board side and Denton immediately took evasive action. But almost at once the starboard inner engine failed. They had been hit again. South of Arnhem three FW 190s appeared out of the mist flying straight at them but fortunately they did not spot the crippled Lancaster. A Canadian Spitfire squadron was chasing the fighters and broke off the engagement to escort the ailing Lanc towards their base at Brussels. *U-Uncle* almost hit some high tension cables but one of the Spitfires zoomed up steeply and Denton saw the danger just in time. Turning to avoid a village Denton picked out two fields with a hedge between them and aimed the Lancaster diagonally across the two. Harry Denton hit his head against the control column as they crash-landed but he managed to climb clear. Everyone of the crew including Potts, who had recovered consciousness, was able to stagger out of the wreckage. Thompson was the first man Denton saw. So pitiable was his condition that Denton did not recognise him. His hands and face were blackened and his clothes were in shreds. Cheerily he called to Denton: 'Good landing Skipper!'

Goebel went off to get help while Denton, Kneebone and Sergeant Wilf Hartshorn the flight engineer made for a nearby cottage, taking the injured men with them. Potts and Thompson were in bad shape and Denton gave them both an injection of morphia. The little Dutch cottage filled with sympathetic villagers. Seeing the pathetic state of Potts and Thompson most of the women wept. The Spitfires had reported the Lancaster's position and soon an ambulance with two doctors arrived and Thompson and 'Ernie' Potts were rushed to hospital in Eindhoven. Potts quickly lapsed into unconsciousness again and he died of his burns the next day. Price was badly burned about the head but was well enough to be flown home to hospital in England 10 days later, where he eventually recovered. Goebel was badly frostbitten and lost all the top finger-joints of one hand but he too made an otherwise full recovery. George Thompson was terribly burned and was too ill to be flown home but with regular injections of a new drug called penicillin he made surprisingly good progress and seemed to be out of danger. His burns however were too extensive and he died on 23 January of pneumonia. He was posthumously awarded the Victoria Cross for his courage. Denton was awarded the DFC. Thompson's courage, said the citation, 'has seldom been equalled and never surpassed.'[7]

On 2/3 January, 514 Lancasters and seven Mosquitoes of 1, 3, 6 and 8 Groups bombed Nürnburg and 389 aircraft raided Ludwigshafen. Four Lancasters were lost on Nürnburg and one Halifax failed to return on the Ludwigshafen raid.[8] At Nürnburg, with the help of a rising full moon and in clear visibility, the Path Finders carried out good ground-marking and the centre of the city, in particular the eastern half, was destroyed. Over 1,800 people were killed and over 400 separate industrial buildings were destroyed. At Ludwigshafen the Main Force used the area of the two I G Farben chemical factories as their aiming point. The bombing was accurate with about 500 HE bombs and 10,000 incendiaries falling inside the limits of the two factories, and 1,800 people were bombed out.[9]

On 3 January the Main Force went out in daylight again when almost 100 Lancasters of 3 Group made 'G-H' accurate attacks through cloud on the Hansa benzol plant at Dortmund and another benzol plant at Castrop-Rauxel. Dick Perry on 218 Squadron recalls:

This was our 23rd trip and it all started in the usual way. Frank Aspden, our navigator, and I worked at the Nav Course in the Briefing Room before the Main Briefing and discussed the problems that we might encounter along the way. On this particular trip, we were leading the Group and were equipped with target indicators along with a 'cookie' and fourteen 500-pounders. The Briefing over, we went out to our various aircraft and prepared for the operation. Takeoff was at 10.13 and our first exercise was to collect the other aircraft before heading out for the target. At 11.06 we were on our way. This was to be a 'G-H' raid and we had been told to expect 10/10th cloud for the bulk of the journey there and back. The route we took was one that we had taken on previous occasions, down to Tunbridge Wells, southeast to Dungeness, across the Channel to Boulogne, onwards to Brussels, then turn and northeast up to Wiesbaden, then south on the bombing run to Castrop Rauxel.

Castrop-Rauxel was Joe Eyles' crew's second trip and it proved eventful, as Walford Jones recalls:

We experienced mechanical trouble. When we were well over France just about to cross the line to which the Allied armies had advanced, I noticed an aircraft on our starboard side sending a signal with an Aldis lamp, which when our Wireless Op read it, was telling us that we were losing fuel. I checked the gauges but saw nothing to worry about but when the engine oil pressure and temperature gauges were checked I was very alarmed as it showed pressure at almost zero and temperature going up at a very fast rate, which if left would cause a fire in the starboard outer engine. On my advice Joe agreed that we had no option but to feather the engine to prevent the fire. I pressed a button in the cockpit, which caused hydraulic pressure to change the pitch of the propellers to such an extent that the engine stopped and also the fuel supply to that engine was stopped, but we had to wait a while before we were sure that a fire had not started before we had taken action, but the absence of smoke gave us hope. When we lost the power of one engine we started to lose speed and the rest of the formation of a few hundred aircraft soon left us behind to fend for ourselves. We were really in no-man's land as Reg our navigator calculated that we were a few miles behind enemy lines but not over Germany. There was no chance of us going all the way back with a full bomb load to The Wash where any bombs we called hang-ups would be manually released from the bomb bay to be dumped in the sea, as the fuel with such a load would be used up and it was doubtful if we could have maintained height.

Going to the target on our own was out of the question as we would have been picked off with no trouble, so after a crew chat Joe decided we should get over Germany just a few miles and just let our load go. This we did but not without one or two shells from ground defences coming uncomfortably close. It was then nose down and head for the North Sea as quickly as possible. There was a bit of anxiety waiting for Reg to tell us we were back over territory occupied by friendly forces just before which we were given a sharp burst of gun fire from Jerry but he was a good way off.

On arriving over the sea Joe put the aircraft down to a couple of hundred feet above the waves, this helped to give the three remaining engines a bit more power from the denser air and would also make any hostile aircraft wary of making an attack as they might not be able to pull out of their dive before going into the sea, but this was not a certain way to prevent attack; if they were keen enough they might take a chance. All our eyes were scanning the sky for a tell tale sign of intruders and our hearts sank into our boots when 'Ducky' our mid upper gunner saw four tiny gleaming specks in the sunlight a few thousand feet above us. After a while it was obvious they had seen us for they were circling right above us but gradually coming lower. We were all very tense and going over the action we should take in such an emergency, the gunners ready to fire. The bomb aimer had gone into the front turret, which he only did if an attack was likely and I started to think about going out onto the wing to float the dinghy if we were to end up in the sea. Our relief was unbounded when one of our gunners suddenly shouted over the intercom that panic stations were over as the intruders were not hostile and had been identified as Mustang fighters of the American Air Force. Were we pleased to see them! Joe climbed towards them and Keith sent an Aldis message. When they realised we knew they were friendly, they took up positions all around us and escorted us back over the UK coast, leaving us with a wave from their cockpit and each doing a victory roll as they passed us on the way back over the North Sea. We landed safely at our base and they were unable to find anything wrong with the engine, but when it went on an air test the same trouble we had experienced repeated itself. We didn't use that aircraft again until a month later but used it on five raids out of the 12 we made during February, it giving no trouble at all.

Dick Perry's Lancaster meanwhile had neared the target:

We picked up the 'G-H' signal as we were abreast of Dortmund and followed it down to the target. That's when we hit the first of the predicted flak. We were a lead aircraft and ran right into it. As usual we pressed on to the target with Harry in the tail giving a running commentary to Robby, which allowed him to dodge back and forth as the flak bursts went past us on either side. Afterwards, I made the remark that it sounded as if we were in a tin can with stones in it. By means of weaving and dodging we were able to reach the aiming point, drop our bomb load and, more importantly, the target indicators; then quickly southwest towards Cologne, west past Ghent and then northwest over Ostend and onwards across the Channel to Chedburgh and home. We landed and were in the mess having the usual dish of bacon and eggs at 3.30pm. We went down to take a look at the aircraft afterwards. Twenty-seven holes of various sizes in the fuselage and a nick out of the control rod serving the elevators! Once again, this was our lucky day.[10]

Harry Pinnell on 218 Squadron recalls:

At Downham Market, when the powers that be built a new officers mess it was built in a hollow, presumably so that any bomb blast would go over the top. My mob started up a motor roller standing on the normal ground. We lost control of it and it crashed through the mess wall. Fortunately it went between two pillars but it still made a big hole. We also managed to get the gunnery leader's Fiat sports car in to the mess by turning it on to its side and all pushing. We then cleared the furniture and succeeded in driving it round the ante room – eight-point turns as well. When I finished my tour what a party we had that night. Footprints on the ceiling – I left mine at Woolfox Lodge.

Dick Perry adds:

At Chedburgh the Mess building was only a short distance from the Nissen huts we slept in which was a great advantage after imbibing at one of the Mess parties. I well remember one party where we all had to discard clothes if we failed to answer questions correctly. I ended up losing my way home in the middle of winter and ending up in someone else's bed in a strange hut. Then there was the night when someone with a motorbike rode round and round the billiard table and finally fell off and had to be escorted to bed.

No night bombing operations were carried out by the heavies on 3/4 January, but on the night of the 4/5th, 347 Lancasters and seven Mosquitoes of 1, 5 and 8 Groups controversially attacked Royan at the mouth of the River Gironde. Upwards of 800 French civilians were killed. Four Lancasters were lost and two more collided behind the Allied lines in France and crashed. The number of aircraft lost in mid-air collisions is not known but it is generally accepted that the numbers were few. On 5/6 January, 23 Halifaxes and eight Lancasters failed to return from the raid on Hannover, the majority shot down by an effective *Tame Boar* operation, while two Lancasters were lost on a raid on a bottleneck in the German supply system in the Ardennes in a valley at Houffalize in Belgium.[11]

On 6/7 January over 600 aircraft set out to bomb an important German rail junction at Hanau and the marshalling yards at Neuss. Many of the bombs dropped by 468 Halifaxes and Lancasters of 1, 4 and 6 Groups at Hanau and 147 Lancasters of 1 and 3 groups at Neuss missed the targets and fell in surrounding districts. Hanau was reported to be '40 per cent destroyed' while in Neuss over 1,700 houses, 19 industrial premises and 20 public buildings were destroyed or seriously damaged. Four Halifaxes and two Lancasters failed to return from the raid on Hanau. *H-Harry*, a

Lancaster on 218 Squadron piloted by Flying Officer Dave Banton failed to return from the raid on Neuss as Jim 'Paddy' Giffin the bomb aimer recalls:

On our run in to the target (Neuss) there was a sudden loud bang and our Lanc was thrown out of control. We lost quite a bit of height before the Skipper, Dave Banton, regained control. Someone said, 'It's getting bloody hot in here' and someone else said 'Yes there's a bloody great fire outside' and indeed there was. The flight engineer tried to extinguish it with the usual procedures but unsuccessfully. I jettisoned the bombs and the fire was extinguished by cutting off the fuel to both port engines The port outer still could not be feathered and when the Skipper tried to maintain height by increasing power to the starboard engines it only caused the aircraft to heel over. We were told to put on our parachutes. We had now lost considerable height and were on one and a half engine power. The emergency exits were opened and there was quite a gale tearing through the aircraft. Flying Officer Larry Lillis the navigator reckoned we were over the battlefront so the wireless operator Sergeant 'Chick' Longley fired the colours of the day and we hoped to make it to Brussels or Ostend where we might be able to land. There was no response to our 'Mayday' calls and we were still losing height. No lights could be seen anywhere although the navigator reckoned we were not too far from Brussels. What we did not know then but learned later, was that Brussels airfield had been attacked about New Year by German aircraft and was out of action. We then decided to abandon. In the darkness the flight engineer's parachute was accidentally opened in the aircraft and with the open escape exits and the wind it was tangled in the aircraft. The order to 'Bail out' had been given so I as the bomb aimer being at the front escape hatch had to go first. I responded to the order, took off my helmet and dropped out. I felt the jerk of the chute opening, looked up, saw the white canopy and looked down where I could see the dark woods swinging slowly from side to side. Suddenly I saw a tree rush up. I locked my knees, put out my hands and was on the ground – frozen hard it was. I sprained my right ankle but was otherwise OK.

I saw a faint light and walked towards it, hoping to find a friendly place and I was lucky. It took a little while to convince the man who I was but finally he took me in. It was a dimly lit room with a big round stove in the centre and a family of young people gathered around but I felt that I was among friends. Soon I was drinking a mug of warm sweet coffee and this was followed by bacon and egg (*spek* and *arran* they called it, for these people were Flemish). News spread and soon the room was full of people. Then someone came in and said 'Comrade, Comrade' and taking me to the door he pointed across the fields. I realised another member of our crew might be there. Before I left, the family looked for a souvenir and I gave them my whistle, small escape compass, which they still have and showed me during my recent visit. I also parted with my gloves and chocolate ration. At the next farm I found Sergeant Stan Brown our mid-upper gunner. He had come to earth beside a barn and surprised the farmer and his son who were milking the cows inside. They took him in and brought a young girl from Rotterdam who could speak English. The farmer's son was sent to inform the gendarme who in turn sent him to inform the Americans who were about two miles away. They loaded up a truck with troops and drove across the fields in their haste to check us out. At that time German saboteurs were being dropped dressed in allied uniforms so the Yanks were taking no chances. They surrounded us with Tommy guns pointed at us but we were able to convince them who we were and they took us to their unit from where I was able to get a signal to the UK and eventually to the station at Chedburgh where an 'Old Christmas Night' party was in progress.

Just as Giffin had bailed out, more drama had been unfolding in the Lanc. Sergeant Sims could not use his parachute so Sergeant Chick Longley agreed to take him out on his back. They, in the darkness, attempted to strap themselves together using their parachute harness. In their struggling to get down into the bomb aimer's exit area. Longley's parachute opened but he managed to gather it in his arms and the two dropped out, but when the chute opened Sims fell off and was killed. Longley thought that the release block of Sims' parachute harness must have been accidentally turned to release. Longley fell in a tree and was only found in the morning after he had laid all night under the tree. His back was broken, either by the fall or by the release block of Sims' parachute. He was taken to No. 101 Hospital Louvaine and then to hospital near Gloucester where a bone from his ankle was grafted into his back and he made a full recovery. Longley was awarded the CGM and lived a full life as an estate agent in the Bournemouth area after the war.

Flying Officer Larry Lillis received a broken nose, lost some teeth and had other facial damage as he struck some part of the aircraft as he left. Sergeant Gillespie, the rear gunner who was flying as a replacement for Sergeant Frank Laity, left by the rear door.

When I met up with him next day I asked him how be managed getting out. He said, 'I was standing at the back door and I thought I would try this handle before leaving. I just touched it and the next I knew was I was flying through the air.' He was lucky for he might have been caught by the tail-plane. David Banton was the last to leave. The aircraft was so unstable he had to cut the engines and throw himself down towards the front escape exit. When he opened his parachute he tumbled partially out of the harness and descended headfirst. He fell among trees, which broke his fall, but he did sustain cuts to his head. He saw a light and walked towards it and was welcomed into the home of people at the Château-de-Sevenel. When he left the aircraft he saw that the altimeter registered 1,200 feet so he was indeed fortunate. The Americans found his harness and showed him that one of the straps was not connected to the release block. He had waited until he was sure that all the crew were out before leaving the aircraft which was most unstable at that time. None of the people who took us in were known by name to us nor did we know exactly where they lived. We spent two days in Brussels and were entertained right royally in the Officers Club where champagne was flowing freely. Dave Banton and I found ourselves wandering the streets of Brussels after curfew time and the snow blowing but we were alive and happy. At that time we did not know how serious things were with others of the crew. We were flown back to UK in a Dakota to Down Ampney near Gloucester and eventually to Chedburgh where the crew was reformed and we went on until the end of the war.[12]

On 7/8 January Bomber Command returned to area bombing with the final major raid on Munich, which was memorable for the sheer beauty of flying along Lake Constance with the snow-covered Alps crystal clear in the moonlight. The raid was carried out by 645 Lancasters and nine Mosquitoes of five Groups. Frank Aspden a navigator on 218 Squadron, recalls:

We were on the whole a pretty steady crew and we had a good name on the squadron, but this was one night when the majority of us did not want to fly. I had a date with a wizard little dame so if the trip were scrubbed early I could make it. We knew it was a 'full tanks' trip and it was therefore a long one, so it was no surprise to me to find when I went to the information briefing that the target was Munich. Dick Perry and I got to work on the charts and flight plans and then the rest of the crew came in for the main briefing. There were many groans when the length of the trip was known and we were all praying for a 'scrub'. However, no scrub materialised and we got out to the dispersal, started up and began taxiing out. It was then that the first ray of hope shone; Johnnie the engineer looked at the brake pressure and found it extremely low, but Robbie, being in a 'press on' mood that night said it would build up in the air and carried on to the taxi post and in due course took off. Then our troubles began to show themselves. My 'Gee' was no good; there was so much grease on the screen that I could not get the pulses and we might have been about 5° east for all the use it was. Then the intercom in the rear turret became so bad that it was impossible to hear Harry's voice, except for the odd word that broke through the interference now and again. Lastly, by the time we had turned on the runway and taken off, we had no brake pressure left at all and it now became apparent that the brake pressure was not building up and that the aircraft was u/s. That meant that we would have to land without instructions; too risky a thing to do at night on a normal length runway and we should therefore have to land at Woodbridge, one of the emergency aerodromes with special long runways. This did not cheer us because we should be dead tired by the time we returned and instead of going straight to supper and bed, we would have a long and weary business of booking in and getting fixed up with billets, blankets etc besides having to wait around for a meal to be cooked.

I could have hugged Johnnie when as we were climbing slowly across the Channel, he called up the Skipper in the intercom and said 'Do you realise that with no air pressure we shall be unable to get into 5th gear?' This meant that we could not climb above 14,000 and 15,000 feet and we should have to abandon the trip. It shook Robbie considerably. For some unknown reason he was dead set on going that night. But it was obvious that it would be folly to press on at 6,000 feet below the main stream and consequent slower speed. So when we got to 14,000 feet, Johnnie put over the lever to go into 5th gear and with bated breath, we waited for the lurch that would mean that we had made it, but I didn't come and as I turned round to shake hands with Reg, the Skipper asked for a course for England. About an hour later we landed at Woodbridge in a far happier state than we thought that we would enjoy that night!

Flying Officer Ken Lee's Lancaster crew on 49 Squadron at Fulbeck in Lincolnshire was one of the 'supporters' for the Path Finder Flare Force (83 and 97 Squadrons). His bomb aimer was Flight Sergeant John Aldridge, who despite the nature of his job for the most part did not think in terms of people being killed but of areas that had to be hit:

Nine of the 33 operations I flew September 1944–April 1945 were on built-up areas. Tom Gatfield, navigator, and I had been working LORAN and obtained some decent fixes and we managed to keep to time. However predicted winds were all to cock that night and we arrived over Munich on time ... but on our own! I went forward into the bomb aimer's compartment to prepare for the bomb run in our supporting role. The sky was one mass of flak bursts and we seemed to be the only aircraft around and we were leaving a contrail at that.

We were well and truly hammered. One piece of flak came through the front Perspex and ripped the sleeve on my battledress blouse. Searchlights also dazzled us and the Skipper nearly stalled the aircraft taking evasive action. Tom called out that the airspeed was 110 knots and falling and there was a shout of 'Get the bloody nose down skip!' Thankfully he did. We were then hit in one engine, which had to be feathered. This was the only occasion on which I removed my parachute from its stowage and laid it on the floor beside me. I looked down at the snow covered landscape and thought: 'Its damned cold down there if I have to jump.'

We had to keep an altitude of about 14,000 feet as our route home was above the Alps skirting Switzerland. We saw the lights of that neutral country. Everything went well till half way across France (by now mostly occupied by our own troops since D-Day) when another engine started vibrating badly and shaking the whole aircraft. The Skipper and Lou Crabbe our flight engineer decided to feather that engine, so now we were on two! We decided that rather than land at an airfield in France we would go for a landing at the emergency runway at Manston in Kent, entailing a short sea passage on two engines. This was managed successfully although the Skipper risked un-feathering the last engine to give us trouble, to get a little more power if required.

The raid on Munich was the 13th op for Squadron Leader Lane's crew on 626 Squadron at Wickenby. Peter Bone reflected that 'perhaps Frank and I were a little trigger-happy'.

Over the target, in the shadowy flickering light from the inferno below, we both saw simultaneously what looked like a night-fighter closing in from starboard. We yelled 'Corkscrew starboard' in unison, whereupon Skipper promptly thrust the Lancaster into a steep dive. As he levelled out however, before climbing again, we both realized that instead of a small aircraft at half a mile, it was a large aircraft at probably twice that distance. In other words, it was almost certainly another Lancaster. Frank and I had both fired a short burst, which fortunately hit empty air but as Skipper said later, 'It's better to fire first and ask questions later'. Frank was, of the two of us, the gen-man, a term that was applied to any member of aircrew who went the extra mile to become as proficient as he could in his duties. Frank studied every aspect of gunnery with relish and kept a detailed diary in which he wrote at length about the latest techniques in use by both Bomber Command and the Luftwaffe. Although he later told me that I was just as keen as he was to read up on such matters, I have no recollection of doing so. I saw myself as the back-up man. I must also acknowledge here how heavily we relied on the expertise and dedication of our ground crews, who worked round the clock, often on the tarmac in all weathers, to keep us flying. Although I was responsible for cleaning and re-aligning my guns after every flight, an armourer was always there to replace parts, unravel snags and give helpful advice to a novice gunner.

The incident over Munich, however, underlined what we had come to realize. Our most useful weapons were not at this stage of the war our guns, as we had been taught at gunnery school but our eyes. The top scorer in training would be of no use whatsoever if he weren't on the ball every second. Another thing I learnt was that when the real test came, I was too busy doing my job to think about air-sickness. But in addition to the night fighters, the radar-controlled anti-aircraft fire was as deadly as ever – probably more so. With the retreating German armies eastwards from France and westwards from Russia, came thousands of guns that had been used against allied tanks. They now reinforced the already formidable defences of German cities, hence the hot reception we received over the outskirts of Cologne as related earlier. But we had had a much earlier reminder of our vulnerability over Stuttgart on our third op.

When we landed 'Able 2' suddenly veered off the runway. We hurtled across a bumpy field in pitch darkness and came to rest in mud, fortunately not meeting anything on the way. Next morning a sliver of flak was found in a very flat tire. If it had penetrated one of the fuel tanks in the wings, we would have become the fireball that we were, by now, used to seeing all around us. We would remain oblivious to the many occasions when a split second separated us from eternity. It was just as well that we remained in blissful ignorance. We listened in the mess to other crews recounting stories of being attacked by night-fighters. It was on the Munich op that a mid-upper gunner in another crew claimed to have shot down a jet fighter. These were just beginning to make an appearance but usually by day and were still very much in the experimental stage, fortunately for us, as the allied air forces had none in service before the war ended. And, fortunately for us, the Luftwaffe jets came too late to have any effect on the outcome of the war.

Bomber Command claimed a successful area raid with the central and some industrial areas of Munich being severely damaged. A Lancaster on 630 Squadron crashed after returning to East Kirkby soon after take-off. Two crew members were killed and five were injured. Ten Lancasters were shot down, three more went down after collisions and a 106 Squadron Lancaster flew into trees near Void-Vacon. A 467 Squadron Lancaster returning to Waddington was lost when it crashed near Eye in Cambridgeshire. All the crew perished in the crash.

The raid on Munich was followed by one on Krefeld and three visits to Saarbrücken. A series of oil targets were then targeted by Bomber Command and on 13/14 January over 200 Lancasters attacked the Pölitz plant near Stettin and reduced it to a 'shambles' for the loss of just two Lancasters. The following night over 570 Lancasters took off for a raid on the synthetic oil plant at Leuna and caused severe damage throughout the facility. On the 15th a benzol plant at Recklinghausen was the target for over 80 Lancasters of 3 Group and again the bombing appeared to be 'excellent' and no aircraft were lost. Another 60 plus Lancasters of 3 Group attacked the Robert Muser benzol plant at Bochum and again all aircraft returned. Just over 300 aircraft destroyed 44 per cent of the built-up area of Magdeburg on the 16th/17th when four separate targets were hit this cold winter's night. Over 230 Lancasters and Mosquitoes of 1 and 5 Groups raided the synthetic oil plant at Brüx in Czechoslovakia and this was a complete success with oil production set back severely. Seventeen Halifaxes failed to return from the raid on Magdeburg but only one Lancaster failed to return from the raid on Brüx. The Krupp benzol plant at Wanne-Eickel was also attacked, by 138 Lancasters of 3 Group. No results were known and one Lancaster was lost. Another 328 Lancasters of 1, 6 and 8 Groups caused much damage to the northern half of the *Braunkphle-Benzin* synthetic oil plant at Zeitz near Leipzig.

On the way home a Lancaster on 582 Squadron at Little Staughton, piloted by Flying Officer P J McVerry RNZAF, that had assisted in the marking of the synthetic oil plant, was attacked by a night-fighter. Flight Sergeant 'Monty' Carroll, the Australian WOP/AG, was sitting with his back against the port side of the aircraft and his feet against the starboard side 'which was not the approved method', when they were hit from below by a night-fighter. 'A shell went through my wireless. We went into a dive and the Skipper pulled the aircraft out by using the tail trim. He said that we would be unable to land because the aileron controls had been shot away.'

Sergeant Nicholas 'Paddy' McNamara the rear gunner, who was from the Irish Republic, had been hit. 'Monty' Carroll went back to get him out:

> I had trouble getting the turret doors open because after the fighter attack they were just jagged metal. It was 48° below and I got frost-bitten fingers because I was only wearing mittens. When we finally got 'Paddy' out we put him on the floor of the aircraft. He said, 'Take your foot off my balls Blondie.' I said, 'What do you mean? I'm nowhere near you. (Paddy had been hit in the kidneys and when we got back the Doc told us that this might have caused constriction.) We decided to put Paddy on a static line and bail him out. The static line was supposed to be over the rest bed position but it wasn't there so I used the trailing aerial instead. I attached it to his ripcord and we pushed him out.

Flight Sergeant 'Jimmy' Denton the bomb aimer went out the front of the aircraft at the same time, the hope being that they would land together and he could attend to Paddy. 'Trouble was', says Carroll, 'it was about 12.30 at night and the middle of winter with snow everywhere. Jimmy ended up landing in some barbed wire entanglement and injured himself. They didn't find Paddy for about another 36 hours. He was dead when they found him.'

The rest of the crew bailed out safely over liberated territory and made it back to Little Staughton where they resumed operations. Monty Carroll, the eldest of six children, would later return to Australia to face questions from his three younger brothers who had an age gap of about ten years, but he did not feel like answering them. 'They couldn't understand. My parents didn't understand. How could they? So you tended to congregate with people who did understand and then all you did was get nervy and drink again while recounting all that had happened. We thought that we could have saved Paddy but I don't think that we could.'

McVerry's aircraft was one of 10 Lancasters that were lost on the raid on the *Braunkohle-Benzin* synthetic oil plant at Zeitz. Lancaster P4-V, better known as *Vicious Virgin/Baby*, and Flying Officer Clyde Willis Byers RCAF's crew on 153 Squadron at Scampton were lost without trace. This Lancaster had arrived on the Squadron in November and was the regular aircraft of Flying Officer Bob Purves' crew. It was on this aircraft that WAAF Iris Price flew a night operation to Germany! Her friend Doris Davies, a crew-bus driver on 153 Squadron recalls:

> On the night of the trip I saw Iris at the dispersal and thought that she had gone out on the bus with the crew to wave goodbye to her boyfriend, Bob Purvis, as she had done many times before. I did not see her again and assumed that she had got another lift or had walked back to the watch tower. However, when I went to collect the crew of *V-Victor* upon their return, I was amazed, when the plane door opened, to see Iris, semi-conscious, being supported by two crew members!

Iris recalled:

> I can remember Bob daring me to go on an op with him, so being the dare-devil that I was I agreed. It was a night operation which made the plan easy to achieve. A friend stood in for me while I was gone. This night I boarded the *Vicious Virgin*, Bob had got me a helmet, mask, parachute and harness. I was in my Battle Dress – normal MT garb. We took off for Germany, via France and Belgium. There were a lot of searchlights and some flak. At this stage I was feeling sick. We arrived over the target, the bombs were dropped and we

turned for home. Mission accomplished I calmed down a bit. Then it happened, I wanted to relieve myself. This I managed to do, eventually, into a bag, which was disposed of down the flare-chute. However in the process of partly undressing and struggling to dress again I lost my oxygen supply and became anoxic. Fortunately the crew were checking on me and returned. The next day I reported to SSQ, put my disposition down to a touch of flu and got two days off duty. At the time neither I nor the crew members dared to tell anyone. Goodness knows what the consequences would have been! The whole business was an experience that I will never forget.[13]

The next Main Force op was on 22/23 January when the benzol plant in the Bruckhausen district of Duisburg was attacked by 286 Lancasters and 16 Mosquitoes of 1, 3 and 8 Groups for the loss of two Lancasters. Another 152 aircraft of 4, 5 and 8 Groups carried out an area-bombing raid on Gelsenkirchen. *Friday The 13th* on 158 Squadron at Lissett, one of the 107 Halifaxes that took part, was flying its 100th op. All aircraft that were dispatched returned safely from Gelsenkirchen. Only four other B.Mk.IIIs are known to have completed 100 or more sorties and two of these, both on 578 Squadron, flew their 100th op jointly on 3/4 March on the raid on Kamen. *Friday the 13th* completed its 129th and final sortie on 25 April on the German coastal gun installations at Wangerooge. After the end of the war the most famous of all Halifaxes was put on display in Oxford Street in London but was scrapped in May 1945.[14]

During the first week of February Dick Perry on 218 Squadron completed his tour:

Wiesbaden on 2/3 February was our 28th against 14 for Les Harlow's crew. I remember that we looked down on those who we considered were still newcomers even though they were half way through a tour. It was an easy trip except for the weather. We used 'G-H' to bomb and there was neither flak nor searchlight to bother us. The big problem came on the way home. Everywhere we looked there were towering cumulonimbus clouds and lightning everywhere. Our only recourse was to fly over the top, which we proceeded to do. One of the things that became evident was that the Lanc was incapable of climbing over the tops of those CuNims. At 22,000 feet we were really wallowing around. By dint of dodging around them we managed to find our way back to the coast and home to base. An indication of how difficult it was, we were in the air for six hours. Our next trip, on 3/4th, our 29th, was much more interesting. We took off in daylight to arrive over Dortmund just after dark. We had just been congratulating ourselves on the fact that we were going to finish our tour with a string of easy trips. Talk about searchlights,

I'd never seen so many as they had up that night and everywhere, aircraft caught in the beams, which coned in on them. Then the 'G-H' went out so, only recourse, bomb visually using the preceding aircraft bomb strikes as indication of target. All was commotion, me directing Robbie, our crew yelling at me to drop the bombs, Harry yelling out that we had a fighter on our tail and do something, Robbie trying to take evasive action and listen to me at the same time. How we got out of that mess unscathed was a miracle and the bombs landed in the target area too. That was not the end of it. Harry fought fighters off all the way back to the coast. Strangely enough, there was very little flak, just fighters and searchlights. At least, for once, 'Gee' was working and we could find our way home. Harry and I took turns navigating on the way back which was interesting, as Robbie was continually dodging fighters. Once again, we were in the air for six hours. Our final trip, #30, was a piece of cake, much to our relief. The trip to Hohenburg was over 10/10 cloud and bombing was on 'G-H'. Harry and I took turns on the 'Gee' coming home. Once again, we had the awful experience of watching a kite blow up in front of us. This was the third time for us, one Halifax and two Lancs unexplained?[15]

Peter Bone's experience on 626 Squadron was one he would never forget either:

Our tour was relatively uneventful. We saw bombers being attacked by night fighters and shot down and others blown up by anti-aircraft fire but we were never attacked or so seriously damaged that we had to bail out or ditch in the sea. All the time we wondered when our turn would come. Survival was, I am convinced, 75% luck, 25% crew discipline. Eighteen Lancasters and 126 six aircrew never returned to Wickenby during our tour, which was longer than most because Skipper had a multitude of administrative duties to perform as Flight Commander. He had been promoted to Squadron Leader in December 1944. Each squadron consisted of 16 bombers so it was impossible to get to know more than a fraction of our fellow aircrew because of the sheer numbers. I think there was another reason; it was easier to handle losses if one didn't know too many 'bods', as we called each other. So, most remained just names on the Battle Order and faces that never became more than just familiar. Most soon vanished from memory. One name and face however, I'll never forget. Roderick Donner had been on my navigation course in Winnipeg a year earlier. He was probably ten years older than most of us and I think I regarded him as a kind of older brother. There was always a friendly grin behind that moustache and he smoked a pipe, which seemed to me to indicate stability. I lost sight of him when I failed the course and became an air gunner. I was pleased when he turned up at Wickenby not long after our arrival. He was now a flying officer and protocol demanded that some distance must be kept between officers and sergeants when not in the air. Whenever our paths crossed in the briefing and crew rooms, he would always call out, 'How's it going Pete?' with the same cheerful grin.

Came the night of 20/21 February 1945. Our crew was on the Battle Order for Dortmund, in the Ruhr. Although I didn't know it, Donner was home on compassionate leave for the birth of his first child. He just had time to bring his wife and baby boy home from the hospital before catching a train back to Wickenby. There he found his crew were on the Battle Order for that night. While he was probably catching a few hours' sleep, I took my guns out of *Tommy Two*, the aircraft we had just used and replaced them with the mid-upper guns of the crew detailed to use T^2 that night. The target was Duisburg but T^2 never came back. I wrote in my diary that night: 'Good bods, Pyatt, Donner, etc. Cleaned bike, wrote home, had crumpets and cocoa for supper in the billet.' And that was all. At the time I was unaware of Donner's personal life and probably gave no thought to whether he was married or not. He was just a 'bod' whom I liked from a distance but who suddenly was gone, like so many others.[16]

No one flew in the same aircraft for long for few of them lasted a whole tour. Our crew became very attached to '*Able Two*', an old warhorse that was approaching its 90th op. In mid-January 1945 our crew had been on the Battle Order twice for an attack on an oil refinery at Merseburg, a fairly long trip to a well-defended target. On each occasion the op had been 'scrubbed' probably because of adverse weather conditions and we weren't put out. Now it was on again. Our crew did the mandatory 'daily inspection' of faithful old A^2, or as we called it, 'Ready, Willing and Able Too'. We were all set to go when we heard that Flight Lieutenant Nelson and his crew would be taking our place. Apparently, they were anxious to finish their tour and Merseburg would be their next to last. Two aircraft were lost on 12 Squadron and one on 626. 'Ready, Willing and Able Two' never came back. 'Very careless' we said. What else was there to say? Seven more faces suddenly no more.[17]

The early months of 1945 saw a tremendous increase in Bomber Command's operations, both in tempo and number, 40 raids being mounted in February alone.[18] On 2/3 February, Bomber Command mounted raids on Mannheim, Wanne-Eickel, Wiesbaden and Karlsruhe by 1,200 aircraft, about 250 being ordered to raid Karlsruhe. Due to adverse weather conditions and extensive *Luftwaffe* night fighter activity near and over the targets operations were only partially successful. Twenty-one aircraft failed to return, including 11 from the Karlsruhe force, and another 13 crashed in liberated French territory. It was a bad night for 189 Squadron with four aircraft failing to return to Fulbeck.[19] Further raids followed, on the Prosper and Hansa benzol plants at Bottrop and Dortmund respectively and on the plant at Osterfeld and the Nordstern synthetic-oil plant at Gelsenkirchen. Bonn too was subject to an attack by 238 aircraft.

On 7 February, 100 Lancasters of 3 Group attacked the Krupp benzol plant at Wanne-Eickel again. Only 75 aircraft were able to bomb in wintry conditions, which scattered the force and the results were unknown. One Lancaster failed to return. Flight Lieutenant Joe Eyles' crew on 218 Squadron were one of the Lancaster crews that flew on the operation, as Walford Jones recalls:

> We had been told in the briefing that the weather at 20,000 feet over Germany would be clear and bright with any cloud at much lower levels. So we set off at about 11am to rendezvous over the East Anglian coast and set up the formation of about 500 planes heading towards the Dutch coast and on to the industrial heartland of Germany. Over the sea and over Holland we flew in bright sunshine but after crossing a short way into the Reich we were suddenly and without warning enveloped in thick cloud. Our immediate thought was that this was a bit of rogue stuff which we would soon pass through so kept to our set flight path, height and speed trusting that all the others around us did the same, for by now we were only able to see the other two craft flying in V formation with us. The other 20 or so that we were leading had disappeared into the mist. This was a very scary situation which after about five minutes caused Joe to decide to try and climb above it into clearer weather. But as we went up we needed more power from the engines, which meant using more fuel and as we were never given a lot to spare I was concerned about having enough to get back home. Also the two others flying within a few yards of us previously were now nowhere to be seen as the cloud, if anything, had got thicker.
>
> We climbed to 30,000 feet at which point it was still thick cloud and the engines were unable to take us any higher. This was a potentially disastrous state of affairs with about 500 fully loaded bombers flying around blind in a very limited sky space and was, if anything, worse than having to deal with the enemy defences which if they were firing at us we could not see but being so high was some consolation. This situation showed no sign of improving so as our navigator calculated that we were not far from the target area the bombs were released and we turned for home still flying blind with no sight of any other aircraft. We were well on our way over Holland before the cloud started to thin and give us some idea if we had

company but amazingly there was not another aircraft in sight, it was as if the cloud had gobbled them all up and we had escaped. What losses had been incurred we never knew but it was inconceivable to think that there had been no crashes in these terrible conditions. Someone in the met office had made a terrible boob leading to this fiasco.

The other crew living in our billet were on this raid as they had been on many of the previous ones, being lucky like us and returning home unscathed, but before long their luck was to run out. It happened during a day when they were flying c nearing the target with qu us when I noticed them ta going into a shallow dive, to our dismay went twistin We hoped they might reco got to a lower altitude and false hope as our last sight with the River Rhine way d was no smoke coming from which we found mystifying the plane the wireless operator who had been in this position before and got out should have been able to give a lead to the others. We were very shocked even though we had seen other planes being shot down, but we knew the people in this one so well and their absence from our billet was very much felt for a long time after and we often speculated about what had exactly happened. Their beds were never filled while we were at Chedburgh.

The noose was beginning to tighten around the German neck. On the night of 7/8 February, 464 aircraft[20] of 4, 6 and 8 Groups were sent to bomb Goch, and 295 Lancasters and ten Mosquitoes of 1 and 8 Groups were given the small town of Kleve, about five miles west of the Rhine and ten miles from Nijmegen, as their targets.[21] Both raids were mounted to prepare the way for the attack of the British XXX Corps across the German frontier near the Reichswald. Goch and Kleve, which were thought to be road and rail junctions, were part of the strong German defences there. At Goch the Master Bomber Wing Commander A W G Cochrane DSO DFC on 156 Squadron, a New Zealander from Rawene, who early in the raid was involved in a collision with another Lancaster, ordered the Main Force to go below the cloud, the estimated base of which, was only 5,000 feet. The attack opened very accurately but the raid was stopped after 155 aircraft had bombed because smoke was causing control of the raid to become impossible. Cochrane made it back to Upwood with a badly damaged wing. Flying Officer John Leslie Beeson RAAF, on 158 Squadron at Lissett piloting *P-Peter* was still at 3,500 feet when he was involved in a head-on collision with *Z-Zebra*, piloted by Flight Sergeant Derrick William Muggeridge on 77 Squadron at Full Sutton, who crashed moments later, 20 kilometres from the target area. All Muggeridge's crew were killed. Beeson tried for two minutes to regain control before ordering his crew to bail out but only three got out in time before the Halifax crashed into forest between Lüllingen and Geldern. The Australian pilot and three other crew members were killed. Two Halifaxes on 347 *Tunisie* Free French Squadron at Elvington and two on 102 Squadron at Pocklington were shot down. Considerable damage was caused in Goch but most of the inhabitants had probably left the town.

Flight Lieutenant F W Powell DFC on the crew of a Halifax Mk III on 640 Squadron at Leconfield was on his 41st operation. He wrote:

A short while after leaving the target we received some unwelcome attention from flak batteries below, which was particularly disconcerting, as we were by then over friendly territory. I fired off a Very cartridge in the colour of the period, which only attracted increased attention from below; the firing only stopped after I had fired two more signals. We had barely recovered from this intrusion when we heard a series of explosions as cannon shells thundered into the fuselage with both the rear and mid-upper gunners confirming that we had been attacked by a Me 262, identified by its jet exhausts as it flashed past from underneath on our starboard side. Convulsed by smoke and the smell of cordite, the aircraft was now in a dive and I recall wondering just how long it would be before the aircraft hit the ground and praying that death would be swift. But after what seemed an interminable period, the pilot levelled out and said he thought he had regained control.

Examination of the aircraft showed that the control cables to the starboard ailerons and rudder were either severed or badly damaged. The Skipper ordered us to prepare to bail out, but the engines were still functioning properly and we decided to try to make the emergency strip at Manston. We now found a new problem as we could not raise Manston and it took another 20 minutes to repair the damaged aerial. By now we had over-flown Manston and with damage to the controls could not easily turn back. We pressed on to Woodbridge who to our relief gave us permission to land. Inspection of the aircraft showed that we had been hit by 30mm cannon shells from below from the rear turret to the bomb bay, but by a miracle all had missed the crew positions. We concluded that the 262 had been lurking in the area and had been alerted to our presence by the Very signals we had made to our 'friendly' flak. Although somewhat concerned when we first heard at the end of 1944 that the jet fighter had become operational, our cause for alarm was to a degree unfounded as the Me 262 did not prove very satisfactory as a night fighter. If the initial strike was not successful, its speed restricted its manoeuvrability and we could usually escape in the darkness or cloud cover.

At Kleve red and yellow 20mm and 37mm tracer shells were criss-crossing from the flak batteries outside the town. Flashes from the exploding blockbusters on the ground were blinding. John Gee on 153 Squadron at Scampton recalls:

Kleve had been virtually destroyed anyway but it was a place where *Panzer* reinforcements might be brought up to resist the army push. It was only just in front of our front-line, so we had to be jolly careful that we didn't bomb our own troops. The weather forecast was good. There was no cloud about. I was the senior officer flying on 153 Squadron that night and was tickled pink to be nominated to take Richard Dimbleby and his engineer and recording equipment. This made us quite a lot overweight, so to reduce it we ditched some gallons of petrol. We sat with them and had a meal before we took off.

Dimbleby was a big chap. When he sat alongside me on the air-craft the flight engineer, who would normally be there, had to stand behind to operate all his gauges and things. You couldn't really get past in the fuselage with all the recording gear. The engineer had to squat down in the fuselage. I couldn't imagine anything worse than squatting in a Lancaster for 4 or 5 hours waiting to operate equipment for probably no more than five minutes. It was only when we got near the target that Dimbleby started to make his commentary. We were flying at 17,000 feet and couldn't see a thing. I thought, 'What are we going to do? We can't drop our bombs on our own troops.' Suddenly we heard the Master Bomber [Wing Commander 'Tubby' Baker] calling us down below 4,500 feet. You can imagine 295 Lancasters coming down from 17,000 to 4,500 feet through cloud. Why there was no collision I just don't know. There were 295 near misses there all at one time. There below us was Kleve and the target was marked by the Pathfinders and searchlights were reflected off the cloud – it was like daylight. And you could see the Lancasters coming out of the cloud like darts. Then we had to bomb the target from 4,500 feet. The bombs were exploding and the aircraft was being bounced all over the place. Richard Dimbleby made his commentary, which was broadcast the next day on the BBC. We knocked Kleve out completely; so much so that when the army advanced the next day there were so many bomb craters and so many broken roads that it quickly came to a halt.

Some 285 aircraft bombed with such devastating results that after the war, Kleve claimed to be the most completely destroyed town in Germany of its size.[22] One Lancaster was lost when it crashed on its run-in, blowing up with its full bomb load.

On 8/9 February Bomber Command returned to attacks on synthetic oil plants, when Pölitz was bombed by 475 Lancasters and seven Mosquitoes. The attack took place in two waves, the first being marked and carried out entirely by the 5 Group method and the second being marked by the Pathfinders of 8 Group. The weather conditions were clear and the bombing of both waves was extremely accurate. Severe damage was caused to this important synthetic-oil plant. It produced no further oil during the war.[23] Ten Lancasters were lost and one crashed near Hjortshog in Sweden. The pilot survived and he was interned but all of his crew died in the crash. Two hundred Halifaxes carried out a smaller-scale raid on the Krupp benzol plant at Wanne-Eickel and 151 Lancasters attacked the Hohenbudberg railway yards at Krefeld, but both these raids were largely unsuccessful. Forty-seven RCM sorties were flown for the loss of a single Halifax on 192 Squadron, which collided with a Lancaster on 625 Squadron on the way home. The Lancaster made it back but the Halifax crashed into the sea with the loss of all the crew. Two other Lancasters were lost. Two Halifaxes on the Wanne-Eickel raid failed to return when one crashed near Dunkirk and the other was abandoned over Belgium. A Halifax on 426 'Thunderbird' Squadron crash-landed near Wetherby in Yorkshire, injuring the pilot and one of his crew. The other five men on board were killed.

There then followed a series of minor operations from 9–13 February, involving Mosquito bombers, mainly while the Main Force was grounded. Bomber Command though was merely building up for an operation that has since gone down in history as one of the most controversial bombing raids of the war.

Notes

1. Middlebrook and Everitt.
2. *Barnes Wallis' Bombs: Tallboy, Dambuster & Grand Slam* by Stephen Flower. Tempus 2002)
3. NA501 *X-X-Ray*, in all probability, fell victim to *Oberleutnant* Peter Spoden of 6./NJG6, for his 18th *Abschuss*. Donmall successfully evaded and reached the Allied lines. Watson and three other members of the crew were taken prisoner; three were killed on the aircraft.
4. *'By Oboe Victor To Cologne'* by Bill Lanning/Little Staughton Path Finder Association. The other crewmember lost was S/L Albert Carter DFC, the second pilot.
5. 2nd TAF and 100 Group Mosquito crews destroyed 14 Luftwaffe aircraft.
6. See *Strike Hard, Strike Sure* by Ralph Barker (Pen & Sword Military Classics 2003)

7. See *Strike Hard, Strike Sure* by Ralph Barker (Pen & Sword Military Classics 2003). One Lancaster was lost from the 146 aircraft of 3 Group that success-fully attacked the railway yards at Vohwinkel. No aircraft were lost from the force of 105 Halifaxes of 4 Group and 18 Lancasters and 16 Mosquitoes of 8 Group that attempted to bomb a benzol plant at Dortmund. Bombing was scattered and none of the bombs hit the plant. Mosquitoes of 2nd TAF and 100 Group on bomber support covered heavy operations over Germany and eight German night-fighters were claimed shot down.

8. *Hauptmann* Kurt-Heinz Weigel of 11./NJG6 claimed two four-engined bombers west and southeast of Stuttgart for his 2nd and 3rd victories. *Hauptmann* Martin 'Tino' Becker, *Kommandeur*, IV./NJG6, claimed a Lancaster south of Mannheim-north of Bruchsal and another Lancaster over Luxembourg for his 44th and 45th victories.

9. *The Bomber Command War Diaries: An Operational reference book 1939–1945.* Martin Middlebrook and Chris Everitt. (Midland 1985).

10. *218 Gold Coast Squadron Assoc Newsletter No.55* August 2009. One Lancaster was lost on Dortmund.

11. Two Mosquito bombers were lost raiding Berlin while two 100 Group Mosquitoes also FTR, making 37 aircraft lost in total. Thirty-one bombers were claimed destroyed by *Nachtjagd*. *Hauptmann* Werner Hopf of 8./NJG5 claimed four Halifaxes (for his 15th–18th *Abschüsse*), *Hauptmann* Werner Baake, *Kommandeur* of I./NJG1 and *Major* Hans Karlewski of *Stab* NJG2 each claimed three and *Oberleutnant* Walter Briegleb *St.Kpt* of 7./NJG2 two. *Hauptmann* Hermann Greiner of 11./NJG1 claimed three Lancasters over Hannover for his 43rd–45th victories.

12. *218 Gold Coast Squadron Newsletter No.32* February 2005.

13. Adapted from the *Bomber Command Assoc Newsletter*, No.28 February 1995.

14. *Handley Page Halifax: From Hell to Victory and Beyond* by K A Merrick (Chevron Publishing 2009).

15. *218 Gold Coast Squadron Assoc Newsletter No.35* August 2005.

16. F/O Roderick William Donner, WO1 Robert Stanley Pyatt RCAF and the others on F/O Donald Rodger's crew of UM-T, KIA.

17. F/L D S Nelson RCAF survived and was taken prisoner. The others on the crew on UM-A were killed.

18. That same month *Nachtjagd* flew 772 sorties and claimed 181 *Abschüsse* for the loss of 47 fighters. 100 Group and 2nd TAF Mosquitoes shot down 18 German aircraft at night and probably destroyed one other. During January–February 1945, *Nachtjagd* crews flew 1,820 sorties, claiming 302 victories against the odds – 117 in January and 185 in February – but 94 aircraft were lost together with the majority of their crews. On the night of 13/14 January, 274 aircraft were dispatched to Saarbrücken and a second force of 218 aircraft attacked the oil plant at Pölitz, near Stettin.

19. Five Lancasters crashed in the same area around the town of Bruchsal, NE of Karlsruhe on 2/3 February 1945 (3 on 189 Squadron – PB848 flown by F/L Norman Philip Blain RCAF crashed in a wood near Heidelsheim South of Bruchsal. All except rear gunner KIA. F/Sgt Don Clement RCAF had a similar escape to Sgt Dyson, being blown from his turret by an explosion, which was possibly caused when the Lancaster was hit by flak when making a 2nd bomb run over the target with its bomb load still aboard. PB743 flown by

F/L John Outram Davies, exploded on its bombing run over Weingarten, SW of Heidelsheim after dropping the 4,000 pounder and part of the load of incendiaries and it may have been hit by a *Schräge Musik* equipped night-fighter. F/Sgt Les Cromarty DFM, crew tail gunner on his 2nd tour, was again the sole survivor when he was blown out of his turret and he landed by parachute. ME298/B on 463 Squadron RAAF came down at Unterowisheim nearby after being attacked by a night-fighter and possibly being hit by flak over Karlsruhe. F/O Richard Kay Oliver RAAF and four crew KIA. They were buried in the British and Commonwealth war cemetery at Durnbach, as were the 6 crew of PB840, the remains of which fell into a wood near Oberowisheim, NE of Bruchsal. It is believed that PB840 was shot down by *Oberfeldwebel* Heinrich Schmidt of 2./NJG6 at 23.21 hours; it was Schmidt's 9th *Abschuss*. 5th Lancaster was PB306 on 467 Squadron RAAF (shot down by *Hauptmann* Friedrich at Karlsdorf at 23.30) piloted by F/L Noel Sidney Caesar Colley. All 8 crew, average age 21, were KIA.

20. 292 Halifaxes, 156 Lancasters, 16 Mosquitoes.

21. In another operation, 177 Lancasters and 11 Mosquitoes of 5 Group attacked a section of the Dortmund-Ems Canal near Ladbergen with delayed-action bombs. Later photographs showed that the banks had not been damaged; the bombs had fallen into nearby fields. Three Lancasters were lost.

22. Middlebrook & Everett. The British attack, led by the 15th (Scottish) Division, made a successful start a few hours later but quickly ground to a halt because of a thaw, which caused flooding on the few roads available for the advance and also because of the ruins, which blocked the way through Kleve. Lieutenant-General Brian G Horrocks the corps commander in charge of the attack claimed later that he had requested that Kleve should only be subjected to an incendiary raid but Bomber Command dropped 1,384 tons of HE on the town and no incendiaries. One Lancaster FTR.

23. Middlebrook & Everitt. 12 Lancasters FTR.

CHAPTER 4

Flying Into The Flames of Hell

I had been a prisoner of war in Dresden for some months before that dreadful night. It was a beautiful city with parks and grand houses – it seemed virtually untouched by war. I quite liked the people of Dresden. They were more softly spoken, civilised people than I had met elsewhere in Germany. The Russians had reportedly already bypassed the city and the people were convinced that the war was all but over. They were certainly more frightened of being caught up in the Russian advance than of any threat from the air. It must have been about 22.00 that I first heard the aircraft. They were so low that I could see them quite clearly. I was on the outskirts of the city and no bombs fell near me, but there was a strong wind blowing and they dropped the incendiaries so that the fires started upwind and then raced through the city. It was as bright as day and I could see the fires burning on the surface of the river and the markings of the aircraft still flying overhead. There seemed to be no opposition. They were now dropping high explosives and I saw the railway station receive a direct hit and blow up.

Sergeant W Morris of the RASC (Royal Army Service Corps)

Whistling loudly the train entered Dresden station. At most of the platforms trains were belching smoke. There were crowds on all platforms. The first impression was of noise, hurrying people, yelling, calling to each other, loud signals and penetrating voices from various loudspeakers. The light was dim everywhere. Globes were covered with something blue, giving only a little light which shone feebly on the masses of people. Carried along by the crowd Marushka (Maria) and Zygmunt Skarbek-Kruszewski and Jurek (George) Zygmunt Skarbek reached the street. Small cream-coloured Dresden trams were ringing their bells non-stop trying to avoid hitting the people. Marushka and her companions were looking for an address given them a long time ago. Near the station in

103

one of the lesser known streets, they found the bookshop they were looking for. In its windows, as in all German bookshops, was displayed the book which was read by hardly anyone – *Mein Kampf* by Adolf Hitler. The book was propped up by a wilting pot plant. It was quiet in the bookshop. The shop was full of books with shelves reaching to the ceiling. Behind these shelves in a narrow darkish room Alma was sitting, typing. They had been looking for her for many reasons. Firstly, she was the only person they knew in Dresden. She was Marushka's friend from Lithuania and for the last few years had worked in Germany and would be able to give them valuable information and tell them the score. Alma was a rather unusual woman. She considered herself a *civis orbium terrarum* (citizen of the world) and went her own ways. Because of her love of books she had gone to Dresden to work in the bookshop. She was an employee of the cultural society of German–Turkestan Friendly Relations. Goebbels had liquidated all cultural life, and many schools, universities, theatres, libraries and other places of education and cultural entertainment closed, but the cultural society for German–Turkestan relationship still existed, even employing quite a few people.

As Alma asked her visitors to stay with her, they decided to spend a few days in Dresden. After a good rest, they went to see the capital city of 'Soksofony' which Lithuanian labourers called Saxoni. There were many Lithuanians there, as the German employment office in Kaunas sent many transports of forced labour to Saxoni. There was also a large group of educated Lithuanians who, fleeing the Front, came to Dresden – people from the theatre in Kaunas, employees from different adminis-tration offices and even some divisions of the Lithuanian Army. In the streets one heard many different tongues and saw different features. People from the 'Ostland' were easily distinguishable. Ukrainers, White Russian and Lithuanian women wore bright, multi-coloured scarves and long skirts. Their men folk wore clean but crumpled tunic shirts and high boots. Being a Sunday, the streets were crowded with masses of gaping people. All these people from the captured East had sewn on their clothes a blue patch with a stamp 'OST'. These three letters covered a multitude of people. They included not only the Russians in their red and white berets but also people from Ukraine, White Russia, Baltic countries and also Georgians, Tartars, and Azerbaijans. They were all imported into Germany for slave labour; the labourer marked 'made in the East'. In this crowd were some dressed worse than others, even in torn clothing. They could not ever afford a Sunday best – those were the Poles. They were excluded from the general 'OST' – they did not belong to the East or to the West but the newly formed German oddity 'General *Gubcrasatian*'. God alone might have known what their position would be in the 'New Europe' of Messrs. Goebbels and Rosenberg. Now they were required by the *Third Reich* for the hardest jobs. On their chests was a yellow sign well-known to all in Germany – a yellow rhomboid with a purple letter 'P'.

Walking along the streets of Dresden, Marushka, Zygmunt and Jurek heard many more languages, some completely foreign to them. The Germans, taking over foreign countries, at the same time decreased their own population as the foreign countries taken by force had to be peopled by the Germans. This was the *Führer's* law – he was the master of New Europe. At this time Dresden was one of the few German cities largely untouched by mass bombing. The most beautiful part of the city was spread along the River Elbe. It was dominated by the famous *Zwinger*, the beautiful arena of ancient jousting knights, which was surrounded by a ring of ornate galleries, balconies and terraces. The fine old baroque was fully displayed amidst the flowers and the greenery. Among the fantastically arched galleries were miniature palaces built on different levels. Large greenhouses with huge windows seemed to catch all the sun's rays. Theirs was a superior world, beyond temptation, beyond understanding of the gaping crowd. From there, arched galleries led to the king's chambers. Only tops of the trees planted on lower levels could reach them. Golden leaves were falling on the marble balustrades where, long ago, crowned heads and princesses watched the knights. All this was a long time ago. The shining armour was put on wooden models, the exquisite gowns of the princesses were displayed in glass cabinets in the museums and the mansions were taken over by Dresden rich commoners. The rattling sound of the armour was replaced by the rich, soft sound of music. The Dresden symphony concerts received here their true sanctuary.

Further down, Marushka, Zygmunt and Jurek looked at the banks of the River Elbe with its large, sloping terraces leading to the *Zwinger*. The open grounds over the Elbe were joined by bridges like clamping buckles. The other side glittered with the mosaic of many coloured houses. To the left of the open space stood the Dresden Opera House, its entrance enclosed with winding colonnades. To the right was the king's church – a beautiful Gothic, its proud tower rising straight to the sky, its wall nearly touching the king's castle. Over the narrow street was suspended an arcade in the shape of a state coach joining the church with the castle, the king's salon with the altar. A large painted gate led to the king's yard. Further on were the boulevards along the river. In their shade were the buildings of the art academy and the museums. Now they were quite empty like tombs in a cemetery covered by autumn leaves. They were declared closed by orders of the *Führer*. Objects of art were buried in the ground and people loving and living for art were fighting for a worse future. Only empty halls, galleries and auditoriums remained. Buildings by famous architects, these sanctuaries of beauty, culture and truth were waiting in the empty stillness the uncertain tomorrow. Would they survive? Would the war respect them?

Achtung! Achtung! The street loudspeakers were calling. 'Large formations of enemy bombers have crossed the frontiers of the *Reich*. Stay tuned'. Soon there followed names of towns in central Germany as the bombers continued on. Marushka and her companions and everyone around them rushed to the shelters. Had Dresden's last hour come?

No.

Soon the 'All Clear' sounded. The bombers had turned to the north. *Achtung!* headquarters announced. 'A large force of enemy Flying Fortresses is attacking our capital city. Churches and hospitals are being hit. The civilian population has received many losses ...'

It was time for Marushka, Zygmunt and Jurek to leave Dresden.

They went to the information office at the *Hauptbanhof*. Travellers were asking and pleading constantly with the officer about the safety of different railway lines. They wanted some kind of guarantee. An old gentleman in a railway uniform was shrugging his shoulders and occasionally addressed everyone, saying 'I can't promise you anything. Trains going to the north are being shot at. If you don't want to take risks, go during the night.' People from the crowd replied 'But that would mean sitting for long times at different railway stations waiting for connections and we all know that stations are being bombed frequently.'

A woman going to Duisburg was very worried. The officer again shrugged his shoulders and said, 'I can only inform you which lines are temporarily closed due to damaged and bombed railway lines. I can't tell you which lines will, or will not, be bombed in the future.' Smiling, he added, 'If you are frightened, the best idea would be not to travel at all. As it is our trains are overcrowded.'

'I have to go. My son is seriously wounded,' the woman said, showing him the wire received from her son. 'He is in Duisburg hospital.'

Marushka at last reached the window with her travel order for Isny, east of Ravensburg.

'You can have two connections,' the officer said in a tired voice. 'One through Munich, the other through Augsburg.' Not waiting for Marushka's question, he continued, 'I would advise you to go through Augsburg as lately Munich has had more air raids.'

She agreed without any further question and he wrote out the tickets: Nürnburg, Augsburg and Memmingen – departure at 22.30.

The same evening they arrived with their rucksacks at the *Hauptbanhof*. The long platforms were poorly lit by a blue light, giving everything a deathly pallor. The top platforms were shrouded in darkness. Sometimes sparks from the noisy engines flickered down onto the platform. Unexpectedly all the lights went out. Only red and green regulation lights and lighted signs showing the way to the shelter stayed alight. A thundering voice from the loudspeaker informed them: 'Enemy planes are over Germany. This is a warning. Keep calm and orderly.'

Marushka got frightened and grabbing Zygmunt's hand, she begged him to run away. But the crowd did not move – they looked indifferent. They knew that announcements would shortly follow advising the path of progress. Germany was large and there were many towns to be bombed. A warning did not frighten anyone. The train soon arrived and there was a rush to the doors. Marushka hesitated and entered the train distrustfully. They had to find their places in darkness. None of the travellers would part with their luggage. One had to be ready just in case any minute the real alarm might come and then ... The unpleasant minutes of waiting continued. Here and there people were lighting matches to look at their watches and count the minutes until departure. Seven minutes to go ... now only five ... now three ... If only the time would hurry on, they could leave this station more quickly, these heavy metal constructions, the ghosts of a permanent tomb. Again the voice from the loudspeaker: 'All Clear.'

The lights came on, a loud whistle blew and the train started moving.

Operation *Thunderclap* was planned to cause as much destruction, confusion and mayhem in Berlin, Leipzig, Chemnitz and Dresden as possible and had been under consideration for several months. It was to be implemented only when the military situation in Germany was critical. The orders had been issued to Bomber Command on 27 January. Stalin was informed of the plan a week later, at the Yalta Conference and he gave enthusiastic encouragement. *Thunderclap* was to have started with an American raid on Dresden on 13 February but bad weather over Europe prevented any US involvement until the 14th. Formerly the capital of Saxony, Dresden had become a centre of art and culture, under the elector Augustus II the Strong during the latter part of the 17th and early 18th centuries. The manufacture of Dresden china, started at Dresden in 1709, was transferred to Meissen a year later. By the beginning of World War Two the 'German Florence and the loveliest rococo city in Europe' was manufacturing a more sinister range of weapons for war. Over 3,700 industrial plants of various sizes worked full-time for the Nazi war machine, among them such giants as Zeiss Ikon AG. The Dresden Zeiss plant alongside the main plant in Jena was one of the principal centres for the production of field glasses for the *Wehrmacht* and bomb sights for the Luftwaffe and periscopes for the U-boats, as well as aiming sights for the Panzer tanks and the German artillery. Telefunken made electrical components used in radar. As an economic centre Dresden ranked sixth in importance in pre-war Germany. It was one of the key centres for the German postal and telegraph system and a crucial east-west transit point with its seven bridges and a huge rail junction[1] and was targeted now because it had become a vital communications and supply centre for the Eastern Front, which had reached the eastern border of Germany after the rapid Soviet advance across Poland. In effect Dresden had become a potential *Festungen* (fortress). The Elbe is over 300 feet wide at Dresden and the highest point in the town at the time was almost 1,000 feet above sea level offering an excellent view of the surrounding countryside.

At the bomber stations in England the plan for Operation *Thunderclap* was made known to crews at briefings. Bomber Command's briefing notes, issued to groups and squadrons on the eve of the Dresden raid said:

> Dresden, the seventh largest city in Germany and not much smaller than Manchester, is also far the largest un-bombed built-up area the enemy has got. In the midst of winter with refugees pouring westwards and troops to be rested, roofs are at a premium, not only to give shelter to workers, refugees and troops alike but to house the administrative services displaced from other areas. At one time well known for its china, Dresden has developed into an industrial city of first-class importance and like any large city with its multiplicity of telephone and rail facilities, is of major value for controlling the defence of that part of the front now threatened by Marshal Koniev's breakthrough. The intentions of the attack are to hit the enemy where he will feel it most, behind an already partially collapsed front, to prevent the use of the city in the way of further advance and incidentally to show the Russians when they arrive what Bomber Command can do.

That morning on 619 Squadron at Strubby airfield in 5 Group, five miles south-west of Mablethorpe, Lincolnshire John Whiteley's wireless operator reported sick and was grounded by the Medical Officer. Then the Flight Commander informed Whiteley that he was taking a pilot who had recently joined the Squadron, for operational experience. 'I told the 'second dickey' that I would also take his wireless operator as a replacement, which I believe, scared them both!'

At Downham Market, Fred White, a navigator who had come though scores of trips to targets like Peenemünde and Nürnburg and 13 raids on Berlin and was now on his second tour, sat through the briefing.

'It was different to the briefings when Berlin was announced when all heads would drop. We hated Berlin. In February 1944 my pilot, Peter de Wesselow completed his tour and so I flew with an Australian called Pelletier for the five flights needed to complete my own tour. Then I was sent to Warboys to instruct. I didn't like it at all. In October Squadron Leader Peter de Wesselow contacted me to ask if I wanted to go back to ops for a second tour on 635 Squadron. I leapt at the chance.' Peter de Wesselow was the 5 Group Master Bomber for the second wave attack on Dresden. He was on his third tour and it was his 72nd operation. They would be in the air for 8 hours and 50 minutes and had to circle the target for about 20 minutes, showing the other crews where to drop their bombs.

'We knew the time on target was between 10 and 10.30pm and joked that we'd catch the Germans as they were coming out of the pubs' recalled Flight Sergeant John Aldridge. 'In hindsight I don't feel good about that but for the most part, we didn't think in terms of people being killed but of areas we had to hit. That was how things were in 1945.'

Most crews looked upon Dresden as just one more operation towards the completion of their tour. This was certainly the view of Eric Thale at Kelstern where the weather was so bad that morning that aircrew on 625 Squadron doubted that they would be flying that night. Thale had completed 17 trips and he had 13 to go. Dresden was to be bombed in two RAF assaults three hours apart, the first by 244 Lancasters of 5 Group and the second by 529 Lancasters of 1, 3, 6 and 8 Groups. At briefing Thale and his crew and all the others were told that 5 Group would open the attack with 250 aircraft to get the fires going, with a time on target of 22.15 hours. Their marking point would be the Ostragehege sports stadium in the centre of the city situated near the lines of a railway and a river, which would serve as a pointer to the stadium for the Marker Force, especially since it was anticipated that visibility might not be too good. There would be diversionary attacks on Böhlen, Magdeburg, Bonn and Nürnburg to confuse the German fighter controllers as to the main target. One hour and forty-five minutes later 1 Group would attack with 500 aircraft. The delay would ensure that all emergency services would probably have been called in from outside Dresden, so the attack would knock those out as well. 627 Squadron would provide nine Mosquito Path Finders and Master Bomber was Wing Commander Maurice Smith, whose call-sign was 'King Cole'.[2] The Main Force call-sign was 'Strongman'.

'The main threat from the enemy tonight' concluded the briefing officer 'will be flak. His fighter aircraft should be chasing the *'Window'* feint force, which we hope will be indicating to the enemy that Frankfurt, Mainz, Darmstadt or Mannheim is the main target. By the time we get into the picture they will be running out of fuel and therefore landing. But just in case, our night-striking Mosquitoes will be patrolling the enemy's rendezvous beacons and airfields.

'Now, any questions?'

No one spoke.

As the target was relatively close to the advancing Soviet lines crews were issued with Union Jacks to put across their chests, in case they were shot down behind the lines, with the words *I am an Englishman* printed on them in Russian. Some thought that they were not much of an asset; rather they would present a better target! Later, as the words of the briefing sunk in, some crews joked that with TOT (Time on Target) at Dresden scheduled for 10.30pm they would catch the Germans just as they were coming out of the pubs. For the most part crews never thought in terms of people being killed but of areas that they had to hit. But not Johnnie Byrne who since losing his first crew in December only wanted German blood. The 20-year-old Lancaster wireless operator had finally received his commission and he was now a Pilot Officer on *B Squared* on 550 Squadron at North Killingholme, piloted by Flight Lieutenant Eric Allen. He taxied out and turned onto the main runway, a green was flashed from the ACP and at 21.39 with throttle pushed fully forward he took the Lancaster off into wind. At Faldingworth Warrant Officer Marian Mykietyn's crew on 300 'Masovian' Squadron climbed aboard their Lancaster and took off at 21.47. Twelve minutes later and while still gaining height, both Lancasters collided over Lincolnshire. The two aircraft exploded and fell at Stott's Farm at Apley three miles south-west of Wragby. Only three of the Polish crew could be identified. The bodies of the two air gunners on Allen's aircraft were found but the rest could not be identified. Johnnie Byrne had been spared death in December and his one purpose since had been to avenge the death of his crew, but it was only for a short time.

It seemed to the *Jägerleitoffiziers* (*JLO*, or GCI-controllers) following the path of the bombers on radar that Leipzig was the likely target, but 50 miles from it, the Lancasters turned towards Dresden. The RAF weather forecasters had promised that large areas of cloud would hide the bombers' approach and at the target itself, clear skies were predicted. When the illuminator force of the Path Finders arrived over Dresden the cloud cover was 9 to 10/10ths up to about 9,500 feet. The Marker Force of Mosquitoes found that the cloud base was at about 2,500 feet. The cloud was not too thick and the flares illuminated Dresden for the markers who placed their red Target Indicators very accurately on the aiming point. At 22.13 hours 244 Lancasters controlled throughout by 'King Cole' commenced the attack , and it was completed by 22.31 hours.

Eric Thale was gratified that the cloud started to break up as they had been promised by the 'met' man:

> Soon we noticed a faint glow appearing in the sky ahead of us. We still had twenty minutes to run. Was that glow ahead coming from Dresden? We switched on the radio and heard the Master Bomber and his deputy. From their discussion we gathered that visibility was excellent. The Master Bomber said that illumination flares were not needed and he ordered the Path Finders carrying them to go home. We were fifteen miles from the target and the whole area was just one sea of flames. Strangely there was no smoke. The fires were burning with such intensity that they were generating their

own winds, which carried the smoke away and kept the target almost clear. Those fires also quickly swallowed up the marker flares. Realizing this, the Master Bomber issued an order to the Main Force – 'King Cole to Strongman: no markers, bomb visually, bomb visually.' Ahead of us the first wave of aircraft were dropping their loads and we saw aircraft below us silhouetted against the fires. As the cookies exploded, a shock-wave ring momentarily appeared in the fire, to be swallowed up again in an instant. We commenced our own bombing run at 01.33 hours, exactly on time. It was very turbulent now, either from the tremendous heat generated below us or from the slipstreams of aircraft ahead. There was a cold draught as our bomb doors opened and the noise level increased. There were odd puffs of ack-ack but few and far between. Bombs away!

Squadron Leader Allardyce, a pilot in the second wave on Dresden, recalled that the Master Bombers 'were remarkable men'. 'He would circle over the target at about 3,000–4,000 feet, usually through a hail of 'friendly' bombs. I well remember one occasion when a voice came through 'Take over number 2 – I shall have a cup of coffee.' Very reassuring. We could see the fires burning 50 miles away. There was little flak and no fighters. This was the longest raid I ever flew and the only raid I ever had any qualms about and that was purely to think of the lovely china being destroyed.'

John Whiteley continues:

One of the responsibilities of the wireless operator on operations was to listen out at half hourly intervals in case there was a recall. After half an hour's flying, my novice wireless operator, through the intercom, reported that he was unable to make his set work. As it was not quite dusk and I could see Lancasters flying in the same direction, I told him not to worry but to keep trying. Half an hour later, I received the same report and again I said, 'Don't worry but still keep trying to make the set work.' Although it was now dark, I felt judders on my Lancaster, caused by the slipstream from aircraft ahead, which confirmed that there had not been a recall. In fact, by the time we reached Dresden, the wireless operator's radio was still unserviceable. Strictly speaking, I should not have continued the operation but should have turned back. There was a fine line between heroism and foolhardiness in such circumstances. I was also very conscious of the indictment of LMF and the inevitable Court of Enquiry.

We approached our target from the northwest flying on a south-east course and, at a height of 17,000 feet, I was able to distinguish the River Elbe about 50 miles from the city. I switched on my VHF radio (quite separate from the wireless operator's set) and listened to the Master Bomber and his Pathfinders whilst they marked the target. I then received a coded message from the Master Bomber to begin our bombing.

Flight Sergeant Ray Base, a Lancaster flight engineer on 115 Squadron wrote:

We arrived over the city about three-quarters through the raid, so things were well alight by then. The marking TIs were mostly red and green and showed up clearly among the fires. It was a very good attack, with the whole city burning, the streets being outlined in fire. Of the fires themselves, the burning buildings were very bright and around the outskirts were large dull red glows from the region of the railway station, gasworks and other industrial buildings.

The vapour trails were lit up 'like white train lines running in a curve straight over the middle of Dresden' when Flying Officer Eric Barton, a Lancaster pilot on 186 Squadron, called his navigator: 'Jock, you've never seen a target; come and look at this one – you won't see it again.' Jock was standing with tears running down his face. 'Christ, you poor bastards, you poor bastards; I never want to see that again Skipper; don't ever show me again ... what poor bastards.'[3] Leaving the target and seeing Dresden burning fiercely one Lancaster crewmember considered that 'we hit the jackpot – fires were visible when 150 miles away.' An American airman who took part later heard the raid described as the 'St. Valentine's Day Massacre' because so many civilians were killed – somewhere around 30,000.

At about half-past nine Karin Busch, a German schoolgirl was sitting sewing a bag for a friend when she heard a roaring noise:

I didn't know what it was – we had no warning at all. Before the 13th of February there had not been any air activity over Dresden. We had warning exercises but that was all. It was considered a safe city and we believed that culture-loving people would never destroy a jewel like Dresden. We felt safe in that knowledge. A few anti-aircraft guns had been placed around Dresden but a few nights before the raid, they were removed. No shelters had been built. The only defence measure was to provide buckets of sand. In case of an air raid, you were supposed to receive a pre-warning and then a full warning but now we heard the full warning and suddenly the town was lit up by flares in the shape of Christmas trees all over the sky. Then hell broke loose. It was terrible, absolutely terrible. We ran into the cellar. My mother grabbed two Japanese lacquer boxes – one had food in it and the other had all our documents – and we ran down. My father and brother, who were both in uniform, began organising people and telling them what to do. It was very hot and we heard all this noise going on when suddenly a bomb fell into the cellar. It didn't go off, but total pandemonium broke out and we tried to climb out. I tried to help my mother out. I held her and tried to force her through but as I did, I lost my grip on her and she disappeared.

Pfc Kurt Vonnegut Junior had been a prisoner of war since 19 December when the 106th Division was cut to ribbons by Hitler's last desperate thrust through Luxemburg and Belgium:

Bayonets aren't much good against tanks. Our ammunition, food and medical supplies gave out and our casualties out-numbered those who could still fight – so we gave up. I was one of the few who weren't wounded. For that much Thank God. Well, the supermen marched us, without food, water or sleep to Limburg, a distance of about 60 miles, where we were loaded and locked up; 60 men to each small, unventilated, unheated box car. There were no sanitary accommodations – the floors were covered with fresh cow dung. There wasn't room for all of us to lie down. Half slept while the other half stood. We spent several days, including Christmas, on that Limburg siding. On Christmas Eve the RAF bombed and strafed our unmarked train. They killed about 150 of us. We got a little water Christmas Day and moved slowly across Germany to a large PoW camp in Mühlburg, south of Berlin. We were released from the box cars on New Year's Day. The Germans herded us through scalding delousing showers. Many men died from shock in the showers after ten days of starvation, thirst and exposure. But I didn't. [4]

Vonnegut was one of 150 'minor beings' shipped to a Dresden work camp on 10 January, where they were imprisoned in an underground slaughterhouse known by German soldiers as *Schlachthof Fünf* (Slaughterhouse Five):

I was their leader by virtue of the little German I spoke. It was our misfortune to have sadistic and fanatical guards. We were refused medical attention and clothing: We were given long hours at extremely hard labor. Our food ration was 250 grams of black bread and one pint of unseasoned potato soup each day. After desperately trying to improve our situation for two months and having been met with bland smiles I told the guards just what I was going to do to them when the Russians came. They beat me up a little. I was fired as group leader. Beatings were very small time: one boy starved to death and the *SS* Troops shot two for stealing food. In 24 hours all of Dresden – possibly the world's most beautiful city – was destroyed. But not me.

The subterranean nature of the prison saved their lives during the bombing of Dresden. 'After that we were put to work carrying corpses from air-raid shelters; women, children, old men; dead from concussion, fire or suffocation. Civilians cursed us and threw rocks as we carried bodies to huge funeral pyres in the city.'

Another PoW in Dresden was Alexander Gregor who was captured in 1942 just outside Tobruk by the 21st *Panzer* Division and saw Rommel in his staff car on the day he was captured. He recalls.

If the RAF had come the day before they would have caught the heavy troop movement passing through Dresden by road and rail. We saw the first wave of the bombing. We were billeted in a ball-room and the guards took us down to the cellar when the bombing started. Boy, did it get hot. Steam was coming through the wooden plugs blocking the air vents and the metal handles began to glow red hot too. We tied handkerchiefs soaked in water from the Guards water bottle over our noses because of the dust, but they were of little use. The smell of burning flesh penetrated even the cellar.

Outside the cellar she had just left, Karin Busch was hit by an inferno of wind and firestorm.

It was like looking into a huge burning oven. I saw my twin brother sitting down, holding his eyes. He couldn't see, so I held him and together we were swept along by the storm. Flames were licking all around us and somehow we found ourselves by the River Elbe. I could see phosphorus dancing on the water, so for people throwing themselves into the river to get away from the fire, there was no escape. There were bodies everywhere and the gas masks that people were wearing were melting into their faces. The massive throng of people was moving aimlessly and we started looking for a cellar to hide in, but in every cellar we looked into, we saw people sitting dead because the fires had sucked the oxygen out and suffocated them. I have no idea how long the hell lasted – time had no meaning when all this was going on.

I looked around and I saw the whole city in ruins. Everything, all the beautiful churches, everything was destroyed. We stood on *Marshallstrasse* with its huge houses – now a mass of rubble with a few chimney stacks standing out. When I called out to someone I thought I knew, one of these chimneys stacks fell down just from the echo of my voice. My brother had lost his sight from the heat. One eye recovered later but the other did not. We found our father and older brother by calling out their names and together we went back to the cellar where we had first taken shelter. Inside, I saw a pile of ashes in the shape of a person. You know when you put wood into a furnace and it burns and becomes red hot and it keeps its shape with an inner glow but when you touch it, it disintegrates? That's what this was – the shape of a person but nothing left of the body. I didn't know who it was but then I saw a pair of earrings in the ashes. I knew the earrings. It was my mother.

As tons of explosives plummeted from the sky, an 8,000°C firestorm similar to that created in Hamburg on 27/28 July 1943 tore through the heart of the Saxon capital, burning an estimated 25,000 to 40,000 Dresdeners alive. *Oberleutnant* Wilhelm 'Wim' Johnen, *Staffelkapitän*, 5/NJG1 described the horrors of Dresden:[5]

> ... the bomber formations appeared over the city and enveloped it in a single sea of flames by dropping phosphorus bombs. Hundreds remained stuck in the melting asphalt and were burnt alive like flaming torches. Hundreds jumped with their clothes on fire into the icy waters of the Elbe or into the 9ft deep water basins from which they could not clamber out. Those who could swim were dragged down into the depths by non-swimmers. The Exhibition grounds in the Dresden gardens were filled with refugees who had taken cover there when the sirens wailed. But even the lawns with their centuries old trees were sprayed with bombs and phosphorus canisters until a forest fire was raging. The burning city was again subjected at 2 o'clock in the morning with a second carpet of bombs, which transformed the centre of the city into a ruined wilderness. The casualties that night are estimated at over 100,000. Most of the bodies could no longer be identified. The human remains were placed on huge steel platforms, sprinkled with petrol and burnt in the open air.

Lothar Metzger, just nine years old, recalled:

> I lived with my mother and sisters (13, 5 and 5 months old twins) in Dresden and was looking forward to celebrating my 10th birthday on 16 February. My father, a carpenter, had been a soldier since 1939 and we got his last letter in August 1944. My mother was very sad to receive her letters back with the note: 'Not to be found.' We lived in a three-room flat on the 4th floor in a working class region of our town. I celebrated Shrove Tuesday (13 February together with other children. The activities of the war in the east came nearer and nearer. Lots of soldiers went east and lots of refugees went west through

our town or stayed there, also in the air raid night 13/14 February. About 9:30 pm the alarm was given. We children knew that sound and got up and dressed quickly, to hurry downstairs into our cellar which we used as an air raid shelter. My older sister and I carried my baby twin sisters and my mother carried a little suitcase and the bottles with milk for our babies. On the radio we heard with great horror the news: *Achtung, a great air raid will come over our town!* This news I will never forget.

Some minutes later we heard a horrible noise – the bombers. There were nonstop explosions. Our cellar was filled with fire and smoke and was damaged, the lights went out and wounded people shouted dreadfully. In great fear we struggled to leave this cellar. My mother and my older sister carried the big basket in which the twins were in. With one hand I grasped my younger sister and with the other I grasped the coat of my mother. We did not recognize our street any more. Fire, only fire wherever we looked. Our 4th floor did not exist any more. The broken remains of our house were burning. On the streets there were burning vehicles and carts with refugees, people, horses, all of them screaming and shouting in fear of death. I saw hurt women, children, old people searching a way through ruins and flames. We fled into another cellar overcrowded with injured and distraught men women and children shouting, crying and praying. No light except some electric torches. And then suddenly the second raid began. This shelter was hit too and so we fled through cellar after cellar. Many, so many, desperate people came in from the streets. It is not possible to describe! Explosion after explosion. It was beyond belief, worse than the blackest nightmare. So many people were horribly burnt and injured. It became more and more difficult to breathe. It was dark and all of us tried to leave this cellar with inconceivable panic. Dead and dying people were trampled upon and luggage was left or snatched up out of our hands by rescuers. The basket with our twins covered with wet cloths was snatched up out of my mother's hands and we were pushed upstairs by the people behind us. We saw the burning street, the falling ruins and the terrible firestorm. My mother covered us with wet blankets and coats she found in a water tub.

We saw terrible things: cremated adults shrunk to the size of small children, pieces of arms and legs, dead people, whole families burnt to death, burning people running to and fro, burnt coaches filled with civilian refugees, dead rescuers and soldiers, many calling and looking for their children and families and everywhere fire. And all the time the hot wind of the firestorm threw people back into the burning houses they were trying to escape from. I cannot forget these terrible details. I can never forget them.

Now my mother possessed only a little bag with our identity papers. The basket with the twins had disappeared and then suddenly my older sister vanished too. Although my mother looked for her immediately it was in vain. The last hours of this night we found shelter in the cellar of a hospital nearby surrounded by crying and dying people. In the next morning we looked for our sister and the twins but without success. The house where we lived was only a burning ruin. The house where our twins were left we could not go in. Soldiers said everyone was burnt to death and we never saw my two baby sisters again.

Totally exhausted, with burnt hair and badly burnt and wounded by the fire we walked to the Loschwitz bridge where we found good people who allowed us to wash, to eat and to sleep. But only a short time because suddenly the second air raid began and this house too was bombed and my mother's last identity papers burnt. Completely exhausted we hurried over the bridge over the River Elbe with many other homeless survivors and found another family ready to help us, because somehow their home survived this horror.

In all this tragedy I had completely forgotten my 10th birthday. But the next day my mother surprised me with a piece of sausage she begged from the Red Cross. This was my birthday present. In the next days and weeks we looked for my older sister but in vain. We wrote our present address on the last walls of our damaged house. In the middle of March we were evacuated to a little village near Oschastz and on 31 March we got a letter from my sister. She was alive! In that disastrous night she lost us and with other lost children she was taken to a nearby village. Later she found our address on the wall of our house and at the beginning of April my mother brought her to our new home. You can be sure that the horrible experiences of this night in Dresden led to confused dreams, sleepless nights and disturbed our souls, me and the rest of my family. Years later I intensively thought the matter over, the causes, the political contexts of this night. This became very important for my whole life and my further decisions.

Elisabeth, a young woman of around 20, sought shelter in the basement of the house where she lived. She wrote:

Then the detonation of bombs started rocking the earth and in a great panic, everybody came rushing down. The attack lasted about half an hour. Our building and the immediate surrounding area had not been hit. Almost everybody went upstairs, thinking it was over but it was not. The worst was yet to come and when it did, it was pure hell. During the brief reprieve, the basement had filled with people seeking shelter, some of whom were wounded from bomb shrapnel. One soldier had a leg torn off. He was accompanied by a medic, who attended to him but he was screaming in pain and there was a lot of blood. There also was a wounded woman, her arm severed just below her shoulder and hanging by a piece of skin. A military medic was looking after her, but the bleeding was severe and the screams very frightening.

Then the bombing began again. This time there was no pause between detonations and the rocking was so severe, we lost our balance and were tossed around in the basement like a bunch of ragdolls. At times the basement walls were separated and lifted up. We could see the flashes of the fiery explosions outside. There were a lot of fire bombs and canisters of phosphorous being dumped everywhere. The phosphorus was a thick liquid that burned upon exposure to air and as it penetrated cracks in buildings, it burned wherever it leaked through. The fumes from it were poisonous. When it came leaking down the basement steps somebody yelled to grab a beer (there was some stored where we were), soak a cloth, a piece of your clothing and press it over your mouth and nose. The panic was horrible. Everybody pushed, shoved and clawed to get a bottle.

I had pulled off my underwear and soaked the cloth with the beer and pressed it over my nose and mouth. The heat in that basement was so severe it only took a few minutes to make that cloth bone dry. I was like a wild animal, protecting my supply of wetness. I don't like to remember that.

The bombing continued. I tried bracing myself against a wall. That took the skin off my hands – the wall was so hot. The last I remember of that night is losing my balance, holding onto some-body but falling and taking them too, with them falling on top of me. I felt something crack inside. While I lay there I had only one thought – to keep thinking. As long as I know I'm thinking, I am alive, but at some point I lost consciousness.

The next thing I remember is feeling terribly cold. I then realized I was lying on the ground, looking into the burning trees. It was daylight. There were animals screeching in some of them. Monkeys from the burning zoo. I started moving my legs and arms. It hurt a lot but I could move them. Feeling the pain told me that I was alive. I guess my movements were noticed by a soldier from the rescue and medical corps.

The corps had been put into action all over the city and it was they who had opened the basement door from the outside, taking all the bodies out of the burning building. Now they were looking for signs of life from any of us. I learned later that there had been over

170 bodies taken out of that basement and 27 came back to life. I was one of them – miraculously!

They then attempted to take us out of the burning city to a hospital. The attempt was a gruesome experience. Not only were the buildings and the trees burning but so was the asphalt on the streets. For hours, the truck had to make a number of detours before getting beyond the chaos. But before the rescue vehicles could get the wounded to the hospitals, enemy planes bore down on us once more. We were hurriedly pulled off the trucks and placed under them. The planes dived at us with machine guns firing and dropped more fire bombs.

The memory that has remained so vividly in my mind was seeing and hearing humans trapped, standing in the molten, burning asphalt like living torches, screaming for help which was impossible to give. At the time I was too numb to fully realize the atrocity of this scene but after I was 'safe' in the hospital, the impact of this and everything else threw me into a complete nervous breakdown. I had to be tied to my bed to prevent me from severely hurting myself physically. There I screamed for hours and hours behind a closed door while a nurse stayed at my bedside.

The second attack went in at 01.30 hours on 14 February by another 500 aircraft of Bomber Command. Calculations were that a delay of three hours would allow the fires to get a grip on the sector (provided the first attack was successful) and fire brigades from other cities would concentrate fighting the fires. In this second attack target marking was carried out by 8 Path Finder Group. By the time of this attack cloud cover had cleared to 3 to 7/10ths but despite this the Master Bomber could not identify the aiming point due to the huge conflagrations and smoke and a decision was made to concentrate bombing on areas not affected. An area was marked by the Path Finders both to the left and to the right to assist in concentrating the bombing and good concentration was achieved. So great were the conflagrations caused by the firestorms created in the great heat generated in the first attack that crews in the second attack reported the glow was visible 200 miles from the target.[6]

For most of the participating aircrew the Dresden raid of 13/14 February was another well executed and very efficient area bombing attack. John Whiteley landed at Strubby at 03.20 hours, having flown his Lancaster for 9 hours 20 minutes.

In order to remain alert for the whole of the operation, I never used 'George', the automatic pilot. Our report at the de-briefing read: 'This aircraft was one of eleven detailed to attack the primary target, DRESDEN. Weather conditions – 10/10 medium cloud, base about

15,000 feet. Marking very good and although assessment difficult due to cloud, considered that the results good, the glow from the fires being visible when 150 miles away.' In the briefing for the Dresden operation, I was told that the raid was to stop the German Army from using the city as a 'staging post' in their efforts to stem the advance of the Russians – surely a military reason. In my judgment, it was a legitimate target.

Flying Officer Robert Wannop, a Lancaster pilot on 90 Squadron recalls that Dresden was the most memorable of his tour:

I understood that large areas of the place consisted of timber build-ings and judging by the load we carried I should say it was correct. Namely 1 × 4,000lb and five 750lb incendiaries. The Squadron was in the second wave so by the time we arrived the fires were well under way. As we approached the glow could be seen – 50 miles away. The target area was almost like day. Down below – 19,000 feet – the town was simply a mass of flames – a pool of fire – it was awe inspiring – breath-taking – I had never before – nor never again will see such a sight. Searchlights flickered aimlessly around – even their usual brilliance lost by the blazing inferno. Around us we could see other Lancasters – it was light enough to formate had we wished. Even vapour trails were plainly visible, an unusual phenomenon at night. The opposition was negligible – like taking candy from a baby. We saw one night fighter as we left the area but he wasn't interested in us – which was a good thing. It was a long trip home, the monotony broken occasionally by a few bursts of 'flak' as we approached too near a defended area. As we flew over Ostend we saw an unusual light shooting rapidly up into the heavens: curving slowly out across the Channel in the direction of London – a V-2.

Some crews felt 'uneasy' but 'did as they were told'. Miles Tripp could not forget what they had been told at briefing; that the city would be swollen by a million refugees and he remembered 'the old newsreels of German dive-bombing atrocities.' The memory left him feeling disturbed:

Forty miles from Dresden fires were reddening the sky ahead … Six miles from the target the other Lancasters were clearly visible; their silhouettes black in the rosy glow. The streets of the city were a fantastic latticework of fire. It was a though one was looking down at the fiery outlines of a crossword puzzle; blazing streets stretched from east to west, from north to south, in a gigantic saturation of flame.'

6 Squadron Lancaster pathfinders of 8 PFF Group over Hanau lit up by the multi-coloured marker
res on the night of 18/19 March 1945, when 277 Lancasters and eight Mosquitoes of 1 and
Groups carried out an accurate area raid. One Lancaster was lost. About 2,000 people were killed.

n 21 March 1945, 178 aircraft including sixteen Lancasters carried out an accurate attack on the
ilway yards and the surrounding town area at Rheine. One Lancaster was lost.

RHEINE M/Y
K-4063
DIST. 23 E

Lancaster I PA226 AL-H on 429 'Bison' Squadron RCAF at Leeming in 1945 with flak damage in the starboard wing. The former codes WL-X, worn while serving on 434 'Bluenose' Squadron RCAF, can be seen under the fuselage codes.

Photographed on 22 March 1945, the battleship *Tirpitz* capsized in Tromsö Fiord by a 14,000lb 'Tallboy' dropped during the raid by Lancasters on 29 October 1944. The hull is covered by snow and there is a hole in the starboard side.

Sergeant F D Moss and his crew on 10 Squadron at Melbourne, photographed in York in 1944. On 5/6 March '45, Moss, now a flight lieutenant, and his crew on Halifax III MZ948 ZA-E were shot down on the operation on Chemnitz. Standing L–R: Flight Sergeant Fred Fearnley (KIA 5/6.3.45); Sergeant Harold William Tasker (KIA 5/6.3.45); Warrant Officer 2nd Class Lindsay Wilkie Webster RCAF (KIA 5/6.3.45); Flight Sergeant C Fowler (PoW 5/6.3.45). Seated L–R; Flight Sergeant Hodgson (PoW 5/6.3.45); Flight Lieutenant Moss (PoW 5/6.3.45); Flight Sergeant Robert Edward Davenport (KIA 5/6.3.45). Sergeant Lionel Leslie Hall RAAF (not in the photograph) was KIA also.

On 21 March 1945, 133 Lancasters and six Mosquitoes of 1 and 8 Groups attacked the Deutsche Vacuum oil refinery at Bremen, seen here from 15,000 feet. No aircraft were lost.

A 22,000lb 'Grand Slam' loaded on a Lancaster I (Special) on 617 Squadron at Woodhall Spa. (*IWM*)

On 21 March 1945, 178 aircraft including sixteen Lancasters carried out an accurate attack on the railway yards and the surrounding town area at Rheine. One Lancaster was lost.

'Grand Slam' earthquake bomb being dropped from Lancaster B.1 Special PB996 YZ-C on 617 Squadron. Lancasters dropped a total of 41 *Grand Slam* bombs operationally. *(IWM)*

Pilot Officer Ernest Yule Yeoman and crew on 158 Squadron were flying Halifax III MZ759 on the operation on Gladbach on 24 March 1945, when it was hit and went down in flames over the target area. Yeoman and three crew were killed but incredibly, three men survived and were taken into captivity.

On 22 March 1945, 227 Lancasters and eight Mosquitoes of 1 and 8 Groups attacked the railway yards at Hildesheim, seen here from 16,000 feet. Four Lancasters were lost. This was the only major Bomber Command raid of the war on Hildesheim and 263 acres, 70 per cent of the town, were destroyed.

This view of completely devastated railway yards at Münster, which was last bombed by Bomber Command on 25 March, was photographed on 7 April 1945 by the advancing British Army. (*IWM*)

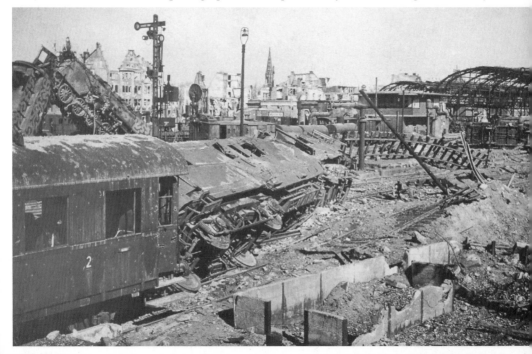

noto-reconnaissance had covered the construction of the huge *U-boat* shelter at the Valentin ibmarine works at Farge on the River Weser north of Bremen. The work was nearing completion hen it was attacked by twenty Lancasters of 617 Squadron on 27 March 1945 and they dropped velve 22,000lb bombs, two of which penetrated the 23 feet thick reinforced concrete roof, bringing own thousands of tons of concrete rubble and rendering the shelter unusable. No aircraft were lost the attack on Farge or on the raid on an oil-storage depot by ninety-five Lancasters of 5 Group. WM)

Lancaster II DS830 OW-S on 426 'Thunderbird' Squadron RCAF which also served on 432 'Leaside' and 408 'Goose' Squadrons and 1668 CU befor being SOC in March 1945.

Halifax B.Mk VII PN240/W o 415 Squadron which complete forty-two operations at East Moor. *Willie The Wolf* was a popular slogan that appeared on several aircraft, including B.Mk.VII NP707 on 432 'Leaside' Squadron RCAF at East Moor. (*Wilfred Tuer*)

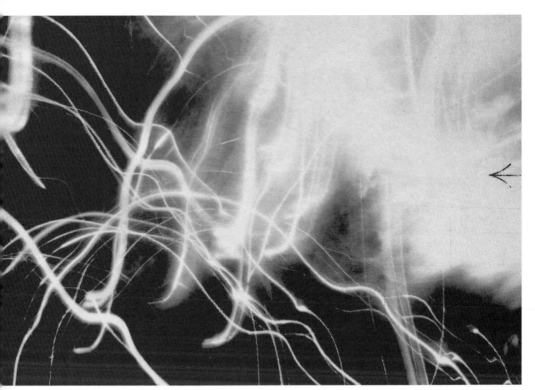

…auen from 17,000 feet on 11 April 1945.

TI (Target Indicator) dropped by a PFF Mosquito falling on Komotau in Czechoslovakia on 18/19 April 1945, the last major raid in a long communications offensive. In all, 114 Lancasters and nine Mosquitoes of 5 Group attacked this town (now called Chomutov). All aircraft despatched returned safely. (*Bill Burke*)

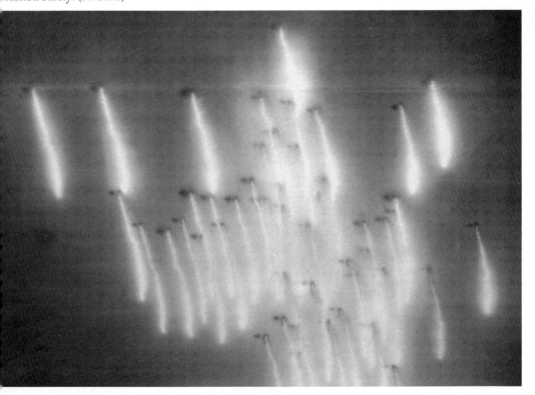

Lancaster over Berchtesgaden on 25 April 1945 when the Berghof, Hitler's home, referred to as the 'Chalet' by the RAF, and the *SS* barracks nearby were the target for 359 Lancaster heavy bombers and 14 *Oboe* Mosquito and 24 Lancaster marker aircraft. Included in the mighty force were thirty-three Lancasters of 9 Squadron and 617 the 'Dam Busters', each carrying a 12,000lb 'Tallboy' bomb. Those who bombed the 'Chalet' mostly missed. A mountain peak between the *Oboe* ground station and the aircraft had blocked out the bomb release signal. Since *Oboe* signals went line of sight and did not follow the curvature of the earth, the further the target, the higher one needed to be, and the *Oboe* Mosquitoes flew at 36,000 feet because of the Alps. Crews heard the first two dots of the release signal and then nothing more. They were unable to drop and brought the markers back. Two aircraft were lost. (*IWM*)

When Allied troops entered Düsseldorf in April 1945 they found the remains of a Halifax lodged against the wall of the city's municipal offices. It appears to be ZA-V of 10 Squadron, which was lost with Pilot Officer John Currie RNZAF and crew on 8/9 April. Currie and four crew who died were buried in the Nordfriedhof at Düsseldorf, though their graves are now at the Reichwald Forest War Cemetery. The two other crew were injured. (*IWM*)

'ar damage.

Cologne at the end of the war.

Unfinished *U-boat*s in a Hamburg shipyard on 3 May 1945. Production was pursued despite the repeated bombing of Germany's second largest city, but only with great difficulty in the final months of hostilities. (*IWM*)

(*left*) Lancaster *Sisco's Scamps Press On!* on 626 Squadron at Wickenby. (*via Peter Bone*)

(*right*) Squadron Leader Dick Lane's Lancaster crew. Standing, L–R: Freddy; Bert, wireless operator; [...]an, flight engineer; Peter Bone, mid-upper gunner. Kneeling, L–R: Frank, rear gunner; Mac, [...]vigator. Unfortunately Dick Lane had already left the squadron when this picture was taken, just [...]er VE Day. (*Peter Bone*)

[...]andoned German aircraft.

Operation *Manna*. Between 29 April and 7 May 1945, Lancasters of Bomber Command dropped food
supplies to starving Dutch in those parts of Holland still occupied by the Germans, who had
declared a local truce. Over 3,000 sorties were flown, delivering 6,672 tons of food. The USAAF
participation was named Operation *Chowhound*.

Lancasters on 635 Squadron start engines at Lübeck during the repatriation of ex-PoWs in Operation *Exodus* on 11 May 1945. (*IWM*)

On VE-Day Flight Sergeant A D M Anderson of Handsworth, Birmingham was flown back from a prison camp in Lancaster PB422. Anderson was the only survivor on the crew captained by Flying Officer Eric Albert Williams DFC that was shot down on the night of 11/12 April 1944 on the operation on Aachen. On 27/28 January 1944 Anderson had been one of four survivors on Pilot Officer Williams' crew on Lancaster W4315 QR-Q, which was ditched off Guernsey after being hit by flak south of Hanover while homebound from Berlin.

Lancaster RA573 on 463 Squadron RAAF at Juvincourt airfield on 6 May where ex-PoWs wearing Mae Wests get ready for the flight home to England. (*IWM*)

Group Captain Leonard Cheshire VC DSO* DFC and Warrant Officer Norman Jackson VC on 106 Squadron at Buckingham palace on 13 November 1945 to received their Victoria Cross awards .

There was no Master Bomber on the air to instruct crews to stoke up the fires so he told 'Dig' Klenner, his tough Australian pilot from Adelaide, to turn to starboard, to the south of the city and when they were just beyond the fringe of the fire he pressed the bomb release, hoping that their bomb load would fall in open country.

On the way back' recalls a navigator, 'our wireless operator picked up a German broadcast accusing the RAF of terror tactics and that 65,000 civilians had died. We dismissed this as German propaganda.' A squadron leader Path Finder pilot at the Air Ministry visited his old squadron the day after the Dresden raid and discovered that 'there was a feeling in the mess that it was a horrible mistake. The firestorm had been horrendous and nobody knew why it had been done. They had been briefed that it was at Russian request but nobody wanted to help them anyway. Both we and the Americans hated their guts.'[7]

Bomber Command lost six Lancasters on Dresden and one Halifax failed to return from the raid on Böhlen. A second crashed on return after being diverted to Chedburgh. There were no injuries to the crew.

Nineteen-year-old Friedericke Clayton lived about 12 miles from Dresden:

On the train [home] I didn't know where I was, it looked like I had entered another country. The shock was tremendous; the smell of burning flesh – I still have it in my nostrils. It was a dull day and the clouds were still hanging over the city. I didn't see anybody, there was no life. It was a dead town, just rubble. It was just devastation and it was a hell of a shock to your system. I lost an aunt and her daughter. On the second day of bombing, the animals broke out of the zoo and ran towards the river and so did the people running away from the fire. One of my aunts lived near the main train station. She lost everything. Her husband was a teacher and she was a housewife. They tried to dig in the rubble to find something, anything, but found nothing. They eventually built their own house out of the debris. The city was gone.[8]

Prisoner of War, Sergeant W Morris of the RASC recalls.

The American bombers came the next day, but there didn't seem much left to destroy. Many Russian prisoners were killed in the bombing, but most of the British survived and we were drafted into the city to help clear up. There was rubble everywhere and even three weeks after the raid the bricks underneath the rubble were still hot to the touch. We came across bodies everywhere as we cleared up the rubbish. There was a network of cellars under the city interconnecting from house to house and the people had obviously used these for protection. Many had apparently died of suffocation as the flames racing overhead had sucked out all the oxygen from the air. One German I met, who had been away from Dresden at the time of the bombing, committed suicide when he saw the state of the city in which his family had been trapped – he knew they could not have survived. It was a sad experience. I wish now it had never happened.

Colonel H E Cook usaaf later reported:

We PoWs were shunted into the Dresden marshalling yards where for nearly 12 hours German troops and equipment rolled in and out of Dresden. I saw with my own eyes that Dresden was an armed camp – thousands of German troops, tanks and artillery and miles of freight cars ... transporting German logistics towards the East to meet the Russians.

Over 300 B-17s of the Eighth Air Force dropped 771 tons of bombs on Dresden on 14 February. The following morning the burnt-out walls of the Frauenkirche gave way under the weight of its stone dome. The final collapse of the church was the symbolic concluding act of the catastrophe; the pile of rubble left behind now marked the centre of an area of almost complete destruction covering twelve square kilometres or more than four and a half square miles. 'Dresden was like the moon now' wrote Kurt Vonnegut.

John Morris from New York City and a Fortress waist gunner in the 91st Bomb Group at Bassingbourn, recalled:

I'm hardly ashamed of having gone to Dresden that day. It was sound strategy to prevent the *Wehrmacht* from falling back to regroup and be lethal again. So we bombed the hell out of the railroad marshalling yards and road hubs along the *Wehrmacht*'s line of retreat, up and down Germany's eastern border. I didn't rejoice at the 35,000 Germans killed there. I doubt there were many Jews in that number. The good burghers of Dresden had shipped them all off to Auschwitz. It is true that the RAF purposely started a firestorm, causing many of the casualities. It was a tactic they frequently tried. But they and we killed more people in other cities on other days. So did the Russians. So did the Japanese. So did the Germans. Dresden was not unique.

Roman Halter was a Polish Jewish slave worker working as munitions worker in Dresden at the time of the attack. He had survived the Lodz Ghetto and selections at the death camp of Auschwitz-Birkenau. He says:

There were cartwheels of fire chasing oxygen and we had to throw ourselves down on the tarmac. The tarmac was already hot. And as we went through people were jumping from buildings. People were jumping around with flame. It was horrendous this vision. We had more sympathy for these people than the SS who only cared about guarding us. But we felt really that they started the war. We knew that England was bombed, that Coventry was bombed and they deserved whatever they're getting. They didn't protest; they felt that if Hitler wins, Europe and the world will be thrown into darkness for a thousand years. And if it had not been for Churchill and the RAF boys we would not have won.[9]

At Chedburgh 'Dig' Klenner and his crew on 218 Squadron were not alone in being 'dog-tired' after the 9.5-hour flight to Dresden and back and they went straight to their hut and to bed. They were on again the following night. Operation *Thunderclap* was not over. At briefing Flight Sergeant Miles Tripp, the bomb aimer on the crew, went into the briefing room to learn the name of the target before rejoining the others who were waiting in another room. The briefing was taken by Wing Commander W J Smith DFC or the 'Vicar' as he was known. 'He was a noted disciplinarian who had logged a few minor sorties against the French coast before taking command of the squadron' recalled Miles Tripp. 'His long face was given a look of pre-war conformity by a neat moustache just as a typical suburban semi-detached house of the period was inevitably fronted by a trim privet hedge'.

The briefing finished with the 'Vicar' giving his customary, 'Good luck chaps' message.'

'Dig' Klenner decided to test the powers of prediction of their West Indian rear gunner, Sergeant Harry McCalla, who was from Kingston, Jamaica. He could predict with uncanny accuracy, hours before a battle order was posted, where they would be flying. He also had a wicked sense of humour. Cookhouse staff at Chedburgh complained that when eggs were on the menu in the Sergeant's Mess, some aircrew tried to get a double ration by going round twice. Harry was cited as an example of this sharp practice. As the only coloured aircrew member on the squadron, his protest that this was a case of mistaken identity and was therefore not guilty, did not carry too much weight but no-one was willing to condemn him and so he got away with it! When 'Dig' asked Harry to predict what the target would be on the night of 14/15 February the West Indian went across to where a map of Europe was pinned to the wall, put out a hand, let it stray across the map until his forefinger reached Leipzig. Harry paused a moment, as if uncertain and then his hand moved on slowly across the province of Brandenburg. It continued moving until his finger reached Chemnitz, the Saxon metropolis west of Dresden; then it stopped. 'I think it'll be Chemnitz' he said. The rest of the crew looked at Tripp.

'He's right' he said.[10]

The raid on Chemnitz, – a round trip of 8 hours 20 minutes – and an oil refinery at Rositz near Leipzig, involved 499 Lancasters and 218 Halifaxes of 1, 3, 4, 6 and 8 Groups, attacking in two phases, three hours apart. Very elaborate diversionary raids were mounted with crews on 95 HCU carrying out a sweep into the Heligoland Bight, 46 Mosquitoes heading for Berlin, 19 to Mainz, 14 to Dessau, 12 to Duisburg, 11 to Nürnburg and 8 to Frankfurt, while 21 RCM sorties were flown in support of the main attack. A further 87 Mosquito patrols were added and 30 Lancasters and 24 Halifaxes carried out mine-laying in the Kadet Channel. The route to Chemnitz was similar to the Dresden route. Over the Continent, layers of cloud stretched from the French coast to east Germany and both parts of the bomber force found the target area covered by cloud. Pathfinder flares disappeared almost as soon as they were dropped and the Master Bomber, a Canadian, kept calling for more flares but few were forthcoming. Eventually he gave up his appeals for flares in disgust. 'Oh hell,' he said. 'I'm going home. See you at breakfast.' Eight Lancasters and five Halifaxes were lost. As well, a Lancaster and five Halifaxes were lost on the mine-laying operation. They included *V-Victor* on 429 Squadron piloted by Flight Lieutenant Ross Conger Charlton, which was shot down by Swedish flak and crashed in the sea off Falsterbo lighthouse. The crew – all Canadians – were killed. At Rositz, 224 Lancasters and eight Mosquitoes of 5 Group attacked the oil refinery. Damage was caused to the southern part of the oil plant. Three Lancasters were lost. Many parts of Chemnitz were hit but most of the bombing was in open country. At Chedburgh the news must have been disappointing for the 'Vicar'. He had told his crews 'and when you come back don't let there be a Chemnitz.'

On 28 March Winston Churchill composed a memorandum for the Chiefs of Staff Committee and the Chief of Air Staff:

> It seems to me that the moment has come when the question of bombing of German cities simply for the sake of increasing the terror, though under other pretexts, should be reviewed. Otherwise we shall come into control of an utterly ruined land. We shall not, for instance, be able to get housing materials out of Germany for our own needs because some temporary provision would have to be made for the Germans themselves. The destruction of Dresden remains a serious query against the conduct of Allied bombing. I am of the opinion that military objectives must henceforward be more strictly studied in our own interests rather than that of the enemy. The Foreign Secretary has spoken to me on this subject and I feel the need for more precise concentration upon military objectives,

such as oil and communications behind the immediate battle-zone, rather than on mere acts of terror and wanton destruction, however impressive.[11]

Harris responded angrily, claiming that 'We have never gone in for terror bombing and the attacks which we have made in accordance with my Directive have in fact produced the strategic consequences for which they were designed and from which the armies now profit.' He went on … Dresden 'was a mass of munitions works, an intact government centre and a key transportation point to the East. It is now none of those things.' Harris added, 'I do not personally regard the remaining cities of Germany as worth the bones of one British Grenadier.'

Marushka, Zygmunt and Jurek Skarbek passed a few suburban stations. It was very stuffy in the train and Marushka opened the window:

It was a beautiful night with a full moon. We were travelling through the Saxonian Alps. The train often entered tunnels cut through deep cliffs, oddly shaped and covered with shrubs. The cliffs seemed to stretch up to the sky, blotting out the view and bringing complete darkness. Then again the cliffs were falling away leaving only boulders covered with a pale glow of the moon. It could be a beautiful country viewed during the day but at night it gave an eerie feeling as if God Himself in an angry mood had tossed down the heavy boulders, breaking them into oddly shaped humps. Now covered with shrubs they made a phantom landscape. The day was full of nervous tension – the compartments became empty. Everyone knew or had heard about the Flying Fortresses and preferred to travel by night. In Nürnburg we saw many ruins and sooty remnants of previous buildings and many ruins around the station. This town was already deeply scarred but still alive and working fully because the *Führer* had so decreed. We continued without interruption – hours passed. We were getting nearer to the wide, blue Danube, which had its beginning somewhere here in the *Schwarz Wald* (Black Forest).

The train was rumbling over a bridge. Through the window we saw an unsightly narrow river full of sandbanks. In the middle of the river stood a boy, his trouser legs turned high up, holding a fishing rod. In Augsburg we had a long wait so we went to sleep. When I woke up the sun was already setting. The train was standing at a small station smelling of freshly cut hay. We could hear the gentle sound of bells coming somewhere from the field as if flowers were tinkling softly in the breeze in this meadow between the hills. Enraptured, we looked at the scenery near the Alps, smelled the forgotten clean air and listened to the tranquil, melodious sounds. The high fir trees were cutting a straight line dividing the well kept fields. The colourful houses of the *Bauer* (farmer) nestled against the hills. The walls of the houses were brightly painted with the shutters painted in another colour and masses of bright flowers made an enchanting view like a fairy tale. From the nearby hill cows were coming home – all alike, dark brown, wide in the shoulders, with a leather collar and a hanging bell. Even the young calves were ringing their bells as they romped around. Now we understood the origin of the ringing which had reached us from the meadows. There were many herds in the wide valley of Bavaria. For the first time we felt the calming influence of a peaceful atmosphere. The melody of the bells, which the breeze, rich in scents of mown grass, was bringing nearer was like a balm for our nerves; nerves which were stretched tightly during tracking through the highways of war. We had the feeling that we were entering a land that had been left behind the main events of a total war. A land steeped in peace; the land of south Bavaria.

In Kempten we had to change trains and continued our journey on a small local puffing train (*Bummelzug*). This little train with only a few small carriages puffed heavily, climbing the hills and whistling madly at each twist of its track. It went happily down the hills but panted heavily and whistled loudly going uphill. On each station stood the funny looking *Schwabs*, locals dressed in shorts like children back home. The farmers on the platforms had very hairy legs, long pipes clenched between their teeth and were dressed in short leather pants supported by embroidered braces, a Tyrol hat with a fancy feather and a bright checked shirt. They were the Swabians. Their women looked just as unusual in short pleated skirts with an apron, also with braces, bright embroidered blouses, hats with a feather and white socks. Their throaty talk and their slang seemed quite incomprehensible and one had to listen carefully to pick up German words. After a sharp bend we saw hills covered with snow. High peaks reaching the sky. On the far horizon was the chain of the Swiss Alps. We had left one Front behind and had approached another, this time from the west.

After four attacks on Wesel preparatory to the crossing of the Rhine by the Allies in the west, 254 Lancasters and six Mosquitoes of 5 Group were dispatched to Böhlen on 19/20 February but the raid was unsuccessful, probably because the aircraft of the Master Bomber, Wing Commander Eric Arthur Benjamin DFC* was shot down by flak over the target and he was killed.[12]

On the night of 20/21 February, Bomber Command mounted three Main Force raids: 514 Lancasters and 14 Mosquitoes of 1, 3, 6 and 8 Groups set out to bomb the southern half of Dortmund, another 173 bombers raided the Rhenania Ossag refinery in the Reisholz district of Düsseldorf, 128 aircraft attacked another Rhenania Ossag refinery at Monheim, and 154 Lancasters and 11 Mosquitoes attacked the Mittelland Canal.[13] Twenty-two aircraft failed to return. Worst hit was the Dortmund force, which lost 14 Lancasters. One of them was *E-Easy*, a 419 'Moose' Squadron Lancaster X at Middleton St. George flown by Flying Officer Laurence Allen Blaney RCAF, which was hit by flak. Blaney and one other man were killed. Sergeant Stan Instone the flight engineer and the four other men survived.

Two Halifaxes were lost on Monheim. Four Halifaxes (one of which landed in France and was damaged beyond repair) and *Q-Queenie*, a Lancaster flown by Flight Lieutenant A D Pelly on 156 Squadron at Upwood, were missing on the Düsseldorf raid. Warrant Officer W G Pearce RAAF recalls:

We were detailed to mark the synthetic oil refinery at Reiszholz in the Ruhr Valley. Still some way short of the target we were caught up by an enemy fighter (later identified as a Ju 88 using upward firing cannon) and the starboard inner exploded and caught fire. The captain soon decided our position was untenable and ordered us to bail out: we didn't need to be told twice. I discarded my flying helmet and oxygen mask (we were at 18,000 ft), picked up my parachute pack from the floor and started to make my way to the rear door on the starboard side of the aircraft, just forward of the tail-plane. I sat on the main wing strut, fumbling to attach the parachute pack to the clips on the front of the harness. This is where the lack of oxygen began to take effect and I thought that I had better get moving. When I eventually reached the door the mid-upper gunner was there before me. He had made the fatal mistake of picking up his parachute pack by the shiny handle, the ripcord, and it had opened in the aircraft. He had, however clipped it to his harness and gathered the canopy in his arms. I watched him jump and saw the canopy which was torn from his grasp by the slipstream pass over the top of the tail-plane and his body beneath. His body was found later on the ground, still attached to his parachute: he had been killed by the impact when dragged back into the tail by his entangled canopy.

Now it was my turn to leave the aircraft, by now somewhat light-headed from the lack of oxygen and not too concerned by my predicament. I looked at the fire in the wing and thought 'that sure is burning well'. The next moment I fell out of the aeroplane and after tumbling for what seemed an age thought 'well I had better pull it now'. I was overcome by a feeling of absolute loneliness, but the cold and the lower altitude soon brought me back to my proper senses. But I could now hear other aircraft swishing past me and was frightened of what would happen if one of them hit me: this did not happen of course. They soon passed and I was left hanging in complete silence.

As I drifted down towards a cloud bank I could see a search-light running around on the underside of this cloud. Again I was frightened of being picked up by this light and becoming target practice for an anti-aircraft battery: again my fears were groundless as the light was switched off before I entered the cloud bank. Below the cloud the darkness was even more complete and I couldn't see the ground. I realised I was drifting backwards and remembering my parachute drill I tried to correct; I wasn't very successful and I hit the ground in an untidy heap. There was very little wind and my parachute quickly collapsed, I had landed in the middle of a paddock, but had hurt my left shoulder and the arm was virtually useless.[14]

The following night 1,110 sorties were dispatched to Duisburg and Gravenhorst on the Mittelland Canal and the first and only large raid on Worms. Forty Lancasters and Halifaxes were lost and another bomber crashed in Suffolk. Normally, station commanders were not permitted to fly on operations. But 43-year-old Group Captain Anthony Caron 'Tiny' Evans-Evans, the Coningsby station commander who at take-off time would insist on waving and even saluting each Lancaster as it took off, had managed to borrow an 83 Squadron Lancaster and get a crew together so that he could make the trip to Gravenhorst. The previous summer this huge 'teddy-bear' of a man had squeezed himself into the pilot's seat of a Lancaster and took a crew on what turned out to be a hair-raising cross-country flight. When he landed the crew had gone to see their Squadron CO and told him that they flatly refused to fly with the station commander ever again. Evans-Evans had not let that worry him and he took a scratch crew on an operation in August to Caen, for which he received a DFC. He believed that this award had too easily been earned when compared to aircrew who flew many ops without recognition, so for his second trip he had rounded up a scratch crew for the 5 Group operation by 165 Lancasters and a dozen Mosquitoes to the Mittlelland Canal. Included on the crew was 22-year-old Squadron Leader William Geoffrey 'Jock' Wishart DSO DFC*, the 97 Squadron Navigation Leader, who had flown 83 trips. Wishart never completed his 84th trip nor Evans-Evans his second; a night fighter shot the Lancaster down over the liberated part of Holland and Pilot Officer E H Hansen RAAF was the only man who survived to tell the tale. Bomber Command claimed that the canal was rendered '100 per cent unserviceable'.[15]

Stan Instone on Flying Officer Blaney's crew who survived the shoot down on Dortmund recalled:

I found myself, a few days later at Dortmund Station under guard and in the company of several captured USAAF aircrew, including a Colonel P-47 Thunderbolt pilot with burns to his throat and a B-17 bombardier with serious shrapnel wounds to his buttocks. Dortmund Station was extremely crowded as trains were not running to any kind of timetable due to air raids and subsequent damage. A middle aged German civilian spotted us and, in particular, the Americans and he became very hysterical, shouting and using threatening gestures and the immediate crowd near us became very aggressive. Fortunately the guards backed us into a corner and stood in front of us with their rifles at the ready. Fortuitously too, a train came into the station and the subsequent scramble to get onto the train relieved the atmosphere. I understood later, talking to the guards, that the chap causing the upset had lost his family in an American raid shortly before. Whilst in Germany I also heard rumours of a single RAF crew lynched in Frankfurt and a story widely believed that a crew were waiting for transport, also a German Officer demanded to know who the pilot was and, when he had identified himself, shot him on the spot.

The two consecutive nights, 20/21 and 21/22 February, proved a profitable 24 hours for several German pilots. On the second of these nights[16] *Major* Heinz-Wolfgang Schnaufer, *Kommodore* NJG4 took off from Gütersloh in a Bf 110C. Employing *Schräge Musik* attacks delivered below the bombers in an *Einsatz* (sortie) lasting two hours nine minutes he shot down two Lancasters at about 11,000 feet to take his score to 109. After shooting down the two Lancasters over Dortmund and returning to Gütersloh, Schnaufer and his crew had a rest period until a *Werkstattflug* (air-test) was called at 18.15 hours. The flight lasted 21 minutes and the Messerschmitt Bf 110 was declared 'serviceable.' *Leutnant* Fritz Rumpelhardt, Schnaufer's radar operator, recalls:

The late night sortie on 21 February was to become Schnaufer's most outstanding achievement in two-and-a-half years' service as a night-fighter pilot. It was always a point of honour with him to be the first in the air after the order to scramble so that he could assess the situation and brief his squadron. Chance played quite an important part in the sortie. I was alone in the squadron mess having my supper, having missed the order 'Heightened Preparedness,' so when the order to scramble came the *Major* was ready but I was not. He did not mince his words about my apparent dilatoriness. In spite of the ensuing mad rush, the rest of the squadron was already airborne, on its way to Düsseldorf. By the time 'EF' lifted off from the aerodrome it was 20.08 hours. Events now turned in our favour. Following the instructions from Ground Control we believed that the others had reached the engagement area but we were puzzled when we could see neither bombers, nor night-fighters nor, in fact, any anti-aircraft fire ahead of us. Schnaufer was debating whether to follow our present track when we suddenly noticed over to the north, probably in the Münster area, a lot of light anti-aircraft fire. Again this puzzled us. Guns of that calibre were effective up to 2,000 metres only, yet the British bombers usually flew between 3,500 and 6,000 metres over the Fatherland. Without further thought Schnaufer altered heading to the northwest to cut off the bombers returning home.

At 2,500 metres we flew through a thin layer of cloud and our radar showed us several targets. Suddenly we were in a condition of 'Shroud'; above us a thin layer of stratus through which the moon shone giving us an opaque screen above which we could see clearly the black silhouettes of the bombers from quite a distance. Schnaufer closed upon a Lancaster flying along unsuspectingly slightly to our starboard at altitude 1,700 metres. We had been airborne just over half-an-hour. The *Major* closed with the target, left to right, from below and delivered the first attack with the two vertically mounted 20mm cannons, just behind him, in the cabin. He aimed between the two engines on the right-hand side. The fuel tanks were located there and this method brings the quickest results. The time was 20.44 hours. The right wing of the bomber was badly damaged; a huge flame illuminated the sky. The Lancaster held steady for a while, long enough to allow the crew to escape by parachute before it fell to earth and crashed.

There followed attack after attack, the sky seemed to be full of bombers! Now the British crews knew we were there and began their violent manoeuvres, twisting and turning in an effort to escape us. Schnaufer had to follow all their corkscrew movements, to remain in a position under the bombers' wings where the return fire could not be brought to bear upon us yet ready to use the *Schräge Musik*. In one case we practically stood upon our wing tip whilst firing. Things became more difficult for us when we crossed the front line and the American anti-aircraft batteries opened up. Within a period of 19 hectic minutes we managed to shoot down seven bombers – without so much as a scratch – testimony to the *Major's* great skill and ability to get in quickly, line up his target and dive away quickly. Normally during this wild fighting I would hardly have had time to note the details thoroughly but because of the 'shroud effect' the pilot did not need my assistance at the radar to guide him on to each target and I had more time than usual to observe the effects. *Oberfeldwebel* Wilhelm Gänsler,[17] our gunner, gave great support as usual but even he could not help when we attacked our eighth Lancaster bomber. At the crucial moment we exhausted the ammunition to the upward-trained guns and as a result had the greatest difficulty in getting away from the concentrated fire from the bomber crew.

We still had our four horizontally mounted cannons in the nose of our fighter but these too refused to function during our ninth attack and we had to stop chasing the bombers. On the way back to base we had to fly again over the American batteries and by now the *Major* was thoroughly weary, almost spent. I called, therefore, upon Dortmund to give us all possible assistance to clear us back to Gütersloh with all expediency and with this help Schnaufer greased our faithful G9 + EF on to the ground. The night's work was done, we were back at base and it was just short of 22.00 hours. Once we had taxied in and shut down the engines, we sat in silence for a couple of minutes, thankful to have got through it and thought about the men who had gone down that night and hoped that they had managed to parachute to safety. Many years later I received a letter from an Englishman, Stanley Bridgeman. He had been a crew-member on Lancaster *Z-Zebra* on 463 Squadron RAAF that was shot down that night at 21.02 hours over Holland. All his crew had managed to escape by parachute. My prayers had been answered in part.[18]

On Thursday 22 February the Alma Pluto Benzol plant at Gelsenkirchen and another oil target at Osterfeld were the targets for two forces in 3 Group of 85 and 82 Lancasters respectively. Crews should have bombed the benzol plant in daylight on Tuesday with a dash in from the northwest and a dash out in the same direction but after briefing the operation was cancelled. On Wednesday crews were briefed for the same target by the same route and again the raid was cancelled. At Chedburgh a crew of young sergeants, anxious to start their tour, left the 218 Squadron briefing room feeling very frustrated. So too did another new crew led by Flying Officer Johnny Muschamp, who according to Flight Sergeant Miles Tripp on 'Dig' Klenner's crew 'looked too young to drive a car, let alone an aeroplane'. This time, after bombing, the Lancasters were to turn southwest and fly over Essen and Krefeld, which to Tripp seemed a 'crazy flight plan for a daylight operation even if the route was covered by cloud.'[19] The Met Man stated that the Ruhr would be entirely covered by thick cumulous cloud and the Intelligence Officer claimed that the unorthodox route would fool the opposition. Both statements were treated with equal distain and scepticism. The weather was wrong. It was a cloudless sky over the Ruhr and at Gelsenkirchen crews were met by a 'hailstorm' of flak. Muschamp's Lancaster fell in a sheet of flame. Sergeant John Simpson the flight engineer recalls:

My crew had joined 218 on St Valentine's Day. In our 'welcome' interview from Wing Commander W J Smith DFC I could not remember him saying much other than to inform us that since raids over Germany were no longer as dangerous as previously the tour had been increased from 30 to 40 operations. Now, one week later three of the crew had been killed and the four survivors were lying in varying states of disrepair in a Police Station in Gelsenkirchen awaiting collection by the *Gestapo*, our Lancaster having been shot down by ack-ack during a daylight raid on an oil refinery in that well defended city. We were on the bombing run over the target when we were hit by incendiary shells almost simultaneously with a shout from the bomb aimer: 'Bombs gone Skipper'. In no time at all the Lanc became a raging inferno. Obviously, it was very badly damaged and with no hope of being able to put out the fire our Skipper gave the order, 'Emergency jump jump; emergency jump jump'. By this time despite all his efforts to retain some control of the Lanc it was already in a deep dive. Four of us with great difficulty managed to bail out – Sergeant Jim Halsall the bomb aimer and me, Bill Porter the navigator and Doug White the wireless operator. Sadly, the Skipper and the two gunners, Sergeants George Hogg and Foster 'Paddy' Darragh did not get out and I later learned that they had been buried in the German War Cemetery at Rheinswold Forest, Kleve. When I was taken into custody, which was immediately on landing in the very ack-ack site which shot us down, I was greeted with the words, 'Tommy for you the war is over.' Ironically, little did they know that what with being bombed at night by the RAF, strafed by day by Americans and starved by the Germans, for me the war was just beginning![20]

On the following day 'a little tragedy' was posted on the 218 Squadron notice boards. Under the heading 'New Arrivals' seven names were listed and directly underneath, under the heading 'Missing in Action' were the same seven names.[21]

On the night of 23/24 February the second in a series of terrifying area-bombing raids on German cities which had thus far escaped the bombing, went ahead. Over 360 Lancasters and 13 Mosquitoes of 1, 6 and 8 Groups carried out the first and only area-bombing raid on Pforzheim, a city of 80,000 people. In just over 20 minutes 1,825 tons of bombs were dropped from only 8,000 feet. More than 17,000 people were killed and

83 per cent of the town's built up area was destroyed in 'a hurricane of fire and explosions'. Ten Lancasters failed to return. *Oberleutnant* Wilhelm 'Wim' Johnen, *Staffelkapitän*, 5./NJG1 was one who vented his anger on the RAF.[22]

> With the attacks on Pforzheim and Dresden, the Allies mad-dog rage for destruction reached its peak. Just as in antiquity the city of Pompeii was destroyed by the sudden eruption of Vesuvius ... the Allies annihilated the cities which had so far been spared, with a burning rain of incendiaries; in particular the cities of Pforzheim, Dresden and Würzburg. Pforzheim was the first of these Pompeii's. The city was laid in ruins and ashes and about 17,600 people met their deaths in a hurricane of fire and explosions. During the attack the fire fighters were powerless but even after the raid the fires could not be put out since the water mains had been damaged and the walls of the houses had collapsed and filled the streets. The ashes lay ten feet high in the streets. This storm of fire reached its peak after ten minutes. It was so powerful that the rain of ashes was carried as far as Stuttgart and the sky turned blood red over a radius of 50 miles. On account of the raging flames and the explosion of delayed-action bombs after the attack, the inhabitants dared not leave their cellars and were suffocated. Any who dared to come out collapsed in the white heat of the huge fires. Thousands of blackened and mutilated corpses lay among the ruins.

Bomber Command's last Victoria Cross was gained on the night of 23/24 February, the award going to Captain Edwin Swales DFC SAAF on 582 Squadron, operating as Master Bomber for the attack on Pforzheim. His citation read:

> Captain Swales was 'master bomber' of a force of aircraft which attacked Pforzheim on the night of 23 February 1945. As 'master bomber' he had the task of locating the target area with precision and of giving aiming instructions to the main force of bombers following in his wake. Soon after he had reached the target area he was engaged by an enemy fighter and one of his engines was put out of action. His rear guns failed. His crippled aircraft was an easy prey to further attacks. Unperturbed, he carried on with his allotted task; clearly and precisely he issued aiming instructions to the Main Force. Meanwhile the enemy fighter closed the range and fired again. A second engine of Captain Swales' aircraft was put out of action. Almost defenceless, he stayed over the target area issuing his aiming instructions until he was satisfied that the attack had achieved its purpose. It is now known that the attack was one of the most concentrated and successful of the war.

Captain Swales did not, however, regard his mission as completed. His aircraft was damaged. Its speed had been so much reduced that it could only with difficulty be kept in the air. The blind-flying instruments were no longer working. Determined at all costs to prevent his aircraft and crew from falling into enemy hands, he set course for home. After an hour he flew into thin-layered cloud. He kept his course by skilful flying between the layers but later heavy cloud and turbulent air conditions were met. The aircraft, by now over friendly territory, became more and more difficult to control; it was losing height steadily. Realising that the situation was desperate Captain Swales ordered his crew to bail out. Time was very short and it required all his exertions to keep the aircraft steady while each of his crew moved in turn to the escape hatch and parachuted to safety. Hardly had the last crew-member jumped when the aircraft plunged to earth. Captain Swales was found dead at the controls. Intrepid in the attack, courageous in the face of danger, he did his duty to the last, giving his life that his comrades might live.[23]

On 24 February, 340 aircraft[24] set out to attack the Fischer-Tropsch synthetic oil plant at Bergkamen just north of Kamen and 166 Lancasters and four Mosquitoes of 5 Group took off to breach the Dortmund-Ems canal near Ladbergen in northern Germany. However, both target areas were covered by cloud and the raid on Kamen, which relied on *Oboe* and H_2S markers, resulted in ineffective bombing. At Dortmund-Ems, the Master Bomber instructed crews to return to base with some of the bombs. These were mainly 1,000lb HEs fitted with delay fuses and it was always considered too dangerous to bring this type of bomb back. After jettisoning some of their bomb load in the North Sea to relieve the weight on the aircraft when landing, the Lancasters headed back to their Lincolnshire bases. An hour later the aircraft on 61 Squadron joined the Skellingthorpe circuit waiting to be called in to land by Flying Control. Suddenly many of the aircrew in the circling Lancasters saw a large flash on the ground indicating an explosion had taken place on the airfield. Within a few minutes Skellingthorpe was closed down to air traffic and the waiting Lancasters were diverted to land at nearby RAF Waddington. After landing at Waddington all the Squadron aircraft were shepherded to the farthest corner of the airfield and widely dispersed away from all buildings and other aircraft. The aircrews were then ordered to leave their aircraft as fast as possible and were taken away to a debriefing hut to await further instructions. The emergency diversion from Skellingthorpe was the result of Lancaster *E-Easy* landing heavily, which activated the short delay fuse in one of the bombs on board. After returning from the abortive operation, *E-Easy* had been parked with other aircraft in line around the perimeter track. The aircrews were quickly taken away for debriefing leaving ground crews working inside and around the aircraft.

Suddenly there was a massive explosion as the whole of *E-Easy's* bomb load went up and completely destroyed the aircraft and damaged several others close by. The initial fear was that the bombs inside the damaged aircraft would also be activated causing a chain reaction. The Squadron armament officer Flight Lieutenant Stewart was quickly driven out to take charge of the situation by the 'B' Flight Commander Squadron Leader Ian Fadden. They found a large area of devastation all lit up by burning fuel. The station's emergency services were quickly on the scene and dealing with numerous fires and taking the injured to the station sick quarters. The initial casualty report was three dead and many more injured. After taking stock of the overall situation and talking to the armourers, Stewart went along to each aircraft forcing open the bomb doors and defusing all the suspect bombs. For this act of extreme bravery Stewart was not even mentioned in dispatches. As one of the Squadron 'erks' said later, 'There ain't no bloody justice.'[25]

As it had escaped destruction until now, a 'G-H' attack was ordered on the Fischer-Tropsch plant on 25 February by 153 Lancasters of 3 Group. One Lancaster was lost and the plant still functioned. So, after night raids on Dortmund, Mainz and Gelsenkirchen and on Mannheim and Cologne, on the night of 3/4 March Kamen and the Dortmund-Ems Canal once again appeared on the Battle Order. Some 234 aircraft – 201 Halifaxes of 4 Group and 21 Lancasters, and 12 Mosquitoes of 8 Group – were detailed to bomb the synthetic oil plant and 212 Lancaster and ten Mosquito crews of 5 Group were to attack the aqueduct, safety gates and canal boats on the Dortmund-Ems canal at Ladbergen. Fifteen Lancasters on 467 Squadron RAAF at Waddington were included in the attack on the canal, which the Australians had twice bombed in November 1944 and again on New Year's Day 1945. The squadron returned to Ladbergen on the night of 7/8 February when they lost their newly appointed CO, Wing Commander John Douglas DFC AFC who the RAAF had found another command once the heat had died down after the debacle in France in September when Lancasters had bombed Canadian troops. Douglas had held the post for just one week since replacing Squadron Leader Ellis, who had been shot down on 1 February. On 20 February, 467 Squadron bombed the canal again and they returned on 21 February, but 10/10 cloud over the target prevented them making a daylight raid. An attack on 28 February was cancelled and early morning attacks were cancelled on 1 March and the 2nd. When bomb and fuel loads similar to those of the previous days were prepared on 3 March, crews had been up early in preparation for a daylight operation, but this was cancelled in favour of the night attack. Squadron Leader Eric Le Page Langlois DFC, whose promotion from Flight Lieutenant had come through only that morning, would lead the squadron on the 18th trip of his second tour. With him was the new gunnery leader, Flying Officer R E Taylor, who had only just joined the squadron.

At around 18.00 hours aircraft began taking off for their targets. The first aircraft over Germany were the 89 Mosquitoes of 8 Group bound for Berlin and Würzburg in northwest Bavaria. At 23,000 feet over Bremen a single 4,000lb 'Cookie' was released at 19.51 hours. The first bomb of the night had fallen and the remaining Mosquitoes carried on to their targets. Berlin was first marked by three H_2S-equipped Mosquitoes at 10.27 hours. Six red and six green 250lb TIs were dropped in three clusters, which fell in a line from the north-east to the south-west across the city. Sixty-four other Mosquitoes then made their way through the searchlights and flak to drop 59 tons of bombs on the TIs. Würzburg was bombed at the same time as Berlin. Six *Oboe* Mosquitoes marked the target with 15×250lb red TIs. These dropped through heavy cloud over, illuminating the River Main running through the target below. The following 24 Mosquitoes each dropped their single 4,000lb bomb in a concentrated area on the east bank of the river. A large fire was still visible when the attackers were 50 miles away. None of the Mosquito crews saw any defences.

Sixteen Lancasters of 5 Group and 15 Lancasters of 1 Group sowed mines in the Kattegat and in Oslo Fiord between 20.15 and 21.08 hours. One of the 5 Group Lancasters aborted the operation but 15 dropped 90 mines in Oslo Harbour. The 15 Lancasters of 1 Group made their way over the North Sea above low 10/10ths cloud to Denmark where the weather cleared. *Major* Werner Husemann piloting a Ju 88G of I./NJG3 was on patrol east of Aarhus and close to the area in the Kattegat where the 1 Group Lancasters were to lay their mines. At 20.29 hours Husemann shot down Lancaster *R-Robert* for his 33rd *Abschuss*. Flying Officer Lee Joseph Robert Gregoire DFC RCAF and his crew on 153 Squadron went down into the Kattegat and became the night's first victims. All were lost without trace. The remaining Lancasters sowed 83 mines and one crew claimed to have shot down a Ju 88.

Perhaps the most unusual of the sorties flown were those flown by 61 aircraft of 100 Group. Twelve Halifaxes and four Stirlings took up positions in a line across the bomber route and at 20.45 hours switched in their *Mandrel* equipment. This effectively shielded the incoming force by jamming the long range *Freya* radars. The 16 aircraft orbited their positions for 45 minutes and then changed direction where they again orbited for 50 minutes before returning to their original stations for another 25 minutes. One Mosquito and seven Halifaxes on 192 Squadron flew a signal investigation patrol to monitor enemy radio transmissions. Although one Halifax returned early when its undercarriage became unserviceable, the remaining aircraft accompanied the 4 Group Halifaxes to Kamen. Five Halifaxes, three Liberators and eight Fortresses set out on other jamming missions, but three aircraft returned early due to mechanical failures. The remaining thirteen aircraft operated *Piperack*, *Carpet* and *Jostle* to jam the defences whilst accompanying the bombers.

From various Operational Conversion Units of 7 Group, 40 Lancasters, 19 Halifaxes and 35 Wellingtons were detailed to fly a *Sweepstake* diversionary flight towards the Frisian Islands. Three Halifaxes cancelled after mechanical failures but the remaining 91 aircraft spent an hour throwing 3,721 bundles of *Window* out over the North Sea. The American contribution to the night consisted of 24 B-24s. Six of these returned early, leaving eighteen aircraft to drop 183×500lb bombs on Emden. The final preamble to the main attacks came again from 100 Group with a feint attack on Meppen. Ten Halifaxes and six Mosquitoes dropped flares and TIs in an attempt to mislead the fighter controllers into diverting their night fighters away from the main force.[26]

Just one minute after the TIs were released over Meppen, the first Main Force attack began on the Dortmund-Ems Canal at Ladbergen. The first markers to fall over the canal were eight 1,000lb green TIs. And then came 305 flares to illuminate the target, and finally Mosquitoes dropped ten 1,000lb red TIs. This main group of markers fell just 300 yards north-west of the aiming point and the Master Bomber orbiting over the target began to issue instructions to the 118 Lancasters of the Main Force. The attack lasted for just over 25 minutes. Eighteen 'Tallboy' bombs dropped by Lancasters on 9 Squadron were followed by hundreds of 2,000lb bombs fitted with 90-minute delay fuses. Under this weight of explosives the canal burst its banks on both sides of the safety gates, flooding the surrounding area and leaving many canal boats stranded. As the bombers left the target area night fighter pilots were being directed on to the bomber stream by their ground control stations. Whilst the *Window* and other countermeasures made detecting the bombers a difficult task, the large number of four-engined aircraft in the comparatively small airspace formed by the bomber stream aided interception and four pilots claimed eight Lancasters in just 18 minutes. All fell in the vicinity of Münster. The first claim to be made was by *Major* Heinz-Wolfgang Schnaufer, *Geschwaderkommodore* of NJG4 and holder of the *Ritterkreuz with Brillanten* (Diamonds), the highest award ever given to a German night fighter pilot. At 21.55 hours he shot down a Lancaster between Münster and Osnabrück – his 117th claim. Nine minutes later another Lancaster became his 118th victim. *Hauptmann* Hermann Greiner, *Gruppenkommandeur* of IV./NJG1, who had 47 day and one night victory, claimed three Lancasters. *Hauptmann* Joseph Kraft, also of IV./NJG1 made his 53rd and 54th claims whilst Major Martin Drewes, *Gruppenkommandeur* of III./NJG1 made his 49th claim. All three of these pilots were holders of the *Ritterkreuz* with *Eichenlaub*.[27]

Whilst the *Experten* wrought havoc among the Lancasters of 5 Group, the Halifaxes of 4 Group approached their target at Kamen. As before, the attack was opened with markers, this time dropped from between 28,000 and 35,000 feet by eight of the *Oboe* Mosquitoes. The 21 Lancasters followed the red TIs with green TIs and almost 98 tons of high explosive, which effectively illuminated the plant for the following 181 Halifaxes. A total of 690 tons of bombs fell on the target in the space of ten minutes. Only searchlights and flak met the bombers who left continuing explosions and spreading fires in their wake. The plant was severely damaged and no further production took place. This night the *Luftwaffe* mounted their Operation *Gisela*, sending about 200 night fighters to follow the various bomber forces to England. In the two and a half hours that the attack lasted, 13 Halifaxes, nine Lancasters, a Fortress and a Mosquito were shot down. More than 20 other aircraft were attacked but escaped with varying degrees of damage. The Dortmund-Ems Canal was breached in two places and put completely out of action but seven Lancasters were shot down. Three of these were on 467 Squadron; amongst which was the aircraft of Squadron Leader Langlois.[28]

Near the target area the gunners on the 619 Squadron Lancaster flown by Wing Commander S G Birch claimed to have shot down a V-1 flying bomb which was probably aimed at the port of Antwerp. Peter Bone on 626 Squadron had cause to recall the threat posed by Hitler's vengeance weapons:

Neither our Skipper or the Squadron Commander chose easy ops for themselves and therefore for us. Nine of our ops were to the Ruhr, which vied with Berlin as the most fiercely defended territory in Germany. Three were to Essen, the home of Krupps, which provided the bulk of Hitler's armaments to all three services. It was two days after our final op to Essen – a daylight attack on 11 March – that we went on leave for a week. Since the previous September, Hitler's second Vengeance Weapon, the V-2, had been falling all over London. These supersonic rockets, each weighing eight tons with a one ton warhead, descended from a height of sixty miles at a speed greater than that of sound and thus gave no warning of their approach. Londoners knew they couldn't remain in air raid shelters all day and night just in case a rocket might fall on them, so there was nothing for it but go about their business by day and pleasures by night. I heard tremendous explosions on several occasions as these diabolical missiles landed and sensed the stress Londoners were going through beneath their legendary 'stiff upper lip'. It was a strange leave. Two evenings after going to a North London music hall to see my favourite dance band on stage, I was sitting in my gun turret while Freddy dropped sea mines on parachutes into the darkness over Oslo Fiord, to harry German shipping.

On the way to the target, I caught sight of the exhaust of a V-2 as it climbed steadily to height over the English Channel. I knew that within a few seconds it would fall somewhere in Greater London. Only a month earlier my mother had been concussed when a V-2 fell in a field next to her church where she was doing some voluntary work. Because of recent rains, the missile had buried itself into the soft earth before exploding. As it was, the church hall was destroyed but the church itself was only slightly damaged. My sister, who had not long before been called out on first aid duty in Central London, after a V-2 had fallen and had been badly shaken at seeing bloodied body parts in the street for the first time, was telephoned by a neighbour to come home quickly. This she did, not knowing what she would find when she arrived. As I watched the V-2's exhaust flame disappear into the night sky, I was reminded yet again that those manning the home front were just as much in the front line as I was. More so because while I was based in the relative safety of the Lincolnshire countryside and was in harm's way only for a few hours every week my parents, sister and brother were, like all their neighbours now in harm's way around the clock. Its range of error was fifteen miles. This was indiscriminate bombing indeed.

Notes

1. Jim Price, a journalist who had previously served in Normandy, who wrote up the raid just before the 50th anniversary of the bombing of Dresden, in January 1995.
2. See *Mosquito Menacing The Reich* by Martin W Bowman (Pen & Sword 2008)
3. *Chased by the Sun.*
4. Letter home to Williams Creek, Indianapolis, Indiana on 29 May 1945.
5. *Nachtjaeger gegen Bomberpulks: Ein Tatsachen-bericht ueber die Deutsche Nachjagd im Zweiten Weltkrieg*, Pabel Rastatt, 1960/*Duell unter den Sternen (Duel Under the Stars)* 1956/Kimber Pocket Edition 1958.
6. In addition to these attacks the 1st Air Division of the US 8th Air Force dispatched 450 B-17s of which 316 attacked Dresden shortly after 12 noon on 14 February. To assist the night operations of Bomber Command various 'Spoof' attacks were made by Mosquitoes on Dortmund, Magdeburg and Hannover and 344 Halifaxes attacked an oil plant at Böhlen near Leipzig at the same time as the first attack. In addition to the above, the routeing and feints carried out by the Main Forces caused night fighter reaction to be minimal. In the case of the 5 Group attack the outward route consisted of no less than eight legs with feints towards the Ruhr, Kassel, Magdeburg and Berlin using '*Window*' at the same time. An indication of the effectiveness of these operations was that out of over 1,000 aircraft taking part only six were lost.
7. Memoirs of S/L Arthur Charles Carter, RAF Museum, Hendon, archive X001-3554.
8. At the time of writing Friedericke Clayton was living in Exmouth, Devon.
9. After the war Roman Halter came to London and received schooling from former Bomber Command pilots. Inspired by the beauty of Dresden, he became an architect.

10. *The Eighth Passenger* by Miles Tripp (Heinmann 1949; Corgi 1971; MacMillan 1978; Robin Clark 1979) and *218 Gold Coast Squadron Association Newsletter No. 17* edited by Margery Griffiths.

11. At Portal's instigation, Churchill was persuaded to withdraw his paper and substitute a new one, dated 1 April 1945: 'It seems to me that the moment has come when the question of the so-called "area bombing" of German cities should be reviewed from the point of view of our own interests. If we come into control of an entirely ruined land, there will be a great shortage of accommodation for ourselves and our Allies; and we shall be unable to get housing materials out of Germany for our own needs ... We must see to it that our attacks do not do more harm to ourselves in the long run than they do to the enemy's immediate war effort. Pray let me have your views ...'

12. The *Bomber Command War Diaries: An Operational reference book 1939–1945.* Martin Middlebrook and Chris Everitt. (Midland 1985).

13. Including diversionary and minor operations aircraft, 1,283 sorties were flown.

14. F/O David Forster Sinfield DFC and F/Sgts Eric Cecil Bangs and Thomas Stanley Carr were killed. The rest were led away into captivity.

15. Nine Lancasters FTR from the raid on the Mittelland Canal and four crashed in France and Holland. 362 Lancasters and 11 Mosquitoes of 1, 6 and 8 Groups took part in the last area bombing raid on Duisburg, which was successful. Seven Lancasters were lost and three crashed behind the Allied lines in Europe. The area raid on Worms resulted in 1,116 tons of bombs being accurately dropped on the town's built up area; of which 39% was destroyed and 35,000 bombed out from a population of about 58,000 people. Some 64% of the town's buildings were destroyed. Ten Halifaxes and a Lancaster FTR. Middlebrook.

16. *Hauptmann* Adolf Breves of IV./NJG1 took off from Düsseldorf airfield on 21 February in his Bf 110 and claimed three aircraft in the Ruhr area to take his score to 16. Another Bf 110 pilot, *Hauptmann* Johannes Hager, *Staffelkapitän* 6./NJG1, claimed two *Viermots*.

17. Gänsler, an experienced *Bordschütze* who had formidable night-vision, had previously flown with *Oberleutnant* Ludwig Becker and had shared in 17 kills with him. He was awarded the *Ritterkreuz*.

18. Lancaster I NG329 JO-Z on 463 Squadron RAAF, flown by F/O G H Farrow RCAF was MIA at Gravenhorst. All the crew survived and landed in Allied territory. Schnaufer's final score was 121 bombers in 130 sorties (114 of his kills were four-engined Stirlings, Halifaxes and Lancasters) and he was decorated with the *Ritterkreuz* with Oak Leaves, Swords and Diamonds. *Leutnant* Fritz Rumpelhardt took part in 100 of these successful attacks and *Oberfeldwebel* Gänsler in 98. Rumpelhardt was the most successful *Bordfunker* in *Nachtjagd*, being credited with 100 *Abschussbeteiligungen*, or 'contributions to claims'. Schnaufer died in a motor car accident in France on 31 July 1950.

19. *The Eighth Passenger* by Miles Tripp (William Heinemann Ltd 1969)

20. *218 Gold Coast Squadron Assoc Newsletter No.28* January 2004 edited by Margery Griffiths. Jim Halsall never recovered from his injuries and he died in 1950.

21. *The Eighth Passenger* by Miles Tripp (William Heinemann Ltd 1969). Both refineries were accurately bombed. There were no losses at Osterfeld.

22. *Duel Under the Stars* (Kimber Pocket Edition 1958)

23. Captain Edwin Swales DFC SAAF, 582 Squadron, Lancaster PB538. Awarded for action 23 February 1945, *London Gazette,* 24 April 1945.

24. 290 Halifaxes, 26 Lancasters and 24 Mosquitoes of 4, 6 and 8 Groups. One Halifax was lost.

25. The three airmen who died in QR-E were LACs B Burnell, C H Higgins and H G Wilson. *Thundering Through The Clear Air: No.61 (Lincoln Imp) Squadron At War* by Derek Brammer (Toucann Books, 1997)

26. *Intruders over Britain: The Luftwaffe Night Fighter Offensive 1940 to 1945* by Simon W Parry (ARP 2003).

27. *Intruders over Britain: The Luftwaffe Night Fighter Offensive 1940 to 1945* by Simon W Parry (ARP 2003).

28. *Intruders over Britain: The Luftwaffe Night Fighter Offensive 1940 to 1945* by Simon W Parry (ARP 2003).

CHAPTER 5

This Is Your Victory

God bless you all. This is your victory! It is the cause of freedom in every land. In all our long history we have never seen a greater day than this. Everyone, man or woman has done their best. Everyone has tried. Neither the long years, nor the dangers, nor the fierce attacks of the enemy, have in any way weakened the independent resolve of the British nation. God bless you all.

Prime Minister Winston Churchill, 8 May 1945

On the evening of Sunday 4 March at Kelstern, Flying Officer Jim Alexander's Lancaster crew on 625 Squadron had a whip-round (officers £1, NCOs ten shillings) for a night out at the Waterloo Inn at Laceby. On stand-downs if crews did not want to go as far as Grimsby, 12 miles away, or Scunthorpe, they went to the village pub near the airfield. Crews knew all the old Air Force songs even if the dirty ones shocked the regulars, who still treated them well even though they were on the ration. The beer was lousy but this could well be their last pint on earth. Men went to war for a few hours and then returned to live a near normal existence. They could go to the cinema, the pub, see friends and family and then go to war again. It was a clean and comfortable way of fighting a war but in many ways perhaps more stressful. Although everyone faced danger on every sortie they always thought it would be the other chap who would get the chop. Alexander's rear gunner, Sergeant Joe Williams, recalled that 'there was an *esprit de corps* of course, but it was based largely on the crews as self-contained units. Attachments outside your own crew were very few and far between. If *G-George* went missing one night, the next morning a replacement aircraft would arrive from the pool and go to *G-George*'s dispersal. A replacement crew would arrive and within a day or two would be flying in a new *G-George*. It was a self-healing process which was good for morale. Those dispersals and beds would be empty only for a few hours. It was as though nothing had changed.'

It always seemed to be the nicest blokes who didn't come back. Jim Alexander's elder brother had been killed piloting a Dakota at Arnhem the previous September. Alexander was a Canadian and there were two other Canadian Flying Officers on the crew: Bill Patrachenko the navigator, and the bomb aimer Floyd Chapman. Flight Sergeant Wyn Morgan was the Welsh radio operator, Cliff Lear the flight engineer and Bob Pyett the mid-upper gunner. Alexander's crew were joined by the squadron CO, Wing Commander John Barter, another flight commander, and the station medical officer.

Rear gunner Joe Williams was a Sussex farmer's lad and was not accustomed to drinking large amounts of alcohol. In the course of the party, as the brown ale and whisky chasers flowed, Joe heard something about a spare parachute that was always stowed behind his pilot's seat. Spare parachutes were a precious commodity for rear gunners who, because of the lack of space in their turrets, had to leave their parachute hanging in the fuselage. Joe later learned he had travelled back to Kelstern in a Ford Popular driven by his Canadian navigator, who had never sat behind the wheel of a car before. On Monday Williams was still suffering the effects of the night in the Waterloo when the station Tannoy instructed all crews to report for run-ups. This was usually the first indication that ops were 'on' for that night and this was confirmed when the Battle Order was posted in the messes, announcing meals at 12.45 and briefing at 13.30.

At the briefing Joe Williams took his seat along with 200 other aircrew on the squadron who learned that Operation *Thunderclap* had been resumed and that they were part of a 760-strong force detailed for a fire raid to destroy the built-up area, industries and railway facilities of Chemnitz. Another 248 Lancasters and ten Mosquitoes of 5 Group would attack the synthetic oil refinery at Böhlen. Alexander's crew, who were on their 22nd operation, would fly in the third wave of the main attack, the route taking the bomber stream across England to Reading and then out over Beachy Head, passing close to Joe Williams' family home between Uckfield and Lewes.

The crew bus dropped each seven-man group at their dispersals. Alexander's aircraft was *Fox-2*, a Mark III Lancaster. It was a tight fit for a rear gunner in his thick, electrically-heated clothing. Williams had to climb onto the Elsan toilet, clamber over the tailplane and slide feet first down a plywood board into the turret. Then Wyn Morgan put a boot into the middle of his back and slid the doors closed behind him. After the pre-flight checks, the engines were started and *Fox-2* moved out to join the Lancasters waiting to take off, each with an all-up weight of almost 31 tons. Radio silence was maintained (only during landing would the 625 Squadron Lancasters use their call-sign 'Peek-Frean', the name of a well-known biscuit manufacturer). Then, after a final check, the throttles were pushed through the gates, brakes were released and *Fox-2* surged down the runway, climbing out over Louth with the tall spire of the parish church passing beneath the Lancaster.

The operation began badly for 6 Group RCAF, which was detailed to dispatch 98 Halifaxes and 84 Lancasters late that afternoon. Unpredictable heavy icing conditions in a very local cloud condition affected aircraft taking off and caused seven Halifax aircraft to crash near their airfields. At Driffield, Flight Lieutenant C M Halpin RAAF took his Halifax off at 16.54 but experienced severe control problems and returned to base, landing at 19.05.[1] At Linton-on-Ouse, where 14 Halifaxes on 426 'Thunderbird' Squadron lined up to take off, American Flight Lieutenant Ivor Emerson RCAF taxied Y-Yoke out to the runway. The Halifax III, which was carrying a crew of seven and a bombload of eight 500-pounders, was airborne at 16.39 and began to gain height with 13 more of its Thunderbird companions. Just 21 minutes after take-off Emerson encountered the very severe icing conditions that had affected other aircraft and Yoke broke up in flight, scattering wreckage onto Nunthorpe Avenue, York only 12 miles distant. In addition to the six crew members that were killed, five civilians also died and a further 18 injured, mostly when an engine sliced through the roof of a local secondary school and demolished the kitchen area. The WOp/AG, 25-year-old Canadian Pilot Officer John Low, somehow bailed out in the nick of time and found himself falling, with all hope of being able to save himself by pulling the ripcord of his 'chute already gone, as he was far too near the ground. Then literally in a flash – a flash followed by a vivid red glow, which lit up the sky over York – the bomber's fuel tanks exploded, blowing Low several hundred feet skywards, parachute and all, and simultaneously opening his chute for him. He landed severely dazed and injured on the roof of a shed and was rescued by Mr. Herbert Youngman of York. Low was the sole survivor. For him the story had a happy ending, for on Saturday 2 June 1945, he married the Bridlington nurse who had helped him back to health.

The 'Thunderbirds' lost two more aircraft just after take-off. Flying Officer Humphrey Stanley Watts RCAF took H-Harry off at 16.42 and the Halifax iced up almost immediately before crashing at Westfield Farm, Kirbymoorside, 6 miles WNW from Pickering on the road to Sowerby, Yorkshire. The six Canadian airmen, including Flight Sergeant Richard Allan Biggerstaff, just 18 years old, and Pilot Officer William Albert Togwell RAF, who was taken home to be buried at Nottingham Road Cemetery, Derby, were killed. Squadron Leader Eric Thomas Garrett RCAF took off in A-Apple six minutes later and was involved in a collision with J-Johnny, a 425 'Alouette' Squadron Halifax flown by Pilot Officer Mark Sylvester Harold Anderson RCAF climbing out of Tholthorpe on the same operation. Both Halifaxes crashed 300 yards west of Manor House on the south side of the Ouse though much of the wreckage from A-Apple was found at Poolspring near Nun Monkton, 8 miles from the centre of York. In the last fateful moments aboard *J-Johnny*, Flight Sergeant A J de Cruyenaere managed to bail out. The other six men died in the aircraft. *S-Sugar* on 425 'Alouette' Squadron iced up in a very short time and was partially abandoned by three men on Flying Officer Arthur Robert Lowe's crew. Lowe was an American pilot serving in the RCAF. He and three of his crew went down with *Sugar*, which crashed 200 yards from Little Ouseburn, 9 miles north-west from Harrogate and badly damaging the church and Moat Hall.

In the light of these crashes, a spare crew was dispatched by the Thunderbirds, making 15 aircraft altogether. Twelve of these actually attacked Chemnitz but one of them, *J-Johnny*, failed to return. All the Canadians and the one American killed in the crashes after take-off were laid to rest in the Stonefall Cemetery in Harrogate although Flying Officer A R Lowe was later taken home and is now buried in Fairview Cemetery, Red Bank, New Jersey.

Halifax III *U-Uncle* on 420 'Snowy Owl' Squadron at Tholthorpe piloted by Pilot Officer Roald Frederick Sollie and carrying twelve 500-pounders, crashed at 17.20 into Hayton Woods near Hazelwood Castle, three miles south-west of Tadcaster minutes after take-off, killing six crew. Ordered to bail out, Flight Sergeant J H Waugh DFM the mid-upper gunner, did manage to pull the ripcord of his 'chute, but when the aircraft crashed directly beneath him, he was shot up into the air and the canopy partially collapsed. Luckily, after a drop of 400 feet, it reopened and Waugh landed safely. He was later commissioned and awarded the DFC to add to his award of an immediate DFM for the destruction of an enemy night-fighter over Oberhausen the previous November. Another 'Snowy Owl' Halifax was lost when *W-William*, airborne from Tholthorpe at 16.28, iced up and crashed at Marrow Flat Farm, just over a mile northeast of RAF Dishforth, killing four of the crew.

Fox-2 on 625 Squadron, meanwhile, lost the starboard outer engine on the climb out from Kelstern. Cliff Lear diagnosed the problem as a blown cylinder head gasket. This engine drove the hydraulic pump, and with-out power Bob Pyett the mid-upper gunner could not fire his guns or traverse his turret. The engine was shut down and the propeller feathered but without it *Fox-2* was unable to climb and began to lag behind the bomber stream. There was a quick crew conference and Jim Alexander decided to press on even though they would have insufficient fuel to make it all the way back to Kelstern. Joe Williams was convinced that this was because a few nights earlier a 625 Squadron crew had aborted and later in the mess it was hinted that they had got 'the wind up'.

Over France as the bomber stream continued to climb, Alexander restarted the faulty engine to enable *Fox-2* to reach its bombing height of 18,000 feet, but it quickly became apparent that the fault was serious and it was shut down again. As they turned through the 'Cologne Gap' between Bonn and Koblenz it was clear that they would not be able to reach their bombing height. As engine temperatures became dangerously high Alexander decided to level off at 15,000 feet.

There was little flak over Chemnitz and *Fox 2* got its bombs away. All went well until northwest of Bergen on the Island of Rügen they were attacked from behind and below by a *Schräge Musik* equipped night fighter. Williams called 'Corkscrew starboard' and opened fire. Their attacker raked the Halifax all along the fuselage with cannon shells and set both wings on fire. The rear gunner could see that the tail-plane was 'falling off in lumps'. Alexander gave the order for the crew to bail out. Williams did not need telling twice. He opened the port-side door of his turret, which was turned to the beam and great sheets of flame were streaming past, wound the turret straight with the manual gear, but could not open the other door. He thought he was going to die. Williams shouted, 'For God's sake, get me out of here' and when he tried the door again it opened. The flames were spiralling down the length of the fuselage and his parachute was burning in its stowage. It was then that he remembered the snatch of conversation in the Waterloo Inn the previous night and the 'spare parachute.' Williams fought his way to the cabin just as the pilot was about to leave, but there was no chute behind the pilot's seat. Jim Alexander, in what he later admitted was the bravest moment of his life, climbed back behind the controls and held the blazing Lancaster steady while his rear gunner located the spare parachute below the navigator's desk, put it on and jumped. Only then did he go himself. Williams heard *Fox-2* plunge into the ground as he swung beneath his parachute. He could feel the burned flesh on his face but it seemed curiously unimportant at the time. Everything was black and white below as the snow-covered ground rushed up to meet him. There was a bang and he was down. Williams landed on high heath land, buried his parachute and Mae West in the snow and blew his aircrew whistle for a while. No one returned his signal. He walked down the hillside and reached an isolated farmhouse where a gleam of light showed from a small outhouse. Williams knocked and opened the door, which was promptly closed again. '*Englander!*' he shouted, at which the occupant emerged and grabbed him by the shoulder. The family were Sudetenland Germans and they tended his wounds and gave him water before he was led away by the local *Volksturm*. Williams was later taken to a house in the village of Hradiste where he met Sergeant A J E Morton, the flight engineer of Halifax *Q-Queenie* on 102 Squadron at Pocklington, who had only just escaped before his aircraft crashed close to the spot where *Fox-2* had been shot down. He believed most of his crew had been killed.[2] Both were taken to the town of Kaadan the following day where the burns on Williams' face were treated and he was placed in a cell. That night the door opened and in came Bob Pyett. The following day they walked four miles to a nearby railway junction where they were joined by Floyd Chapman, and Cliff Lear and Wyn Morgan who were confined to hospital due to their injuries. The prisoners began a long train journey across Germany, through Nuremburg to Frankfurt where they were sent to *Dulag Luft*. There the interrogator told Williams that he knew he was on 'C Flight' and then proceeded to name the squadron and that he must know Sergeant H —— who he said 'was through here a few days ago'. And he added, 'Unfortunately he hurt his arm when he bailed out.' This was most likely Flight Sergeant J E Hughes or Sergeant W J Harrison, who were the only two survivors on Flying Officer H W Hazel DFC's crew, shot down on the raid to Leuna on 14/15 January.

Later, Williams and a number of other allied aircrew were taken to a transit camp at Wetzlar. The others were sent on to *Stalag Luft III* while he remained behind for treatment for his burns. On 30 March the camp was evacuated and so began a long, tiring march which was to take him back to Nuremburg where he joined a column of 300 prisoners being marched towards Moosburg in Bavaria. He was delighted to discover the group included Bill Patrachenko (who had driven the Ford Pop from Laceby) and Floyd Chapman. Joe still had his escape map with him and on 5 April they simply crawled away from their group. There was a burst of Tommy-gun fire but they got away and made tracks for the Allied lines near Nuremburg.[3] Joe Williams was to keep a diary of his days on the run, a diary written on a toilet roll. For ten days they walked, hid and dodged German troops and American bombers. At one stage they managed to pass themselves off as Hungarian troops. Finally they met up with the Americans in the town of Marktbreit. Williams arrived home on 22 April, three weeks ahead of the rest of the crew.[4]

Two more bombers crashed in England on return. *K-King*, a 582 Squadron Lancaster at Little Staughton flown by Flying Officer John Charles Gould crashed at 01.00 near Bellingdon, two miles northwest of Chesham in Buckinghamshire, when a Target Indicator that had failed to release exploded, with the loss of all but one of the crew. Sergeant G Hart was blown clear and managed to parachute to safety. *C-Charlie*, a 429 'Bison' Squadron Halifax III at Leeming, crashed at Halling four miles south-west of Gillingham in Kent. The American pilot, Flight Lieutenant Mardyth Wesley Sanderson RCAF and crew – all Canadians – died in the aircraft. Low on fuel, two Halifax aircraft on 578 Squadron at Burn put down at Bovingdon airfield where *U-Uncle* swung on landing and ran into *K-King* that had arrived 26 minutes earlier and was now parked just off the runway. There were no injuries but both aircraft were written off. As well, *L8-P*, a 347 *Tunisie* Free French Squadron Halifax at Elvington flown by Lieutenant J J Santi FFAF crash landed at Friston airfield in Sussex. *L-London* on 432 'Leaside' Squadron at East Moor was shot down into the sea off Walton-on-the-Naze, Essex by a British coastal battery. Squadron Leader Edwin Alfred Hayes RCAF and all his crew perished. Pilot Officer Douglas Cooke died just 30 miles from his home at Leigh-on-Sea and Flight Lieutenant John George Clothier RCAF, a former air gunner, was beginning his third tour of operations having re-mustered as a pilot. Both air gunners were 19 years of age.

Lancaster *L-London* on 432 Squadron flown by Pilot Officer J Kitchen RCAF, which had taken off from Croft at 16.35, bombed from 16,500 feet at 21.54 and was almost immediately involved in a mid-air collision with a Halifax that was in the process of being shot down by a Ju 88. The night-fighter crew then turned their attention to the Lancaster, causing much damage to the hydraulic system and starboard wing. Accurate return fire, however, succeeded in driving away the enemy fighter, possibly damaged, and Kitchen succeeded in getting his badly mauled aircraft back to Carnaby in Yorkshire where it was written off in the ensuing emergency landing.

Altogether, Bomber Command lost 21 aircraft[5] shot down *en route* to and returning from Chemnitz. Flying Officer John Albert Hurley on 102 Squadron had taken Halifax *Q-Queenie* off from Pocklington at 17.33 and it crashed near Volyne on the Volynka about six kilometres SSW of Strakonice in Czechoslovakia. Hurley and three of the crew were killed. All the rest of the crew were confined in hospital with injuries. This was the first Halifax VI lost on a Bomber Command operation and for 102 Squadron it was their third *Q-Queenie* to be lost in succession. On 10 Squadron at Melbourne two Halifax IIIs failed to return. Five of the crew on *E-Edward* flown by Flight Lieutenant F D Moss were killed. Flight Sergeant Fred Fearnley who was manning the mid-under gun turret, was 39 years old. Moss, although apprehended, avoided captivity and reached the American lines. All seven men on Flight Lieutenant Andrew Douglas Stephen's crew on *N-Nan*, including Flying Officer Richard Eric Heap, a regular who had gained a DFM on a previous tour with the Squadron, and Flight Sergeant Kenneth Vincent Rees, who had joined the RAF as an apprentice clerk in the late 1920s, were killed on the aircraft, which crashed near *Stalag IXC* at Mülhausen. All the bodies were recovered from the wreckage by PoWs. Two weeks later, on 20 March, despite an order from the Germans forbidding a burial service, funeral proceedings were conducted by the Senior Chaplain, Reverend J R Bamber MA.

After reaching the target and dropping its bombs *N-Nuts* on 420 'Snowy Owl' Squadron was shot down by an enemy fighter to take the Canadian squadron's losses to three on the night. At 21.45 *H-Harry* and its all-Canadian crew bombed the AP from 16,000 feet and homeward bound ran low on fuel so Pilot Officer J H Menary RCAF decided that since Allied land forces had recaptured France he would divert to Juvincourt airfield. At about 01.30 *Harry* emerged from low cloud and while flying through thin patches of mist, clipped a pole standing on high ground. Seconds later the Halifax crash-landed on soft earth eight kilometres north of the airfield. Flight Sergeant R A Nicol sustained a bruised right leg and Flight Sergeant D McClellan emerged from his turret with a cut forehead; the rest escaped with a bad shaking.

The loss of 94 personnel killed and 21 taken into captivity was one of the heaviest blows ever suffered by the Canadian Group in a single night. But if it was a tragic night for the Canadian Group, it was no less so for Chemnitz, for despite 10/10ths cloud, necessitating the use of sky markers, the bombers left fires, which still raged 36 hours later. The old town centre was almost completely obliterated; most of the buildings were gutted and few if any factories in the area escaped. The Siegmar factory, which manufactured tank engines, was destroyed.[6]

In a separate attack, 248 Lancasters and ten Mosquitoes of 5 Group attacked the synthetic-oil refinery at Böhlen, which was covered by cloud. Four Lancasters were shot down, one force-landed at Nuneaton and one other came down in the River Witham near Boston, killing four of the crew. Most crews who survived knew what it was like to be struck by enemy fire. All experiences are different but the split second actions to save the aircraft and lives followed by the struggles to stay in the air are similar. G-George on 463 Squadron flown by Flying Officer A G Belford RAAF was struck by heavy flak approaching the AP, which shot away one aileron, almost severed the main wing spar, dislodged one of the fuel tanks, tore a hole in the fuselage, wrecked the main long range navigation electronics and damaged other flying controls. Losing height rapidly in the uncontrollable aircraft Belford was about to order the crew to bail out when he learned that the two gunners, Flight Sergeant's P Jobson RAAF, who was wounded in the left eye, and P R Shipperd who had also been wounded, were both unable to move. Belford decided that by using brute force, limited flying controls and emergency navigation systems he could nurse the aircraft to Juvincourt. It took four and a half hours to cover the 600 miles and remarkable navigation to find the airfield in heavy cloud and rain. Two attempts were made to land and on the second the aircraft touched down on a wheel and a wing tip. The starboard wheel collapsed and then the other wheel was torn off in a shell hole. George then finished on its belly and no lives were lost.[7]

Attacks on Salzbergen, Wesel and Sassnitz on Rügen Island in the Baltic followed. Then it was the turn of oil refineries at Hemmingstedt near Heide and Harburg while Dessau, Hamburg and Kiel too were also hit before the attacks switched to day and night attacks on other German towns and cities and oil targets again. The raid on the Deutsche Erdoel refinery at Hemmingstedt on 7/8 March involved 256 Halifaxes of 4, 6 Groups and 25 Lancasters and five Mosquitoes of 8 Group. There was slight heavy flak with about three searchlights, some light flak and considerable fighter activity in target area. Four Halifaxes were lost. The Met recce Mosquito duly completed its mission and the Master Bomber, a 35 Squadron Lancaster flown by Squadron Leader Daniel Bulmer Everett DFC** was heard giving the 'basement figure' at 6,000 feet. White flares commenced falling on time and provided fair illumination with a tendency to spread somewhat south. Marking with Green TIs began at approximately 21.55 hours with a generally good concentration but the Main Force attack was early and these green markers were being bombed before visual identification of the target could be established. Yellow TIs were dropped and instructions issued, but unfortunately the Master Bomber was lost soon after. Squadron Leader Everett, who was on his 90th op, and all his crew, were killed. Control was therefore taken over by the Deputy Master Bomber. He identified the target and having dropped Yellow markers near to the aiming point, was able to issue the necessary bombing instructions. This accurate marking was reinforced by Red TIs. Although early bombing generally appeared to have been somewhat scattered, later bombing probably improved. Some fires were left burning in the target area, but no further satisfactory identification of the plant was obtained and bombing fell two to three miles from the target.

On 8/9 March, Bomber Command forces attacked Hamburg and Kassel and on the 9th the North and South plants of the Emscher Lippe benzol plant at Datteln were bombed by 159 Lancasters of 3 Group. Flight Lieutenant B J Aldhous' crew on 90 Squadron, who were flying their last operation of their tour, led the bomber stream. They carried two huge Roman Candles in the rear turret, one to be fired electronically to notify the stream to formate closer together and take no further evasive action or any weaving, the second to be fired four minutes from the target on the run up with bomb doors opened at the same time. This had first been tried on the Wesel operation on 19 February by the CO, Wing Commander Peter Francis Dunham DFC when his Lancaster blew up after taking a direct hit at 23,000 feet killing all the crew. On 9 March it was the turn of Sergeant A F C 'Mick' Smith in the rear turret to fire off the Roman Candles. He was convinced that he would not be returning from air operations that day. Aldhous too had a premonition that it would be their last op. With a grin he just said: 'This is it Mick.' Just after 'Bombs Gone' their Lancaster was hit by flak bursts and set on fire. Mick Smith was the only one of the eight men who survived.[8] No other aircraft were lost.

Next day it was again the turn of the Scholven/Buer synthetic oil refinery, which was attacked by similar numbers of Lancasters in 3 Group. No aircraft were lost. Another daylight raid, on Essen by 1,079 aircraft – 750 Lancasters and 293 Halifaxes and 36 Mosquitoes – of all bomber groups, took place during the bright afternoon of Sunday 11 March. It was the largest attack of the war. For Flight Sergeant Arthur 'Tommy' Thompson, pilot of Z-Zebra on 463 Squadron, Essen was his first operation since his arrival at Waddington. Even that was notable:

We were standing outside our barrack block with another crew waiting for room allocation, when the first female Warrant Officer we had seen cycled along the road. She was wearing a tight skirt so we all had a glimpse of her 'passion killers' regulation issue navy blue long knickers and she was clearly embarrassed at the 'wolf-whistles' she received. Little did I realise that a chance meeting later that night with the same WAAF Warrant Officer Muriel Welsh at the 'Horse and Jockey' in Waddington village would determine my future life. We were together throughout my stay at Waddington and two years later we married at Ormskirk Parish Church, the start of a happy family life.

Within a week of arriving at Waddington we were preparing for our first operation, but an encounter with a German night fighter, whilst travelling in an 'open back' truck from our aircraft dispersal along the perimeter track to the crew room, nearly put an end to any operations. The German night fighters flew back to England with the returning RAF main force and shot down 20 of our bombers in the vicinity of their own aerodromes. We had just returned from a training exercise and as one of the fighters swept across the 'drome with all guns firing, we could see the tracer bullets pass within a few feet of the back of our truck – a very near miss and this was on the ground! I have never seen a WAAF driver accelerate so quickly. Incidentally they hit the 'bomb dump' but it was only incendiary bombs which went up. There had always been dangers in flying training but we would now have anti-aircraft fire, German fighters and collisions with other aircraft to contend with. However it was going to be a 'wonderful' and everlasting experience for the people who survived.

Our crew was five British and two Australian. Our bomb load was 5.5 tons. In approximately 40 minutes 4,660 tons of bombs were dropped on sky markers through complete cloud cover. It was an accurate attack, which paralysed Essen until American troops entered the city. German statistics state that the pre-war population of Essen had fallen from 648,000 to 310,000. No losses for 463 Squadron.[9] The actual flight time was 5 hours 30 minutes. As we bombed over 10/10 cloud, which was 10,000 feet high we did not see the ground, but turning for home after passing over the target it was very noticeable that the heat from the fires on the ground were causing the cloud top to 'billow' upwards. Unfortunately, the same evening the aircraft which we had flown the previous day – JO-N – was taken up by a 'new' crew prior to ops and they collided with a Hurricane fighter whilst carrying out a night time fighter affiliation exercise. All seven bomber crew plus the New Zealand fighter pilot were killed. A great pity that after two years of training they died before their first operation.

It had taken 'Tommy' Thompson two years to become an operational pilot. At the outbreak of War in 1939 he was a draughtsman at Chloride Batteries at Swinton, Manchester and was in a reserved occupation. He was studying Electrical Engineering at Bolton Tech with three colleagues from work and they decided to volunteer for the Army Territorials and tried to persuade 'Tommy' to do the same, but he decided to wait and see how the war developed before making a decision about joining up. All three were immediately called up and all eventually became prisoners of war in Burma, their health suffered terribly and one died from Beri Beri in his early thirties. During pilot training at Regina, Canada, 'Tommy' witnessed his first casualty, a Canadian pupil pilot:

Before our arrival he had spun into the ground from 1,000 feet on a left hand turn in the circuit. Miraculously he had walked away from the crash and the Commanding Officer agreed that it was just tenseness on the controls and he could continue flying training. However just after our arrival we witnessed his 'demise' as he made the same mistake again and this time, his luck had run out. He was returned to camp in a 'body bag' as the aircraft had burst into flames on impact. On leaving Regina we travelled approximately 100 miles west, to No. 39 Service Flying Training School at Swift Current to continue training, this time on the twin engine Oxford aircraft. It was enjoyable to fly, with excellent forward vision. We flew most of the days, either dual with an instructor or solo, we also did night flights both dual and solo and I had my first solo flight on a twin-engine aircraft after 11 hours flying. I was presented with my 'Pilots Wings' on satisfactory completion of the course. However the award was marked by tragedy in that during the course I was directly involved in an accident which killed one of my friends and although I was completely blameless it is something which stayed with me. We were close formation flying with 3 aircraft stepped to the right (starboard) at the same height. I was in the lead aircraft and I decided on a gentle turn to the right, no signals given as per standard practice. The pupil pilot in the second aircraft, directly behind and to the right of me also turned, but the third aircraft behind him did not turn and the leading edge of his wing collided with the trailing edge of the second aircraft. The pupil and the instructor in the third air-craft disappeared from view. The second damaged aircraft returned to base as the trailing edge of the wing is less important than the leading edge. When the third aircraft did not return we took off again to search the area and eventually we found the pieces of wreckage scattered around the ground and the two bodies, which were returned to base for burial, but no pupil was allowed to attend the funeral ceremony.

My second raid was on the Monday afternoon, the day after Essen in JO-O. This time it was Dortmund and in almost identical conditions, 10/10 cloud with 1,108 aircraft dropping 4,850 tons of bombs, a record that stood to the end of the war. Our fighter escort added to the numbers and it was estimated that more than 2,000 British aircraft were airborne during the attack. Later investigations on the effects of the bombing, record that the raid put the city out of the war. The trip was 5 hours 50 minutes carrying 5.5 tons of bombs.

On 13 March when 'Tommy' Thompson's crew had a day's, rest 354 aircraft attacked Wuppertal and Barmen without loss. Bomber Command had now dispatched 2,541 sorties by daylight to Ruhr targets in a three-day period.[10]

'Tommy' Thompson continues:

When turning on to the runway to take off, it was nice to get a wave from the small number of airmen and WAAFs who had gathered by the control van. Muriel was there on a number of occasions when convenient and when take-offs were in daylight. On night ops we often took off at dusk, the idea being to spend all the time over enemy territory in darkness; of course the distance of the target was a deciding factor on take-off time.

Benzol plants at Herne and Gelsenkirchen were bombed on the night of 13/14 March and the next day, 169 Lancasters of 3 Group carried out 'G-H' attacks through cloud on plants at Datteln and Hattingen near Bochum. On the night of 14/15 March, 230 aircraft of 6 and 8 Groups attacked Zweibrücken to block the passage through the town area of German troops and stores to the Front. The same task was carried out at Homberg by 161 aircraft of 4 and 8 Groups. The raids were successful. Two Halifaxes were lost on the Homberg raid. Another 244 Lancasters and 11 Mosquitoes of 5 Group bombed the Wintershall synthetic oil refinery at Lützkendorf near Leipzig in central east Germany. It was 'Tommy' Thompson's third raid:

I flew JO-T. It was a long tiring trip: 9 hours 50 minutes with the continual 'throb' of four Rolls-Royce engines with no sound proofing in the aircraft, a full fuel load of 2,154 gallons and 4.5 tons of bombs. There were 255 aircraft on the raid and 18 were lost, fortunately none from Waddington. We were hit by anti-aircraft fire on the bombing run but luckily none of the holes in the aircraft were in vulnerable areas. It was annoying to be told when crossing the east coast that Waddington was fog bound and that we had to divert to Alconbury, a US Air Force station. But it was nice to enjoy a few hours sleep with all the American comforts and interesting to have a look round their Fortress aircraft, complete with ashtrays! We then returned to Waddington later in the morning for a day's rest.

Eight Lancasters were lost on Lützkendorf. On 227 Squadron at Balderton no word was heard from *J-Johnnie* or *P-Peter*, better known as *Polly Pepperpot*, which was lost with all the crew. 100 Group lost two Mosquitoes and two Fortress IIIs on 214 Squadron during *Jostle* radio countermeasure duties in support of the Main Force. *Hauptmann* Martin 'Tino' Becker of *Stab* IV./NJG6 and his *Funker Unteroffizier* Karl-Ludwig Johanssen in a Ju 88G-6 claimed nine bombers, the highest score by a German night-fighter crew in any single night. *A-Apple* on 207 Squadron returning to Spilsby crashed at Little Rissington in Gloucestershire. All seven crew died. Next day one of Bomber Command's smallest targets, the Mathias Stinnes benzol distillation plant at Bottrop and another benzol plant at Castrop-Rauxel were attacked in daylight by 188 aircraft. Both raids were believed to have been successful. One Halifax failed to return from the attack on Bottrop and another Halifax made it back with the starboard fin and rudder shot off and both elevators jammed, and made a forced landing at Manston. In a separate operation, 16 Lancasters on 9 and 617 Squadrons attacked the Arnsberg viaduct without loss. On 15/16 March, 267 bombers made an area attack on Hagen and another 257 Lancasters and eight Mosquitoes raided the Deurag oil refinery at Misburg on the outskirts of Hannover. Six Lancasters and four Halifaxes failed to return from Hagen, which suffered severe damage in the centre and eastern districts. Three of the Halifaxes lost were from the two French squadrons in Bomber Command. Four Lancasters were lost on the Misburg raid where the main weight of the raid fell south of the oil refinery. One of the losses was *A-Apple* on 153 Squadron at Scampton flown by Pilot Officer 'Ted' Parker, which exploded on the bomb run. Parker was about to call up his bomb-aimer on the intercom when suddenly he was all alone and falling through the sky. His Lancaster had disappeared. Parker pulled his ripcord and the parachute opened. No trace of the aircraft or its crew was ever found.

The night following, 16/17 March, 231 Lancasters of 1 Group and 46 Lancasters and 16 Mosquitoes of 8 Group were detailed to attack the southern and southwestern districts of Nürnburg in the last heavy Bomber Command raid of the war on the city. Würzburg, an old cathedral city famous for its historic buildings and which contained little industry, was the destination for another 225 Lancasters and 11 Mosquitoes of 5 Group. It was 'Tommy' Thompson's fourth raid: 'Another long night raid of 8 hours in JO-W. We carried two tons of HE bombs plus 15 cans of incendiaries to create a 'Fire Storm'.' Altogether, 1,127 tons of bombs were dropped with great accuracy in just 17 minutes and 89 per cent of Würzburg's built up area was destroyed. Estimates were that between 4,000 and 5,000 people were killed.

At Kirmington in Lincolnshire, 26 crews were on the battle order for Nürnburg. The squadron had flown a couple of short practice bombing trips the days before, which were aborted due to bad weather but the briefing after lunch on 16 March probably caused widespread indigestion. Nürnburg was known to be heavily defended and crews were warned to expect heavy flak, with the possibility of fighters before they reached the central marshalling yards, which was their target. Flying Officer 'Bud' Churchward RCAF's crew would fly Lancaster RF154 AS-B, better known as *TARFU* ('Things Are Really Fucked Up'). Alf 'Chalky' White the wireless operator was from High Wycombe, Ted Hull the flight engineer was from Romford. Lloyd 'Lefty' Etherington RCAF was the navigator, Chuck Goddard RCAF the bomb aimer and Bob Green was the rear-gunner. Sergeant Jack Goldstein was the mid-upper gunner. Jack's real name was Jacob. He was Polish and had been in Warsaw. He was brought to England by his mother Feigele ('Fanny') with his older brother Levy (later known as Lou) and his sister Annie, just before the outbreak of WWI, his father Yosef having emigrated to London with his brother-in-law a short while previously. The family settled in the East End and grew to 11 children in all, five boys and six girls. All the boys would serve in the forces during World War 2. Jack Goldstein was 27-years-old when war was declared but he could not enlist owing to his Polish birth. He had to wait until 22 January 1944 when the Government decided to allow all 'friendly aliens' to join the forces. A year later, on 5 January 1945, he arrived at Kirmington. By the time of the Munich raid he had completed 15 operations, including the raid on Dresden on 13 February.

Late that day *TARFU*'s tanks were filled up to the brim with 2,154 gallons of fuel and in the bomb bay were loaded a 4,000lb high explosive bomb and six 1,000lb incendiary clusters. They were due at Nürnburg at 21.34 hours. By 21.30 they were at 20,000 feet and on their approach to the target, which they could see in flames ahead of them. There had been some trouble with the rear guns *en route*, firing short bursts spontaneously, and again at this time. There was some flak and then fighter flares to both port and starboard. They were within seconds of releasing their bombs. And then it happened. Jack Goldstein shouted 'Corkscrew p— ' it was thought he was going to say 'port' but he did not get that far. By the time Bob Green the rear gunner yelled 'Corkscrew Skipper for Christ's sake!' it was too late. There were shells ripping through the fuselage and starboard wing root, which caught fire. The port wing was also on fire and the bomb bay had been hit, letting off the incendiaries and setting light to the aircraft floor. The extinguishers were emptied but to no avail. There was no option but to abandon the aircraft. Chuck Goddard got out first through the front escape hatch and then Ted Hull went out. 'Lefty'

Etherington first became stuck in that hatch by his parachute, but after a struggle he managed to escape. In the rear turret the guns had elevated and jammed Bob Green's foot and he manually cranked his turret round to 'beam', opened the turret doors, leaned out and pulled the ripcord; the opening parachute pulled him out. His boots were left behind. The way out for Alf White was through the normal rear entrance towards the tail; as he made his way there, he passed Jack Goldstein still slung in his harness in the mid-upper gun turret and slapped his legs in case he had not heard the pilot's order to bail out. Throughout this time 'Bud' Churchward struggled to keep the Lancaster on an even keel. He saw the three get out through the front hatch, but would be unable to see the others exit via the rear. When he thought they were all gone, he gave a roll call to check, receiving a response only from the rear gunner. After Bob Green told him he was going, 'Bud' asked if there was anyone still there. Not hearing any more, he assumed all had jumped. So he bailed out but Jack Goldstein went down in the burning aircraft, which crashed near Kammerstein, south of Nürnburg. German records show that at 21.31 the Lancaster was shot down by *Feldwebel* Schuster of I./NJG5 in a Junkers Ju 88.

Alf White was captured immediately, as his parachute took him onto the lawn of Nürnburg Prison! 'Lefty' Etherington landed about 10 miles southwest of Nürnburg. He was badly burned and by the following morning he was badly in need of medical attention, so he gave himself up in a small village near Kammerstein. Ted Hull was seriously burned about the face and he was captured early the next morning. All three men were taken to Munich for interrogation and then to Nürnburg PoW camp, as were Chuck Goddard and 'Bud' Churchward, who was not captured for several days, but who ended up in a prison in Stuttgart before being marched east. When he was captured on the morning after the crash, Ted Hull was taken to a nearby camp where he was interrogated by two SS officers for about an hour. They accused him of being Jewish and coming from 'a Jewish squadron'. He was told: 'Your mid-upper gunner is a Jew and so are you.' Evidently, the German authorities had identified Jack Goldstein as being Jewish by his identity tags which gave a person's religion. Ted was in a bad way, but was interrogated three times along the same lines. He cannot recall how long he was in that camp and was clearly in a state of shock as well as suffering from his untreated injuries. In his mind he thought he saw Jack Goldstein amongst a small group of men being taken by armed guards to some pits, which he took to be mass graves.

In all, 30 aircraft were lost on the night of 16/17 March mainly to German night fighters, which found the two Bomber Streams on the way to the targets.[11] Six were lost on Würzburg. *TARFU* was one of 24 Lancasters of 1 Group which did not return from Nürnburg.

'Fanny' Goldstein learned that Jack was 'missing' by means of a telegram on 17 March. It took her many weeks, even months, before she accepted that he was really dead and to her dying day at the age of 87 on 7 January 2001, she never stopped grieving.

On 17/18 March when there was no Main Force activity, a sweep by 66 Lancasters and 29 Halifaxes was made over Northern France to draw German fighters into the air, and formations of Mosquito bombers carrying 'Cookies' visited targets in Germany. On 18 March, 100 Lancasters of 3 Group carried out 'G-H' attacks on benzol plants at Hattingen and Langendreer. Both raids appeared to be accurate and no aircraft were lost. That night 324 aircraft of 4, 6 and 8 Groups carried out an area bombing raid on Witten in good visibility. Some 1,081 tons of bombs were dropped, which destroyed 129 acres, 62 per cent of the built-up area and severely damaged the Ruhrstahl steelworks and the Mannesmann tube factory. Eight aircraft, including six Halifaxes, were lost. Another 277 Lancasters and eight Mosquitoes of 12 and 8 Groups carried out an area raid on Hanau. Fifty industrial buildings and 2,240 houses were destroyed and an estimated 2,000 people were killed. Just one Lancaster was lost.

Benzol plants in Germany were attacked on successive days and nights, 17, 17/18 and 18 March and 19 March. On the last of this series of raids 79 Lancasters of 3 Group attacked the Consolidation benzol works at Gelsenkirchen. All except two aircraft returned. *P-Peter* on 90 Squadron at Tuddenham piloted by Flying Officer Paine, force-landed near Mönchengladbach with three engines on fire after being hit by flak approaching the RP and again within seconds of the bomb run. *L-Love* on 218 Squadron was 'borrowed' by Pilot Officer Ivor 'Johnnie' Johnson, a Londoner who lived in Ludgate Circus with his parents in the top flat of a building of which they were caretakers for the Methodist Church. Don Moore a 20-year-old miller's son and the flight engineer and youngest on the crew recalls:

We were airborne at 13.00 hours with the usual load of a 4,000lb 'cookie' and 14 × 500 GPs. Climbing to 20,000 feet we approached the target in clear skies at 16.02 to be hit in several places by a barrage being aimed in our direction; nothing serious, but that was our share, or so we thought! Coming away we encountered much heavier flak and eventually we got caught in the middle. We all ducked. The nose went in and a bloody great draught was blowing down the aircraft. Both inboards were on fire and we successfully feathered the propellers but the extinguishers failed to put out the flames. No one fancied bailing out just then, so we decided to do a high speed dive, which fortunately extinguished both fires. Lady luck was smiling for us. Just at that point I felt something wet trickling down my legs. I felt very embarrassed, thinking that I had wet myself. Putting my hand down it came away red and smelly. I thought 'Hell; I've been hit!' But no it was the hydraulic fluid from the front turret!

We now had the aircraft under reasonable control and ahead and below we could see the smoke line of the battle. We were still at about 14/15,000 feet and with most things under control we decided to ride it down over British lines. The aircraft was getting progressively heavier on the port side and requiring a lot of aileron to keep it up. Then the starboard outer coughed and spluttered and eventually cut out; there was no fuel getting to it. George Robinson the newly commissioned WOp who was from Coventry opened the cross feed for me and I got it running again; much joy! We could make it OK! Then the cockpit around the WOp's position developed a fuel leak, so we shut the cross feed and of course lost the outboard engine! Max power on the port outer, it was singing like a bird! We were going downhill all the time, but had passed the battle line so at least we thought that we were not going to be PoWs! Then the poor old port outer started to overheat. Coolant started to blow away and finally it seized. So we became a four engine glider! Control was very difficult and I was helping 'Johnny' to keep the wings straight. By then we were getting quite low down, but on the nose appeared a landing field. The top escape hatches were jettisoned and all except me and Johnny went to crash stations. Everything electrical had been switched off when the fuel came into the cockpit so we had no radio to call Aircraft Control. I stayed up front to help with the controls until it was too late to go back to crash position. Instead I pulled out the lightweight foot bar in my position and braced against that.

'Johnnie' did his finest landing – the nose hatch came up and earth with it – up through their legs and out through the top escape hatch. *L-Love* came to a halt. We abandoned the aircraft and assembled well clear. The mid-upper gunner, Flight Sergeant Roger 'Mac' Makin from Chesterfield, was not there. At 23 'Mac' was the oldest on the crew and recently married. Flight Sergeant Harry Christian our Liverpudlian navigator had been an apprentice draughtsman at a structural engineering works and he and I went back into the aircraft to look for 'Mac' but he was not there. He had bailed out of the back door just after we touched down when we were still doing 70 knots and was forlornly walking along the grass from the horizon! It was at Brussels-Evere airfield on which we had crashed at about 17.30 hours. Americans collected us and took us into Brussels. Everyone was celebrating the freedom of Brussels and we joined them! At midnight we were picked up by the Redcaps and put in a cell in a local Police station for the night . Next morning, together with our hangovers, we were taken to an American Intelligence Unit where we met up with two other shot down crews. All of us were taken to another airfield and flown back to Down Ampney near Swindon in a C-47 at 11.20 and we were collected by Flight Lieutenant Blenkin DFC and crew in C-*Charlie*.[12]

On 19 March also, 19 Lancasters of 617 Squadron attacked the viaduct at Arnsberg a few miles north of the Möhne Dam and 18 Lancasters of 9 Squadron, the bridge at Vlotho (Bad Oeynhausen) near Minden. At Arnsberg five Lancasters carried 'Grand Slams' and the other 14 had 'Tallboys'. The first bomb was a direct hit on the viaduct and the rest went into the centre of the smoke that gushed up. When the smoke cleared crews could see that a 40 feet gap had been blown in the centre of the viaduct and there was a pile of rubble in the river bed. The attack on Vlotho was not successful.

Next day, when 153 aircraft bombed Recklinghausen and 99 Lancasters of 3 Group attacked the railway yards at Hamm, both without loss, 14 Lancasters of 9 Squadron attacked the railway bridge at Arnsberg. On 21 March it was the turn of the Arbergen railroad bridge near Bremen to suffer the same fate. Twenty Lancasters on 617 Squadron were detailed and two scored direct hits with their 'Tallboys' and two piers collapsed. Another one was thrown 15 feet out of alignment and earthquake shock threw a span off another pier. Flak got a direct hit on Flight Lieutenant Barney Gumbley DFM's Lancaster on the run up and the New Zealander and his crew were killed. Next day 82 Lancasters of 5 Group attacked a bridge near Bremen and 20 aircraft on 617 Squadron were detailed to bomb a bridge at Nienburg. Wing Commander 'Johnny' Fauquier DSO** DFC sent four aircraft in to bomb while the rest circled and the first two earthquake bombs hit each end of the bridge. The span lifted bodily and still intact into the air and seemed to hang there for a second and in that very moment a third bomb hit it right in the middle. Early the next morning 128 Lancasters of 1 and 5 Groups were detailed to attack two more railway bridges in the Bremen area. The first three bombs dropped by 617 from 16,000 feet at Bad Oeynhausen scored direct hits. The next two were near misses followed by what looked like another direct hit. On the Bremen operation two Lancasters were lost.

It seemed that the German defences were powerless in the face of the relentless bombing of German cities. One of the reasons was that by this stage of the war Bomber Command's tactics of deception and radio counter-measures had reached a fine perfection. On 20/21 March no less than three feint attacks took place in support of the Main Force attack on the synthetic oil refinery at Böhlen, just south of Leipzig, by 235 Lancasters and Mosquitoes. The *Window* Force left the Main Stream soon after crossing the front line and made for Kassel, which was bombed. Further on, when closer to the true target another *Window* Force broke off and bombed Halle. The third feint force was provided by the *Mandrel* screen which, after the passage of the heavies, re-formed into a *Window* Force and attacked Frankfurt with flares. The Main Force's zero-hour was set at 03.40 hours on the 21st. At about the same time 166 Lancasters headed for the oilfield at Hemmingstedt in Schleswig-Holstein far to the north of the first target. This attack was to commence at 04.30 and together with the other attack involved Bomber Command's main effort.

The evening diversions had begun at 21.14 hours with a large-scale nuisance raid on Berlin when 35 Mosquitoes of the Path Finder force bombed the city. Just after 01.00 hours the main Böhlen force crossed the English Channel on a south-easterly heading, while a few miles to the south a feinting formation, comprising 64 Lancasters and Halifaxes from training units, crossed the Channel on an almost parallel course. Here complications for the German radar operators began. By 02.05 an 80-mile long *Mandrel* screen comprising seven pairs of Halifaxes on 171 and 199 Squadrons was in position over northern France, throwing up a wall of radar jamming through which the German early-warning radar could not see. Shortly after crossing the coast of France, the Böhlen force split into two streams. Hidden behind the *Mandrel* screen 41 Lancasters broke away and headed off to the northeast. Meanwhile, 14 Mosquito fighter-bombers on 23 and 515 Squadrons fanned out in ones and twos and made for German night fighter airfields. Once there they orbited over-head for hours on end dropping clusters of incendiaries and firing at anything that moved. At 03.00 the training aircraft, which had by now almost reached the German frontier near Strasbourg, turned about and went home, their work done. At the same time, the two formations making their separate ways to the Böhlen refinery burst through the *Mandrel* jamming screen. Seven Liberators on 233 Squadron and four Halifaxes on 171 Squadron went five minutes (about 18 miles) ahead of the larger Böhlen force, laying a dense cloud of *Window*, which effectively hid the bombers following them. Once over the Rhine, the more southerly of the two streams of bombers turned northeast straight towards Kassel. So far, there was no way in which the fighter controller could tell the real target for the night. At the time the bomber forces crossed the German frontier *Major* Rüppel, *Jägerleitoffizier* of the Central Rhine defence area, seriously under-estimated the strength of the two approaching formations. He thought each force involved about 30 aircraft and that both might be *Window* feints. As the reports from the ground observation posts began to come in however, it became clear that the southernmost of the two was much larger than he had estimated. No amount of jamming could conceal the roar of 800 aircraft engines. The spoofs, diversionary attacks and counter measures helped keep losses down to nine Lancasters. One was lost on the attack on Hemmingstedt. Three aircraft of the support and minor operations forces were also lost. *Nachtjäger* claimed 11 Lancasters shot down.

'Tommy' Thompson on 463 Squadron at Waddington recalls:

We did not take part in the night raid on Bohlen, but Flying Officer R S Bennett RAAF's crew occupying the seven beds opposite in the billet did so. They should have been back in the early hours, but when I woke in the morning I could see that the beds were still empty and I feared the worst. Initially they were just missing but by mid-morning all their gear had been removed and later that day all seven beds were occupied by a new crew. We later learned that all seven had been killed and they are buried in the War Cemetery in Berlin. My best pal who was opposite was rushing around making up his bed before heading off to briefing and I jokingly said 'You'd not need to bother tonight.' Little did I know that I would never see him again. It was always the practice on a night raid to make up our beds beforehand, so that after the usual breakfast of egg, bacon, sausage and fried bread we could slip into bed without disturbing anyone else in the billet. Although we were issued with flying rations, boiled sweets etc. we always had a good meal before and after an op.

On 21 March 178 aircraft of 4, 6 and 8 Groups carried out an accurate attack on the rail yards at Rheine and the surrounding town area for the loss of one Lancaster. One hundred and sixty Lancasters of 3 Group raided the railway yards at Münster and a railway viaduct nearby for the loss of three bombers. Another 133 Lancasters of 1 Group and six Mosquitoes of 1 and 8 Groups headed for Bremen and accurately bombed the Deutsche Vacuum oil refinery without loss. That same evening 151 Lancasters and eight Mosquitoes of 5 Group set off to raid the Deutsche Erdölwerke refinery at Hamburg and 131 Lancasters and 12 Mosquitoes of 1 and 8 Groups sought a benzol plant at Bochum. Five Lancasters were lost; four of them from the Hamburg force, and a RCM Fortress, which was supporting the Bochum force, also failed to return.

On 22 March raids on railway targets continued when 227 Lancasters and eight Mosquitoes of 1 and 8 Groups raided Hildesheim railway yards. Some 263 acres – 70 per cent of the town – was destroyed and 1,645 people were killed. Four Lancasters were lost. Another 130 Halifaxes, Lancasters and Mosquitoes of 4 and 8 Groups bombed Dülmen in an area attack, which was without loss and 124 Halifaxes, Lancasters and Mosquitoes of 6 and 8 Groups bombed rail and canal targets at Dorsten, which also was the location of a *Luftwaffe* fuel dump, again without loss. One hundred Lancasters of 3 Group carried out a 'G-H' attack on Bocholt, probably with the intention of cutting communications. All returned safely.[13] Another 102 Lancasters of 5 Group in two forces attacked bridges at Bremen and Nienburg without loss. The bridge at Nienburg was destroyed though no results were observed at Bremen where one of the pilots who took part was 'Tommy' Thompson. It was his fifth raid:

I flew JO-O, a five hour trip with six tons of bombs. Luck was with us on our bombing run. With the bomb doors open we could hear the shrapnel from the anti-aircraft shells 'pinging' on the bomb casings. We got our bombs away but could not shut our bomb doors as the hydraulic lines had been fractured. The extra drag meant that our air speed dropped and we were miles behind the main bomber stream, but fortunately the German fighters had disappeared. We had another lucky escape when the German anti-aircraft guns on the islands off the Dutch coast had a 'go' at us. After using emergency air for our undercarriage and flaps we landed safely at Waddington. What a relief! In the end damage to the bridge at Bremen was not as great as expected. There were hundreds of near misses.

Crews liked to fly in the same aircraft and half our ops were in JO-O. Naturally aircraft were quite often unserviceable due to damage or mechanical defects and this applied to 'our' JO-O after the Bremen raid. After repairs the aircraft had to have an air test before we could use it again on Ops. Another crew carried out this test on our behalf, but they made a major mistake when deciding to fly the aircraft with three engines stopped. Without a full bomb load and a part fuel load the Lancaster could be flown on one engine but it would gradually lose height. It was essential that this engine was the one with the electric generator for re-starting the other three. Unfortunately they stopped this engine and therefore they were on their way downwards with no chance of reaching the 'drome on one engine. They managed a belly landing on a nearby road. All the crew walked away from the aircraft which was a 'write-off'. We were allocated a replacement for JO-O later.

On Saturday 23 March, 128 Lancasters of 1 and 5 Groups attacked bridges at Bremen and Bad Oeynhausen and hit both of them, losing two of the Lancasters. At 15.30, 80 Lancasters bombed the little town of Wesel, which was an important troop centre behind the Rhine front in the area about to be attacked by the 21st Army Group massing for the Rhine crossings at dawn. 'Tommy' Thompson's crew were one of the first to bomb. 'Photographs showed that our 6.5 tons of bombs were "spot on" the target markers and we were commended for this. Unfortunately we were a minute or so early and we should have delayed our bomb drop. For this we were punished by being sent up the following day on a 1.5 hour high level bombing practice; rather harsh we thought.'

More than 400 tons of bombs were dropped on the German troops and many strong points were destroyed. Five hours later at 22.30, only a short time before Field Marshal Sir Bernard Montgomery's zero hour, as the

1st Commando Brigade followed by the 51st Highland Division closed in, 195 Lancasters and 23 Mosquitoes of 5 and 8 Groups followed it up with another attack to complete the work of the afternoon. In exactly nine minutes, well over 1,000 tons of bombs went down from 9,000 feet on those troops who had crept back into the ruins to await the British Commandos' attack. In all, more than 1,500 tons of bombs were dropped in the two attacks – a weight of bombs which had already almost completely wiped out cities eight times the size of Wesel. The effects on the defenders was devastating; the bombing was completed at approximately 22.39 hours and the British Army was crossing the river in assault craft, aided by searchlights before the bombers had left the area. A message of appreciation from Montgomery to Sir Arthur Harris was received. It said:

> I would like to convey to you personally and all in Bomber Command my grateful appreciation for the magnificent co-operation you have given us in the battle of the Rhine. The bombing of Wesel last night was a masterpiece and was a decisive factor in making possible our entry into the town before midnight. Please convey my thanks to all your crews and ground staffs.

On 24 March attacks were made in good weather on the railway yards at Sterkrade, the town of Gladbeck and the Harpenerweg and Mathias Stinnes benzol plants at Dortmund and Bottrop because the Ruhr industries were still supplying fuel and munitions for the fighting front, which was now just 15 miles away. Three Lancasters were lost on the Dortmund raid and one Halifax failed to return from the attack on Gladbeck. Next day Bomber Command flew 606 sorties against the main reinforcement routes into the Rhine battle area and Hannover, Münster and Osnabrück were heavily hit. At Binbrook the Lancasters on 460 Squadron RAAF taxied out in the half light of early evening, a time when it is often difficult to distinguish silhouettes, for their 13th operation in 24 days. Crews understandably, were all pretty tired though they did not realize it at the time. In the rear turret of Keith Bennett's aircraft, just as he was turning onto the perimeter track, 18-year-old Peter Firkins caught sight of a Lancaster bearing down upon them, its two churning engines coming into line somewhere about the position of his turret. Firkins yelled 'Look out!' over the intercom. He had visions of two full bomb loads going up so he swung his turret to the beam to beat a hasty retreat, only to jam his rather bulky frame in the small door. The two Lancasters came to a grinding halt, the two engines of the other Lancaster severing Bennett's fuselage amidships. Bennett, unable to raise Firkins on the intercom, climbed out of the escape hatch above the cockpit and ran down the top of the fuselage to see if he had an extinct rear gunner, only to discover a jammed one! To make matters worse, the Lancaster with which they had collided was a flight commander's and 'his ill humour took considerable time to assuage'.[14] Firkins believed that fate had once again taken a hand, just as it had a few days earlier on the trip to Bremen when they had returned on two portside engines and out of fuel as they approached for an emergency landing. The engines had died as the Lancaster rolled down the runway. It had been the longest two and a half hours of their lives. Had they gone on the Hannover raid they might in all likelihood, have 'bought it'. Three Halifaxes were shot down by flak on the raid on Münster and a 166 Squadron Lancaster flown by Squadron Leader Kenneth Graham Laverack was brought down after being struck by a bomb over the target at Hannover.

On 26 March 'Tommy' Thompson had 'rather a shock':

I was lying on my bed having a late afternoon 'kip' when I was shaken by a loud explosion. Initially I thought it was plane down on the 'drome. I was first out of the billet and round the side of the block to find a body on the ground with most of its stomach missing, not a pleasant sight just before dinner. He was a bomb aimer and we accepted the explanation without further discussion that he was trying to dismantle a hand grenade (a Mills Bomb). He is buried at Wigan cemetery. The following day we were on our 7th op, in JO-S; a short daylight trip, 4.5 hours carrying 6.5 tons of bombs to Farge on the German border to bomb the oil storage depot. It was an easy trip. We then had a rest for a fortnight during which time two 463 Squadron aircraft were lost on a further raid on Lützkendorf. One crew bailed out safely and on the other crew, six were killed and one survived. When we returned we flew three more operations as a crew. We carried out our 8th op in JO-O, our new replacement aircraft, a long night raid to bomb the rail yards at Pilzen in Czechoslovakia and were diverted to Boscombe Down for a short stop whilst fog cleared at Waddington. Our 9th op and last long night raid at 8 hours and 40 minutes was to bomb the railway town of Komotau in Czechoslovakia. Our bombsight was U/S and so we brought or bombs back, diverted to Colerne until fog cleared at Waddington; a long wasted journey. Our last operation was to be on the rail yards and port area of Flensburg, a German town near the Danish border, but the Master Bomber eventually ordered the raid to be abandoned as the target was completely cloud covered and marking was impossible. We brought our bombs back. Most of the flight was over the North Sea and it was interesting to carry out low level flying just above the sea.

Late March had ended with raids on Paderborn and Hamm and on the U-boat oil-storage depot at Farge and the Hermann Goering benzol plant at Salzgitter. On the 31st, 469 aircraft attempted to bomb the Blohm und

Voss shipyards at Hamburg where new types of U-boats were being assembled. The target area was completely cloud-covered and most of the bombs that were dropped fell over a wide area of southern Hamburg and Harburg. Eight Lancasters and three Halifaxes failed to return. Two of the Lancasters on 419 'Moose' Squadron RCAF that were lost and a missing Halifax on 415 'Swordfish' Squadron at East Moor were reported to have been shot down by Me 262 jet fighters. *C-Charlie*, the missing Halifax, was flown by Flying Officer George Albert Hyland, an American. He and his crew were lost without trace. For some weeks 419's gunners had been sniffing jet exhaust in the air trails over Germany. One pair had skirmished briefly with Me 262s. It was not until 31 March however that 6 Group squadrons were drawn into anything like a large-scale battle when about 30 Me 262s of JG7 vectored on to the last gaggle, which, being 10 minutes late over the target, found itself without the planned fighter cover. The jets materialized out of the overcast at 10,000 feet and with their great rate of climb, closed the remaining 10,000 feet vertical gap in a matter of seconds. In all, 28 crews on 419 did battle with the Messerschmitts one or more times. *H-How* flown by Flight Lieutenant Harry Alfred Metivier who had logged half a tour went down and he and his crew, most near the half-way mark of a tour were subsequently presumed dead. *Q-Queen*, flown by Flying Officer Donald Stuart Maxwell Bowes and his crew, all of whom had reached or passed the half-way mark of a tour, was the second missing aircraft. Three men survived to become prisoners-of-war but Bowes and the other members on the crew were killed. Gunners on the five crews that returned fired at the jets nine times, but on only three of these occasions were their aircraft actually being attacked. Their inability to lay-off and maintain correct deflection because of the jets' tremendous speed was therefore, not surprising, and despite the 1,200 rounds that they fired, no claims were made by 419 Squadron. None of the returning Lancasters showed damage of any kind. The bombing results achieved on this raid can hardly be said to have justified the losses. Overcast conditions necessitated the exclusive use of sky-markers and though these were fairly well grouped, the bombing concentration was considered, at best, only moderate. The only visible results were puffs of grey smoke pushing through the cloud during the later stages. Common to every crew report were remarks concerning the gaggle leader's unnecessary time wasting on the final leg, an error which was no doubt the reason for the gaggle's subsequent vulnerable position. Bomber Command commented that an officer of more senior rank should have led the gaggle (pilot of lead aircraft was a Flying Officer).

During March Bomber Command had flown a record 53 day and night operations. April began with two attacks by Lancasters and Mosquitoes on what were believed to be military barracks near Nordhausen east of Göttingen, which were in fact, being used to accommodate a number of concentration camp prisoners and forced labourers who worked in a complex of underground tunnels where various secret weapons were constructed. Three Lancasters were lost on the raids. Sergeant Bill Perry, wireless operator on a 61 Squadron Lancaster, saw *F-Freddie* on 49 Squadron go down on the bomb run:

> The plane was a quarter to half-mile away on the starboard side. His bomb doors were open, although I didn't see his first 500-pounders drop out. I did see the 4,000lb 'cookie'. It seemed to come out and stop, hanging there for a split second, keeping pace with the Lancaster. Then it tipped over and I watched a 500lb hang-up come out and hit it. It must have struck one of the fuses on the big bomb. I saw it explode and the back half of the aeroplane seemed to disappear. I couldn't believe it. I watched the wings and the cabin area go down in one piece, like a great leaf, almost to the ground, before it vanished into smoke or haze. No one survived. Getting out would have been impossible with G-force, unless somebody had been blown out by the explosion.[15]

On 4/5 April synthetic oil plants at Leuna, Harburg and Lützkendorf were bombed. Severe damage was caused to the Rhenania oil plant at Harburg and Bomber Command claimed 'moderate' damage at Lützkendorf. A total of 11 Lancasters and Halifaxes were lost. A benzol plant at Molbis near Leipzig was attacked by 175 Lancasters and 11 Mosquitoes of 5 Group on 7/8 April and the night following, 440 aircraft of 4, 6 and 8 Groups carried out the last raid on Hamburg by Bomber Command when they raided oil-storage tanks in the shipyard areas. Seventeen Lancasters on 617 Squadron blasted the U-boat shelters in the already devastated city with 'Grand Slam' and 'Tallboy' bombs. Three Halifaxes and three Lancasters failed to return from the raid. The Lützkendorf oil refinery, which had escaped serious damage the previous night, was rendered 'inactive' by 231 Lancasters and 11 Mosquitoes of 5 Group. Six Lancasters failed to return.

Next it was the turn of 1, 3 and 8 Groups, which raided Kiel on the night of 9/10 April when 591 Lancasters and eight Mosquitoes bombed the *Deutsche Werke* U-boat yards. The pocket battleship *Admiral Scheer* was hit and capsized and the *Admiral Hipper* and the *Emden* were badly damaged. Three Lancasters were lost and a Halifax III on 462 Squadron RAAF failed to return from a diversionary operation to Stade when it crashed in France.[16] A Halifax and a Lancaster were lost on 10 April when 230 bombers attacked the Engelsdorf and Mockau rail yards at Leipzig. *Nachtjagd* pilots claimed six Lancasters, a Halifax and a Mosquito on 10/11 April when 307 Lancasters and eight Mosquitoes of 1 and 8 Groups attacked the rail yards in the northern part of Plauen and 76 Lancasters and 19 Mosquitoes bombed the Wahren railway yards at Leipzig. All the bombers returned safely from the raid on Plauen but seven Lancasters were lost on Leipzig where the eastern half of the yards was destroyed. A RCM Halifax III of 100 Group[17] and a 571 Squadron Mosquito B.XVI, one of 77 engaged on a LNSF operation to Berlin also failed to return.

More attacks on rail yards took place on 11 April when Nürnburg and Bayreuth were the targets for the Halifaxes of 4 Group who in part were supported by Path Finder Lancasters and Mosquitoes of 8 Group. On Friday the 13th of April, 34 Lancasters on 9 and 617 Squadrons set off to attack the *Prinz Eugen* and the pocket battleship *Lützow* in harbour at Swinemünde but the raid was abandoned because of cloud at the target.[18] The following night over 370 Lancasters and more than 100 Halifaxes carried out a heavy raid on the port area and the U-boat yards at Kiel but the bombing was 'poor' and two Lancasters failed to return. On 14/15 April, 500 Lancasters of 1 and 3 Groups and 12 Mosquitoes of 8 Group took part in an operation on Potsdam just outside Berlin. Although Mosquito bombers of the LNSF had attacked the 'Big City' almost continually this was the first time the *Reich* capital had been attacked by heavies since March 1944. One Lancaster was lost to an unidentified night-fighter over the target.[19]

Trevor Priestley on 218 Squadron recalls:

Sunday 22nd April 1945 was the last of the 'Big Raids'. The squadron operated against Bremen in support of the British XXX Corps at the request of General Horrocks.[20] The Germans in Bremen had been asked to surrender and had refused so the army were about to enter the city. The briefing officer informed us that the town was full of troops and the success of the operation would make things a lot easier for our land forces. The latest information was that our troops were 2,000 yards from the target area. On our return, we saw a column of smoke two fields off the end of the runway. An aircraft [Flight Lieutenant Donald Seymour 'Tubby' Spiers] had crashed whilst attempting overshoot procedure. Five of the crew died instantly and a sixth member died of his injuries the next day. Only the rear gunner survived and he spent 14 months in hospital. The driver of a passing bus along with a Land Army girl who was a passenger made a desperate attempt to rescue the crew for which both were awarded the MBE.

Two days later part of 218 Squadron were detailed to attack the rail centre at Bad Odesloe, a small town on the North German Plain, not far from Luneburg Heath where a few days later Field Marshal Montgomery would accept the unconditional surrender of most of the German armed forces. Australian pilot Reg Johnson was listed to fly *H-How* but he refused to do so because he had found the aircraft unfit to fly. While he was vigorously protesting, as was his right, another Australian, Flight Lieutenant Robert Lance Jenyns RAAF appeared and said 'I flew it yesterday; I'll take it.' *H-How* was the last aircraft to take off and it crashed into the field next to the WAAF site with the loss of all on board. Some of the bombs, ammunition and full load of fuel exploded. 'So' continues Trevor Priestley, 'within a period of 36 hours, 218 had lost two aircraft out of which there was only one survivor and not due to enemy action, and this was at a time that it was all supposed to be 'a piece of cake'. We did not realise that this aircraft was the last to take off with bombs for Germany.'

Bomber Command's last bombing operations were the obliteration of Wangerooge[21] and a failed attempt at destroying Hitler's 'Eagle's Nest' at Berchtesgaden in daylight on 25 April by 359 Lancasters and 16 Mosquitoes, and the oil storage depots at Tonsberg in southern Norway on the following night.

Peter Bone flew on the Berchtesgaden raid:

Berchtesdaden was really a political gesture. It was thought that Hitler may have gone there to make a last stand for the Fatherland. It was a sparkling spring morning and we all felt somehow that it would be our final op, our 25th. While some bombed the infamous Eagle's Nest itself, where Hitler had planned his New Order, our aiming point was the *SS* barracks, which gave us great pleasure. There were just a few half-hearted puffs of anti-aircraft fire over the target but I saw one Lancaster slowly spiralling down, trailing white smoke.

Flying Officer H G Payne on 460 Squadron RAAF at Binbrook ran into moderate heavy flak and crashed in the vicinity of Salzburg. All seven crew survived but the bomb aimer was wounded. Flying Officer Wilfred Tarquinas De Marco and crew on 619 Squadron at Strubby, 15 miles north-north-west of Skegness had just released their bomb load and were holding steady for the bombing photograph when the Lancaster was hit by anti aircraft fire and brought down at about 05.30 hours. Three of the crew were able to escape by parachute although Sergeant F J Cole discovered that when he reached for his parachute it was 'pulled'. Flight Sergeant J W Speers, himself wounded, gathered Cole's chute in his arms and then let it go as he kicked Cole out! Flight Sergeant Arthur Shannon broke a leg when he landed into a hostile reception but was mercifully spared by the intervention of an *SS* officer. De Marco and the rest of the crew were killed.

Lancaster I RA542 JO-Z and Flying Officer A Cox's crew on 463 Squadron RAAF at Waddington failed to return from the 5 Group raid by

119 Lancasters on the oil storage plant at Tonsburg, south of Oslo. Jack Wainwright was the navigator:

> Having climbed over a cold front we reached the Norwegian coast at a point near Kristiansund and altered course for the target at a height of 16,000 feet. Within a couple of minutes the aircraft was hit in the starboard wing and cabin, causing severe damage, injuring the pilot, Sergeant G W Simpson the flight engineer and Flight Sergeant R Smurthwaite the bomb aimer who had been lying in the nose and was blown back as far as the navigation 'office'. Obviously we had been hit by an unidentified German night fighter equipped with *Schräge Music*. Following an undignified dive to around 11,000 feet we saw the night fighter waiting for us on the port beam preparing for a straight in attack for the kill. It carried out two further attacks causing very little additional damage. Flight Sergeants F W Logan and W D Hogg, our magnificent gunners, succeeded in firing off every round at him and then he veered off.[22] We were unable to bomb but stream safety required us to overfly the target, where, instead of turning west for return to the UK we turned east to clear the stream then south towards Denmark. After discussion, the captain decided that in our physical and mechanical condition we would not make it to the UK. We jettisoned our bombs (less two which 'hung up') together with other sensitive equipment and documents in the sea and continued flying south.
>
> Eventually we saw the lights of Gothenburg in Sweden and turned to port. At no time had we ever been briefed, of available airfields in Sweden, and having lost all maps we were in state of flux! Ninety minutes after the attack we eventually landed by headlamps of cars on a grass airfield at Jonkoping. Here we were interned, the last crew member arriving back in the UK in July 1945 following hospitalisation.[23]

After Berchtesgaden Peter Bone and the rest of the crew had no more ops left to fly:

> It had been 'a piece of cake' we said a few hours later, when we happily caught sight of Lincoln Cathedral in the spring sunshine. How many times had I looked down on the majestic 800 years' old Norman cathedral, bathed in the amber reflection of an autumn sunset, as we circled before setting course for Germany? And again, shrouded in misty winter dawns as we let down through the clouds on our return. Our aircrew had spent many leisure hours in Lincoln, though never altogether because although we bonded very closely in the air, our crew had diverse leisure interests; some liked to go pub-crawling before taking in a dance, while others, including

myself, preferred to see the latest Judy Garland movie or the show at the vaudeville theatre. I liked to tag along with Freddy, our bombardier, married at 33 with three children, who in happier days had augmented his income as a plumber by playing trumpet in summer concerts on the pier at the seaside resort on the south coast where he lived. Freddy knew some of the vaudeville artistes who performed twice nightly at the Theatre Royal. After the second show there was always time for baked beans on toast or fish and chips before catching the station transport back to base.

Just before our tour ended, Wing Commander Molesworth had been posted and was replaced by Wing Commander Dixon. We flew with him on two ops and thought he was efficient and agreeable but he had come from a training squadron and he became very unpopular with the squadron after VE Day when, to counteract the inevitable drift towards slackness after months of a necessarily strictly regulated regime, he brought in lots of what we called 'bull' – daily morning parades, tidy living quarters, battledress that didn't look like it had been slept in. One morning several of us were ambling along to the cook-house with our caps tucked in our belts, when a staff car approached. It screeched to a halt and out jumped the Station Commander. 'Take their names, sergeant', he barked to his driver. Now we were for it. We had foolishly decided to have a lay in instead of being on the morning parade. We were put on a charge but to our surprise the Wing Commander quashed it because of our good flying record.

'Good for Dixon,' we said.

Then another surprise. Skipper confided to us that he had run afoul of the Wing Commander, who objected to the rather saucy insignia (*Sisco's Scamps Press On!*) that Flying Officer Ensiso's crew had had painted on the nose of their aircraft. Skipper had disagreed, pointing out that it had no doubt contributed to the crew's morale throughout their tour of duty. The Wing Commander thereupon ordered Skipper to have the offending insignia removed, or he would have him posted off the squadron forthwith. Skipper chose to leave and that day he was gone. 'The miserable so-and-so' we said of Dixon, or words to that effect. That is why the photograph of our crew standing outside our Nissen hut doesn't include Skipper, whose skill and discipline in the air had contributed so much to our morale and survival. It was all very unsettling. We had no wild farewell party, no crew photograph in best blue in front of a Lancaster. We six sergeants were left, rather like orphans, to our own devices until after another two weeks' leave we were, one by one, posted off the squadron. There were probably hurried, awkward goodbyes but I can't recall any. I was the last to go. Only nine months earlier I had told my diary, 'I guess we'll get used to this makeshift place.' Now, as I packed my kit in early July, I wrote, 'My last night at dear old Wickenby.' Squadron Leader Lane's crew was no more. Three months later on 14 October 1945, a year to the day from my first op, Wickenby ceased to exist as a bomber squadron.

During the final week of the war there began an operation to deliver food to the starving people of western Holland. The Dutch first heard of the plans for Operation *Manna* around noon on 24 April when it was announced by the British Broadcasting Corporation that the operation was commencing that day. Trevor Priestley on 218 Squadron recalls:

Throughout the winter of 1944/45 the food situation in western Holland had become most difficult and 3,600,000 people were facing death by starvation. This situation had arisen for a number of reasons. The Germans had flooded large areas of some of the best agricultural land in Europe. Frequently electricity, gas and coal supplies were cut off, trains and tramcars were being sent into Germany. Men were being sent into Germany for forced labour. There was a curfew. In January the first cases of oedema/dropsy appeared. The diet of nurses and physicians who were going without food to help the patients in hospitals consisted of one slice of bread and one cup of tea substitute for breakfast, two potatoes, a little bit of vegetable and some watery sauce for lunch; one or two slices of bread with a cup of coffee substitute and a plate of soup for dinner. In May 1945 hunger oedema had affected 10% of the populations of the cities. Males, young and elderly were at most risk from dying. In Amsterdam 30,000 people suffered from malnutrition, in The Hague 20,000, and in Rotterdam 55,000 suffered from oedema/dropsy. During May 1945, 250,000 people had to be taken into hospitals and in addition 200,000 men and women needed daily care at home. Lack of available transport compounded the situation. People were eating tulip bulbs, nettles etc. Scavenging for food was a major occupation. Typical of stories of the search for food was two girls who on four separate trips on their cycles covered a total of 1,000 miles. These journeys were discouraged by the Germans who confiscated food so collected. Crossing in and out of 'Fortress Holland' was forbidden. A friend of Arnold Dawrant ate tulip bulbs and stole food from the Germans under their noses by smuggling the food out in laundry trolleys. On one occasion taking so much food that he could not push the trolley up a gradient, two German soldiers helped him to push it. In Holland it is estimated that between 16,000 and 20,000 people died of starvation during the winter of 1944/45. This in spite of all that the Dutch were doing to try to help themselves by organising soup kitchens and so on. A day's ration for the population as a whole by April 1945 consisted of two potatoes, three slices of bread, some meat substitute and a slice of skim milk cheese. It is not surprising that there was little sympathy for the Germans when you remember that these were the people who had exterminated 105,000 of the 140,000 Dutch Jews. During the early part of 1945 an effort was made by the Swedish Red Cross and the International Red Cross at Geneva to get some relief through to Holland. Two small Swedish vessels got through in January and a Portuguese vessel operated for the International Red Cross managed to get through during March 1945. 38 Group Bomber Command was instructed to prepare a plan for relief flights with their Halifax and Stirling bombers during March 1945 but nothing came of this. Throughout the winter there had been appeals from Queen Wilhelmina, the Dutch Government in exile and others for some action to feed the Dutch. All this was kept highly secret so as not to give false hopes to the Dutch people.

On Thursday 26 April, pilots and bomb aimers from each flight on each squadron together with armourers were detailed to attend a 'demonstration' at Stradishall. Sacks were loaded into panniers, winched up into the bomb bay of a Lancaster and then dropped on to the ground. This was repeated just in case anyone had missed anything. Apart from the general impression that the panniers had been designed by Mr Heath Robinson I cannot recall any constructive suggestions being made. However as is usually the case with the forces there were the inevitable rumours. The favourite being that we were going to drop food to our PoWs in Germany. Oddly enough two days earlier the BBC Overseas Service had advised the Dutch that food was about to be dropped by Allied aircraft and warning them to keep clear of the dropping areas. With a day's notice the Dutch authorities had to arrange crews that had to gather the food from the fields. This was not a small operation. For example at Terbregge, the only drop zone where horse-drawn carts could not enter the field, it was necessary to have a crew of 4,000 men ready to carry the food from the field by hand.

Early in the morning of 28 April two crews at Ludford Manga were briefed together. One crewmember recalls:

Our Lancasters were at that moment the only two bombers on the airfield that did not have secret radio equipment installed. At the briefing we were informed that our bombers had been filled with food, to be dropped over Holland. The ground personnel had pulled all the food in through the bomb bay by climbing through a small opening of the bomb doors and simply stacked the food on the bomb doors. We were chosen to make a test run. We were very excited about the drops. The Germans were still occupying Holland when the drops begun. We had to fly low to the targets, to be able to drop the food without damaging it. We were told to carry no ammunition for our guns and we had to stay within a strictly defined corridor while over Holland for our approach and away from the target area. We were not only excited about the food drops we were also scared. We had been flying over Holland at altitudes of 15,000 to 20,000 feet on our way to targets in Germany and all of a sudden we were asked to fly at 400 feet, while the German soldiers were still manning the 88mm and 105mm flak guns near the corridor we had to fly through. Our two bombers had to fly through a corridor that the Germans had prescribed. If our mission was a success and we could drop our food without being shot at, operation *Manna* would be launched. The weather was really bad. We were not able to get our heavily loaded bombers off the ground due to the bad weather on the morning of the 28th and the mission was postponed.

The clouds began to break in the early morning of Sunday the 29th and the people of Holland heard the BBC announce, 'Bombers of the Royal Air Force have just taken off from their bases in England to drop food supplies to the Dutch population in enemy-occupied territory.' Crews at briefing greeted the news about the operation with astonishment. The typical reaction was 'bloody nonsense' when informed that arising out of negotiations with the Germans through the International Red Cross the Germans had opened up corridors over the area to let them through. There would be no shooting on both sides; 246 Lancasters were on their way preceded by 18 Mosquitoes who would mark the target with red markers.

At Ludford Magna the two Lancasters took off:

Crossing the Channel we flew on instruments because it was still misty. Over the continent the weather cleared and we could see where we were. Crossing the Dutch coast the anti-aircraft guns were pointing directly at our planes. I recall seeing German flags on many buildings as we approached the target for the drop. I saw German soldiers standing guard at railroad bridges over canals. We approached the target area at less than 400 feet above the ground. At that altitude we could see the people on the ground quite clearly. For the drop we had to lower our flaps and wheels in order to slow down the aircraft. The target area was open ground just outside Utrecht. There were no parachutes attached to the load, just free-falling boxes. We saw tanks trying to keep their masterpiece on us. We were looking right down a number of barrels. All the guns were still manned since the war was still going on. We were very lucky that they observed the truce and held their fire. We were however hit by small arms fire. When we returned from our mission, the ground personnel discovered that a 9mm pistol had slung a small hole on the right side of the aircraft, near the tail. There were very few people on this first mission. Nobody knew that we were coming. Then we saw our drop zone for the day, the Racetrack Duindigt. We could fly in directly, without circling. The Australian pilot was flying echelon on my port side. No agreement had yet been signed when the first Lancasters approached Occupied Holland. At an extremely low altitude of 100–1,000 feet the large four-engined bombers would have been an easy prey for the many anti-aircraft guns the Germans could still deploy in the besieged Fortress Holland. Even if the Germans had opened fire and killed hundreds of young Britons and other Allies, they would have had the right to do so. The responsible commanders of the RAF know the risk they took, know the terrible tragedy that could have happened over Holland if the Germans had opened fire. Above all they know that any German reaction would be legitimate. The commanders knew it, so did the pilots and their crew members. I dropped first when we were over the racetrack, while the Australian dropped almost the same moment. I had waited a little bit too long with the drop, partly overshooting the drop zone. Half of the load slammed into the beaches on the end of the racecourse. I hadn't noticed that my load had dropped on the wrong place, until a Dutchman told me forty years later that he had seen the two Lancasters drop on that first day. He happened to be on the racecourse and he saw he first bomber (me) dropping too late. The first part of the mission had been a success. We had to follow the corridor back to the North Sea. The second part of the mission didn't provide any problems. As soon as we were back over the North Sea, our radio operator transmitted the message to our base that the mission had been successful.

Two hundred Lancasters would appear over Holland at 2 o'clock bringing food to the starving population of Holland who reacted en masse on this news. A 17-year-old student at the time, Arie de Jong, wrote in his diary:

There are no words to describe the emotions experienced on that Sunday afternoon. More than 300 four-engined Lancasters, flying exceptionally low suddenly filled the western horizon. One could see the gunners waving in their turrets. A marvellous sight. One Lancaster roared over the town at 70 feet. I saw the aircraft tacking between church steeples and drop its bags in the south. Everywhere we looked, bombers could be seen. No one remained inside and everybody dared to wave cloths and flags. What a feast! Everyone is excited with joy. The war must be over soon now.

Trevor Priestley recalls:

> The orders were to fly in loose, low-level formation. The drop zones were clearly marked. We came in low enough to see the expressions on the faces or the people in the fields. It gave us a real thrill to watch these people as they waved and cheered us on. Of course we couldn't hear them over the noise of our engines, but on their faces you could see they yelled their lungs out. I can speak for the whole crew when they say it brought a lump to our throats. At that time we knew little about the plight of the Dutch people, so we could only imagine what horror it would be to live under the *Nazi* regime for five years. To see the people waving at us and to see 'Thanks Boys' and 'Many Thanks' spelled out with flowers gives you a warm glow. Just sitting there and looking at them brought tears to my eyes and I'm not ashamed of it, either! To think that today we did good instead of blowing towns and people to hell makes me realise that there is still some good left in this world.[24]

Ron Warburton, flight engineer on Flying Officer Alf Cowley RAAF's crew on 218 Squadron, adds:

> Alf was an exceptional pilot and I was grateful that he was flying the aircraft I was in. He started his war in the Australian army in the Middle East, where he was promoted to sergeant and awarded the DSO. He returned to Australia for leave and re-mustered to the RAAF and was sent to Canada to train as a pilot. He was exceptional in his training and was commissioned prior to his return to the UK. We were the lead aircraft in the first *Manna* operation taking food to the Dutch. We had organised a parcel of chocolates and sweets, with a small label saying 'Good luck, from Alf Cowley and his crew' which I dropped out of my window as the food panniers dropped. We turned to head for home and as we flew north we were fired on by the ack-ack battery. The Germans had promised us safe passage. Suddenly the control column was forced back and Alf needed assistance to keep the aircraft level. I called Bob the bomb aimer to help and went back to the fuselage. The wires which operated the trimming tabs were in a mess, having been sheared off by the shells. I sorted them out so that Pete and Norman Boult, our mid upper gunner who was on his second tour, could hold them then one by one pulled them calling to Alf to say what had happened when each one was pulled and so identified which was which. Norman and Pete sat down and operated the wires upon Alf's instructions so that we could fly home.[25]

Trevor Priestley continues:

Monday 30th April, we were on 'Battle Order' to drop food at
Terbregge on the outskirts of Rotterdam. Briefing was much the
same as we had had the previous day. I particularly remember
us being informed that not a single child below the age of one year
was alive. Malnutrition had caused still-births, elderly and young
people were dying. It is impossible to say what an impression this
and subsequent flights made upon us all. On Tuesday 1st May we
went to Ypenburg airfield to the east of The Hague, on 3 May and
again on 7 May to Duindigt race course to the north of The Hague.
On each occasion there was what might be described as a carnival
atmosphere on the ground. It seemed as though the whole population was waving with Dutch flags, sheets and anything they could
lay their hands on quickly. On each trip as we crossed the coast we
saw the Germans stood at their posts with their AA guns, some
actually following us in their gun sights. We were low enough to see
their faces. It all seemed a bit bizarre. Flying over a rather high
hospital in The Hague nurses and patients were waving from the
roof. Our Skipper took us down very low over a small coastal vessel
to the south of Rotterdam the crew unfolded a huge Dutch flag and
all waved it together.

After the first drop we parcelled up our sweet rations and I had the
job of trying to drop them as near as possible to groups of children.
We printed on the parcels Vor et Kinde. I was most flattered when
two of the WAAFs from the cookhouse asked me to drop their sweet
ration for some Dutch kids. We also dropped newspapers, printing
on the wrapper Gut Morgen Nederlander par RAF. At least they would
have a good laugh if nothing else at our pathetic attempts at the
Dutch language. In the middle of the rear turret there was what was
officially called the clear vision panel. Only the RAF could have
given such a technical name for what was just a clear hole. In the
excitement of the first trip our rear gunner took off his RAF scarf – a
recent present from his current girlfriend – and waved it through the
hole. He promptly lost it in the slipstream. At Rotterdam some of
the red markers dropped by the Pathfinder Mosquitoes fell on three
farmhouses setting them on fire. The fire engines were in attendance
as we dropped our food. So many aircraft were fired upon that
'Butch' Harris decreed that the Manna trips were to be counted as
operations. However I am not aware that any RAF aircraft were lost.
When aircrew were not actually flying the Manna trips they were
loading aircraft panniers with food irrespective of rank. I never
heard of anyone skiving off. It was later found that in spite of all
efforts the distribution of the food was a problem due to the very
limited transport available.

In certain areas the distribution of the food did not commence until 16 May, a week after the end of the war in Europe – lager drinkers – Heineken Brewery. It is also regrettable that some people were killed by the falling food. The Germans, Dutch police and civilian volunteers tried to keep people off the drop zones. After the first two days the Germans left the Dutch to sort out that problem. I have never seen any figures as to how many people were killed but it does not require much imagination as to how lethal a large tin of corned beef could be. Queen Wilhelmina in her excitement of the moment promised that the Dutch would be awarding a medal to all the British and American aircrews who had taken part. This never materialised, probably as she did not appreciate the numbers involved.[26]

Thousands of Dominion airmen overseas were counting the days until they would be home with their families. There had been rumours of a possible early repatriation for some units, including 428 'Ghost' Squadron RCAF at Middleton St. George. There was even talk of ferrying their Lancasters home, or perhaps a posting overseas. Word had come down that 23-year-old Flight Lieutenant W G 'Billie' Campbell was one of the pilots scheduled to fly his Lancaster back to Canada. Campbell of Strathclair, Manitoba was hopeful that Flight Sergeant Walter Ward his 20-year-old Scottish flight engineer would accompany him across the Atlantic. Ward had been on the crew since 26 OTU at Wing, Buckinghamshire. He was also a pilot.

Flight Sergeant Ted Wright, the boyish-faced tail-gunner and son of a Winnipeg Royal Canadian Mounted Police officer, himself a RAF pilot in the First World War, wrote a letter to his mother Alfreda on 25 April:

Well, Mom, I've been a flight sergeant for a few months and never knew it. I just found out today. Well, Mom, I'm not sure but I think this squadron is going to the east. I wonder if you could send me a Sheaffer pen and pencil set. I lost a fellow's pencil and want to get him another. Write soon. Ted.

Although he had the intellectual capacity, Teddy was a free spirit and resented being restricted in any way. From time to time he would just take off, doing odd jobs to earn pocket money. Five days before Canada declared war on Germany, 10-year-old Teddy Wright was just beginning Grade 5 classes at Sir Charles Tupper School in Halifax. A few months later, he and his three siblings, Ada, Patricia and Richard, registered at West Kent School in Charlottetown. They lived in Montreal and in Ottawa until May 1937, when Mr Wright was posted to various locations in the Maritimes by the Mounties. While in the Maritimes, Teddy had tried to join the navy or merchant marine, but his father would have none of it. Teddy worked for a few months in the winter of 1943 for the Knights of Columbus Canteen in Halifax before following the family to Winnipeg when they moved there in May 1943. It was Superintendent Wright's final RCMP posting before his retirement in 1946. On 18 November Teddy walked into No. 6 RCAF Recruiting Station. Instead of granting him an interview, the recruiting officer should have sent him straight home to his mother, because the self-confident, fair-haired youth had only recently celebrated his 15th birthday and the minimum age for enlistment was 18. It remains a mystery how the relatively small-framed, 129lb, 5 feet 6 inch teenager was able to fool the recruiting officer.[27]

On 30 April, Campbell's crew set off at 10.59 in *Y-Yoke* their Canadian-built Lancaster X on a cross-country training practice. Sergeant Johnnie Kay, a former member of the RCMP continually checked his navigation charts after the bomber became airborne. Kay, at 26, was the only married man in the crew. His wife and three-year-old son lived in Brooks, Alberta. The wireless operator, 20-year-old Warrant Officer Tom Lawley got in contact with RAF Station Hixon in Staffordshire to confirm the arrival of KB879 in the area. Lawley, formerly a machinist apprentice, was a native of Hamilton, Ontario. Flight Sergeants Lester Tweedy, 19, from Lougheed, Alberta and Wright, both air-gunners, were instructed to remain alert throughout the training flight because *Luftwaffe* intruders into English air space were still an occasional threat. The seventh member of the crew was Flight Sergeant Stuart Berryman, another Hamiltonian and an air bomber who had just celebrated his 23rd birthday.

The pilot of a second Lancaster, flying slightly above, was alarmed at the erratic behaviour of KB879. His tail-gunner, Sergeant Ronald Cranston, had alerted him to this after they had been in the air awhile. Flying at an altitude of 18,000 feet, Cranston had a relatively clear view of Campbell's aircraft, 3,000 feet below. 'At first it appeared to be flying with a side-slipping motion,' he later told investigators. 'After another 20–25 minutes I noticed the aircraft going down in a spiral dive with white vapour trails or smoke coming from the starboard engine. It appeared that nothing was done to counteract the dive. No parachutes appeared to open and no part of the aircraft seemed to fall off.'

Y-Yoke dived into the ground at RAF Hixton. All seven crew members died. Ted Wright was ejected out of the aircraft on impact and later found, as if in a sitting position, some distance from the aircraft. He was the first casualty to be identified. Within days, the dreaded 'We regret to inform you' telegrams began arriving in Canada. The bereaved families questioned why their sons, who were so close to coming home, would now never return. They were devastated. In Winnipeg, RCMP Super-intendent James Wright got the bad news at work and then hurried home to break it to the family. Though he was able to comfort them, he personally never got over the loss of his son, Ted. The funeral for six of the crew took place at the Regional Cemetery at Chester (Blacon) on

4 May. Only Walter Ward can be said to have returned home. He was buried with full military honours in his native Selkirk, Scotland. One month after the tragic incident that snuffed out the lives of Campbell and his crew, the first group of Lancasters on 428 Squadron returned to Canada. On the last day of May, 15 aircraft lifted off from Middleton St. George and headed across the Azores toward Yarmouth, Nova Scotia. One Lancaster aborted shortly after takeoff. Another crashed near the Azores but there were no casualties. All other ground personnel and non-active aircrews on 428 Squadron returned to Canada by sea.

In 1946, a letter from Commonwealth War Graves Commission arrived at the Wright residence. The CWGC was preparing an inscription for a stone tablet to be placed on Teddy Wright's grave. The reply from Mrs Wright surprised commission officials. On his original attestation papers, Wright had given his date of birth as 7 November 1925 but his mother provided the commission with his actual date of birth. As stated on his birth certificate, he was born in Montreal on 7 November 1928. He was 16. Ted Wright is believed to be the youngest aircrew member killed in the Second World War.

On 6 May Peter Bone was home on leave, pasting together a map showing the routes and destinations of his tour of operations, when the BBC interrupted a *Music While You Work* programme to announce: 'The German State Radio has just announced that Hitler is dead.' He had shot himself in his Berlin bunker:

> The next day Berlin fell to the Russians and on 8 May I joined the rest of my family in celebrating Victory Europe Day. What better way than to light a bonfire in the back lane, just as bonfires had been lit on the hilltops across Britain in times gone by, to celebrate great victories, like Drake's routing of the Spanish Armada in 1588 and Nelson's defeat of Napoleon's fleet at the Battle of Trafalgar in 1805. We invited some neighbours to our bonfire but there was no dancing. No-one got drunk. I don't think we even spoke much. I think we were all suddenly tired. We seemed content to watch the flames gradually die down. Around midnight people started to drift away with self-conscious 'good-nights'. By 1 o'clock, Eden Way, the suburban street that had been thrust into the front line in 1940 and had remained steadfast alongside its men and women in uniform was fast asleep, safe in the knowledge that it would not be brutally awakened by stomach-churning air raid sirens, ear-splitting anti-aircraft guns and screaming, shattering earth-shaking bombs. Its war was over. Up to 60,600 people throughout Britain had been killed. Next day I had to face the fact that I had, deliberately, over-stayed my leave by two days. When I got back to the squadron I found that everyone else on the crew had returned on time on the

evening of VE Day – I couldn't believe it! I also found that I would be charged with a breach of King's Regulations. On the following Sunday morning after church parade and a Thanksgiving service at the end of the main runway I was solemnly marched before the examining officer who, to my surprise, turned out to be Skipper. After hearing the charge and my explanation – I said I felt a bit like Bob Cratchit telling Ebenezer Scrooge that he was late because he had been making a little merry on Christmas Day – Skipper declared the charge should never have been brought and dismissed it.

Although there were no more bombing operations, we continued to fly. There were rumours that the squadron would be among those sent out to the Far East to help the Americans finish Japan off. I think only Frank was keen on going. In the meantime, we went to Brussels to bring back newly-liberated prisoners of war, soldiers who had been captured at Dunkirk in 1940. We crammed twenty-four 'brown jobs', as we called them, into every corner of *Tommy Two*. As we crossed the English coast they began to sing *'There'll be bluebirds over, the White Cliffs of Dover'* and I in my mid-upper turret joined in. It was a wonderful moment.

How effective were our efforts? No answer will ever satisfy every critic. Albert Speer, Hitler's Minister for Armaments and War Production, told him in a memo in January 1945, before the bombing reached a crescendo in March that 'the heavier bombs used at night were now doing much more permanent damage than the lighter ones which fell in daylight.' Our Lancasters and Halifaxes carried about twice the bomb load of the American Flying Fortresses and Liberators for the simple reason that, by taking advantage of the cover of darkness, they dispensed with all but minimal armament. The fire-power of their six machine guns was really no match for the cannon fire of enemy night fighters with greater range. In contrast, the Fortresses and Liberators, by flying only by day, had to be heavily armed to ward off and shoot down the day fighters and therefore, the bomb load had to be sacrificed. We in Bomber Command held the American crews in the highest respect, for their casualties were often horrendous, notably at the beginning when they had to fly without long-range fighter escort because there wasn't any. Our heavier bombs therefore in the last year of the war were clearly causing damage that was no longer being cleared away in preparation for rebuilding. An army of between one and two million slave labourers conscripted from the *Nazi*-occupied countries had, throughout the war quickly cleared away the rubble after air raids and production would only be disrupted for at the most a month or two. Harris saw no point in bombing say Essen, until the factories were up and running again. Then he would return. In the meantime, he would send his bombers to anyone of dozens of other targets that needed attention. But now, in the final months of the war, certain industrial cities did not need to be revisited. The attack on Munich in January 1945, our thirteenth op, was the last major attack by the 'heavies'. Munich was no longer an asset to the German war effort. Likewise, the attacks on Dortmund and Duisburg in February were the last by heavy bombers and the daylight attack on Essen in which our crew took part in March, was the last by the heavies, when a thousand of them dropped 4,661 tons of bombs. Out of a pre-war population of 648,000, only 310,000 were left. The number who would have left if they had been able to would never be known. Critics have often sneered that civilian morale was never affected by the bombing by either side. My own experience was that Londoners' morale was severely tested in the *Blitz* and even more so by the V-1 and V-2 attacks and I think it is reasonable to suggest that more German civilians would have fled the cities but for fear of the dreaded SS, Hitler's jack-booted bully-boys.

German civilian morale in the industrial cities probably began weakening during what Harris called The Battle of the Ruhr. Between March and July 1943 forty-three major attacks were made, two-thirds of them on the Ruhr. Morale probably nose-dived after the failure of Hitler's last attempt at a counter-offensive in the West – the Battle of the Bulge – around New Year's, 1945, when the Russians were rapidly approaching the German Eastern frontier. Surely any thinking German knew then that the war was lost. Open rebellion was impossible in a police state but apathy likely reigned in the remaining months of war.

If Britain had decided in 1940 to continue to adhere to the Geneva Convention, it is reasonable to speculate that at best the war would have gone on much longer. At worst, Hitler could well have defeated an unprepared Russia by 1942, having at his disposal millions of tons more of all kinds of armaments produced unhindered by allied air attacks. The thousands of fighter aircraft, anti-aircraft guns and searchlights with the thousands of personnel to man them, that Bomber Command forced Hitler to retain in Germany to defend his cities, would have been available to his armies in Russia. With Russia defeated, he could then have returned to occupy at leisure an isolated Britain, for America, however reluctantly, would almost certainly have turned its back on Europe to devote all its energies to defeating the Japanese. There would have been no D-Day in 1944, no liberation of Europe and no VE Day in 1945. My own fate, at best, would have been deportation to become a slave labourer somewhere in German-occupied Europe or Russia. My sister would very possibly have been deported too, to be forced into prostitution for the German armed forces. My young brother would have had to join the Hitler Youth, to learn how to spy on and denounce his parents. The stakes were therefore very high. Against such a regime as *Nazism*, adherence to the Geneva Convention would have been akin to fighting with one arm behind our backs. To do so in such circumstances would have been nonsensical unless one was prepared to be subjugated for the foreseeable future. When diplomacy has failed, as was the case in 1939, the aim must be to win a war with *every* means at one's disposal. Yes, war is evil and killing is evil. But sometimes the only way to overcome a great evil is to resort to a lesser evil. There is no black or white in war, only graduations, with much grey in between.

For centuries up to 1940 German wars had always been fought on foreign soil. For the first time in modern history, war was brought to the German homeland, to its very doorstep. Unavoidably, it took the lives of thousands of its civilian workers and tragically, the lives of many innocent children, in air attacks that were ten times as heavy as the Luftwaffe raids on Britain. Germany learned a harsh lesson, that its homeland was no longer immune from the ravages of war. That it has become Europe's most vibrant democracy suggests the lesson was well learned. Those of us who took part, however reluctantly, in the bomber offensive, did so in the knowledge that they had contributed significantly to the defeat of the most odious, the most barbaric, regime in modern times and to the restoration of democracy in Europe.[28]

Flying over Germany after VJ Day, seeing what bombing had done to German cities, Bill Anderson expected to reap a certain grim satisfaction from the sight of the 'Nazi paid back in his own coin':

On the whole it seemed that the tide of war had rolled across the countryside and left it still green. Until we came to the Ruhr. The first town we saw was Krefeld. It had only suffered one major raid. That was enough. Round the outskirts of the town, houses were still standing and many of them had roofs. But the heart of the built-up area was just devastation – ugly scars where buildings once stood; great heaps of brownish-purplish rubble and naked walls, with holes here and there filled with water, for it had been raining. Nothing had been cleared away; it had simply been given up as hopeless. Amongst the rubble ran rows of trees proudly flaunting their green. These were all that remained to mark out the avenues down which the people had walked. Nobody was walking there now, only a couple of jeeps and a lorry were picking their way through the ruins.

From Krefeld, we flew across Duisburg, once the largest inland port in the world. Now it was silent with its great docks scarred and blistered. Then we came to Essen. I had always wanted to see Essen, the hated town that had claimed so many of my friends. It used to mean an odd hollow feeling at briefing and the thought of those searchlights and the flak and the fighters used to colour the grass, at take-off an especially lovely green and make the long shadows running across the black fenland fields even more beautiful than usual. Essen in those days was an unreal place, a place where people went and did not always come back, though you might stand outside the mess kicking up the gravel path and listening for those last aircraft as long as you liked. Essen as I saw it just after VE Day was a terrible reality. The destruction beggared description. Take a brown and rotten bird's nest falling to pieces with decay and smear it over the ground. Get a few bits of dry, jagged bone and stick them up out of this mess. There you have an idea of what we saw when we flew over the middle of Essen town; a picture of utter desolation with its rubble and the shells of the shattered houses. We flew round silent, appalled at the awful destruction. But there was real satisfaction in the sight of Krupp's works, a few miles to the north of the town centre. The huge factory that had lived by destruction had died by the very forces that it had let loose. Huge sheds were smashed, their sides and roofs caved in drunkenly. Things that were gasometers or storage tanks were torn open or crumpled and there were great areas coveted by a twisted network of girders that might have been anything. Acres and acres of tortured ground, covered with rubbish and tattered ironwork, all black with fire or red with rust. Only the tall chimneys had survived most strangely and they stood silent witnesses, pointing their fingers to the sky from which death and destruction had fallen.

We flew on past Bochum to Dortmund through miles of shattered buildings and torn factories and then on to Hamm. The famous marshalling yards had largely been repaired. Only in a few places had the damage been too great. But the bomb craters packed along the edges told the tale of the battering that Bomber Command had given the yards. Then we turned and flew back past Kamen. There was an oil refinery there. Now there was nothing but a handful of tall chimneys standing amongst rubble and rusty ruin. The RAF hit it one night and the USAAF hit it one day.

Our journey back was along Wuppertal, a long, thin area devastated in two raids, one for the east end and the other for the west. Then on to battered Düsseldorf, where there were many people strangely busy amongst the ruins like ants about a nest turned up with a spade. Afterwards we flew down the Rhine and left the Ruhr behind. We used to call it 'Happy Valley'. The joke was no longer funny.

So we came to Cologne. They say that Cologne was a lovely city. Now it was in ruins. Flying over it, you began to realize what the Romans meant when they said a city had been laid waste. The heart of Cologne, as in so many German towns, was marked out by a wide road running round in a sort of ring. Within this ring Cologne was like Essen; just dreary brown and purplish rubble with a little grass beginning to grow amongst the shells of houses where the damage was long-standing. And in the middle stood a colossal, gaunt edifice – the famous Cathedral, looking all the taller since the buildings around it were flattened.

We flew home past Jülich, a little town that had been a key point in the German defences. It had been obliterated in fifteen minutes, so that there was no Jülich at all.

During the next two days we flew over other parts of Germany. Here and there we would come across pretty little villages with bright red roofs nestling among the trees quite untouched. And around them were cornfields, where the people were gathering in the harvest. But every time we came to a large town with factories, the terrible tale was repeated. There we saw how the German people had reaped another sort of harvest. Around the outside might be houses with roofs on but the middle would be just heaps of brownish rubble with a few stark walls. Here and there would be roads driven through the mess, roads which had once run quite straight but now had to deviate at times to avoid the bigger piles of rubbish. And sometimes roads had been started but given up as hopeless. In a few merciful places, the damage had been done several years ago and Nature with her green had softened the gaunt outlines of the skeletons of the houses.

After three days' flying round Germany, we set course back to England. We crossed the Kent coast in cloud and came out into brilliant sunshine on the north bank of the Thames not far from Southend. And at once the contrast hit us. There below us was something that we had not seen in Germany, a huge oil plant, well within bomber range, quite intact. Then we came to London and seen through our opened eyes, it was almost as wonderful. True, there were grim scars but the rubble had been cleared, the gaps levelled, the houses roundabout were wearing their roofs and there were flowers growing in the little gardens. Had we seen such a town in Germany, we would have known it had not suffered even one major RAF raid. For if it had, there would have been that dreadful core of damage.

One of the crew of our aircraft had lost his home in London one night. His mother had been crushed and had lived for a few days. Yet looking at those London streets beneath him, he told me that he had never realized before how lucky England had been. For he had seen Germany. So that he could realize how we ought to thank God that it had never happened over here the way it had happened in Germany.

Yet appalling though the devastation might look from the air, it was even worse from the ground. For there one saw the people. Barefooted, starving, picking wretchedly at the rubbish that had once been their homes. They looked at the Air Force boys woodenly and without feeling. There was no hatred. Because they knew that England was in an even worse state. Had not London in the days of the doodlebug been a sea of flame for months?

Ely Cathedral, a reassuring wartime landmark for homecoming bomber crews, was the setting for a special RAF service on 15 August 1992 marking the foundation of the Path Finder Force 50 years earlier. Mrs Lys Bennett, widow of the late Air Vice Marshal 'Don' Bennett, was in the congregation with about 800 former air and ground crews. The Reverend Michael Wadsworth, who lost his father in Path Finder operations over southern Germany in 1944, gave the sermon. He said that of 93 seven-man Lancaster crews posted to the unit between June 1943 and March–April 1944 only 17 survived.

'Nevertheless, there was a strange alchemy about bomber operations,' he said. 'They were a special breed.'

Notes

1. The following day the aircraft was declared beyond the capacity for local repairs and the airframe languished at Driffield for another month when it was SOC.
2. Halifax DY-Q RG502, flown by F/O J A Hurley (KIA) crashed near Volyne. Apart from Morton, two others survived and they too were taken prisoner. The four crew who died were interned in Praha War Cemetery.
3. See *Round The Clock* by Philip Kaplan and Jack Currie (Cassell 1993) and *Maximum Effort: The Story of the North Lincolnshire Bombers* by Patrick Otter (Archive Publications Ltd/Grimsby *Evening Telegraph* 1990). In summer 1981 Joe Williams and Bill Patrachenko returned to Czechoslovakia with Joe's wife and son to retrace their steps. Near the village of Medenec they met Eric Holl who, as a boy of 15 in March 1945, remembered an aircraft crashing in woodland nearby and took them to a spot where he said the wreckage of an aircraft had remained until 1964. He also told them that the 'Messerschmitt' had crashed nearby, the first indication that Joe had shot down the night-fighter which had attacked *Fox-2*. He had often wondered why the fighter had not attacked again. Now he knew the reason.
4. *R-Robert* was the other loss on 625 Squadron. Sergeants C H Bartlett and J H Porter, the two air gunners, were killed. Their pilot, F/L A D Cook, and Sgt W Allen, who was seriously wounded and Sergeants S L Lowe and T H Scowcroft were confined in hospital until liberation and on 3 April 1945 they and F/Sgt F W Brooks returned to England.
5. 13 Lancasters and 8 Halifaxes.
6. *The Parachute Went Up! and it saved their lives* by Philip Moyes (*RAF Flying Review* May 1960).

7. *218 Gold Coast Squadron Assoc Newsletter No.38.*

8. *The Lancaster at War 2* by Mike Garbutt and Brian Goulding (Ian Allan 1979).

9. Three Lancasters FTR.

10. *The Bomber Command War Diaries: An Operational reference book 1939–1945.* Martin Middlebrook and Chris Everitt. (Midland 1985).

11. *Oberleutnant* Erich Jung, *St.Kpt* of 5./NJG2 in his Ju 88G-6 Werke Nr 620045 4R + AN with his *Funker Feldwebel* Walter Heidenreich and flight mechanic *Oberfeldwebel* Hans Reinnagel destroyed eight Lancasters, some by Jung with his *Schräge Musik*, some with his forward-firing guns. Heidenreich, who had taken part in 12 kills with *Oberleutnant* Günter Köberich who had been killed in an American raid on the airfield at Quakenbrück in April 1944, shot down the 3rd victim. All these kills took Jung's personal score to 28 kills. *Hauptmann* Wilhelm 'Wim' Johnen, *Kommandeur* of III./NJG6 claimed his 32nd and final victory of the war, a Lancaster, SE of Würzburg.

12. *218 Gold Coast Squadron Newsletter.* Johnny Johnson, seconded to the Indian Air Force to train its pilots to fly Dakotas, was killed in a crash in 1946.

13. *The Bomber Command War Diaries: An Operational reference book 1939–1945.* Martin Middlebrook and Chris Everitt. (Midland 1985).

14. See *Out of the Blue: The Role of Luck in Air Warfare 1917–1966* edited by Laddie Lucas (Hutchinson 1985)

15. *Bomber Boys* by Mel Rolfe (Grub Street 2004, Bounty Books 2007). Flying Officer Arthur Benjamin Fischer RAAF and crew were all killed.

16. *Leutnant* Arnold Döring and *Hauptmann* von Tesmar of IV./NJG3 and *Hauptmann* Heinz Ferger of III./NJG2 were the *Nachtjagd* pilots who claimed the Lancasters.

17. NA240 on 462 Squadron RAAF, which was flown by P/O Alfred Desmond John Ball RAAF and it was the one claimed by *Hauptmann* Herbert Koch of I./NJG3 northeast of Anholt. Ball and everyone in his crew except one died.

18. A return raid two days later was equally unsuccessful when cloud again covered the target. Finally, on 16 April a raid by 18 Lancasters on 617 Squadron on the *Lützow* was more successful. One Lancaster was lost and all except two aircraft were damaged, but 15 Lancasters managed to get their 'Tallboy's and 1,000lb bombs away and a near miss tore a large hole in the bottom of the pocket battleship and the *Lützow* sank in shallow water at her moorings.

19. *Nachtjagd* scored its final heavy Bomber Command aircraft kill on 16/17 April when *Oberfeldwebel* Ludwig Schmidt of 2./NJG6 shot down a Halifax, which was engaged on a Bomber Support operation in the Augsburg area. Halifax III MZ467 Z5-C on 462 Squadron RAAF at Nordendorf, 12 kilometres north of Gablingen at 03.44 hours. F/O A M Lodder RAAF was thrown clear and he and 2 of his crew were PoW. 5 KIA. *Oberleutnant* Witzleb of III./NJG1 claimed a Mosquito but none were lost.

20. The bombing was on the south-eastern suburbs of Bremen where the ground troops would attack two days later. Altogether, 767 aircraft were dispatched but the Master Bomber ordered the raid to stop after 195 Lancasters had bombed. The whole of 1 and 4 Groups returned without bombing. Two Lancasters FTR. *The Bomber Command War Diaries: An Operational reference book 1939–1945.* Martin Middlebrook and Chris Everitt. (Midland 1985).

21. Four of the five Halifaxes lost on the Wangerooge raid were the result of collisions and the two Lancaster Xs on 431 'Iroquois' Squadron RCAF that were lost off Nordeney were also the result of a collision. There was only one survivor, from one of the Halifaxes, and 28 Canadian and 13 British airmen were killed in the collisions. The fifth Halifax lost was L8-E on 347 (Free French) Squadron piloted by S/Lt Roger Louis, an Algerian. All the crew were killed.

22. Their attacker was a Ju 88G-6, one of about 12 Ju 88s and Bf 110s based at Kjevik airfield near Kristiansund primarily to intercept Stirlings of Transport Command supplying weapons and equipment to the resistance movement. Nine Stirlings had been shot down without loss until the night of 25 April when a Ju 88G-6 crashed at Iveland about 59 kilometres west of Arendal.

23. Cox and the flight engineer were injured by shell splinters and suffered frostbite. The bomb aimer was more seriously injured. The seventh member on the crew was F/Sgt F E Parent. The final Bomber Command losses occurred on 2/3 May on the raid on Kiel when two Halifaxes on 199 Squadron in 100 Group collided on the bomb run and a Mosquito on 169 Squadron was lost carrying out a low-level napalm attack on Jagel airfield. Both crew were killed. There were only three survivors from the two Halifax losses. Thirteen airmen were killed. See *Confounding The Reich* by Martin W Bowman. (Pen & Sword 2004).

24. *218 Gold Coast Squadron Assoc Newsletter No. 35* August 2005.

25. 'Some years later Alf was located and was feted in The Hague on the Anniversary celebrations. During the speech-making a chap forced his way to Alf s side and asked if he was Alf Cowley and when told yes, he produced the letter and said he had been a child in the school by the field where we dropped the food and had picked up the parcel.' *218 Gold Coast Squadron Newsletter No.55* August 2009.

26. 'The Dutch people have always appreciated the significance of this operation. When the one and only flyable Lancaster bomber in Europe flew over Holland by way of celebration 40 years after *Manna*, Schiphol airport was closed for half a day. It is difficult to imagine this happening anywhere else in the world.' *218 'Gold Coast' Squadron Assoc Newsletter No. 31*. 2,835 Lancaster and 124 Mosquito flights were made before the Germans surrender at the end of the war allowed ships and road transport to enter the area. Bomber Command delivered 6,672 tons of food during Operation *Manna*. *The Bomber Command War Diaries: An Operational reference book 1939–1945* Martin Middlebrook and Chris Everitt. (Midland 1985).

27. In 1940 the Canadian government introduced the National Registration Certificate. All Canadians 16 years of age and older were obliged by law to carry this certificate with them at all times. The penalty for non-compliance was $20. It could also be used as proof of birth date but the underage would-be soldiers still managed to slip through. Roy Hadwyn of Lindsay, Ontario was tall for his age. He joined the RCAF at the age of 15 and a year later was an air-gunner on a Halifax bomber crew. When discovered, he was shipped back to Canada, but he was not discharged. F/Sgt Eric Fedi of Winnipeg who also joined the RCAF at 15 was a seasoned 17-year-old battle veteran mid-upper-gunner when he was killed on 7 September 1943.

28. 73,741 casualties were sustained by Bomber Command of which 55,500 aircrew had been KIA or flying accidents, or died on the ground or while PoWs; a casualty rate that compares with the worst slaughters in WWI trenches. Operational bomber losses were 8,655 aircraft and another 1,600 were lost in accidents and write-offs. Approximately, 125,000-aircrew served in the front-line, OTU and OCUs of the Command and nearly 60% of them became casualties. Almost 9,900 more were shot down and taken prisoner to spend one, two or more years in *Oflags* and *Stalags* in *Axis* held territory. Over 8,000 more were wounded aboard aircraft on operational sorties. Bomber Command flew almost 390,000 sorties, the greatest percentage of them by Lancasters, Halifaxes and Wellingtons. Theirs, of course, were the highest casualties.

Appendices

Appendix 1 Bomber Command Victoria Cross Recipients

Name	Sqn	Aircraft	Action	Award
Learoyd, Acting Flight Lieutenant Roderick Alastair Brook, pilot	49	Hampden	12.8.40	20.8.40
Hannah, F/Sgt John, WOP/AG	83	Hampden	15/16.9.40	1.10.40
Edwards, Acting Wing Commander Hughie Idwal DFC	105	Blenheim	4.7.41	22.7.41
Ward, Sergeant James Allen RNZAF, 2nd pilot	75 RNZAF	Wellington	7.7.41	5.8.41
Nettleton, Acting Squadron Leader John Dering, pilot	44	Lancaster	17.4.42	28.4.42
Manser, Flying Officer Leslie Thomas RAFVR pilot	50	Manchester	30/31.5.42	20.10.42*
Middleton, F/Sgt Rawdon Hume RAAF pilot	149	Stirling	28/29.11.42	15.1.43*
Gibson, Acting Wing Commander Guy Penrose DSO* DFC* pilot	617	Lancaster	16/17.5.43	28.5.43
Aaron, F/Sgt Arthur Louis DFM pilot	218	Stirling	12/13.8.43	5.11.43*
Reid, Acting Flight Lieutenant William RAFVR pilot	61	Lancaster	3/4.11.43	14.12.43
Barton, Pilot Officer Cyril Joe RAFVR, pilot	578	Halifax	30/31.5.44	27.6.44*
Cheshire, Wing Commander Geoffrey Leonard DSO* DFC RAFVR pilot	617	Lancaster	8.9.44	
Thompson, F/Sgt George RAFVR, WOp	9	Lancaster	1.1.45	20.2.45*
Palmer, Acting Squadron Leader Robert Anthony Maurice DFC RAFVR pilot	109	Lancaster	23.12.44	23.4.45*
Swales, Captain Edwin DFC SAAF, 'master bomber'	582	Lancaster	23/24.2.45	24.4.45*
Bazalgette, Acting Squadron Leader Ian Willoughby DFC RAFVR 'master bomber'	635	Lancaster	4.8.44	17.8.45*
Jackson, Sergeant (later Warrant Officer) Norman Cyril RAFVR flight engineer	106	Lancaster	26/27.4.44	26.10.45
Trent, Squadron Leader Leonard Henry DFC RNZAF pilot	487 RNZAF	Ventura	3.5.43	1.3.46
Mynarski, Pilot Officer Andrew Charles RCAF mid-upper gunner	419	Lancaster	12/13.6.44	11.10.46*

* Posthumous award

189

Appendix 2   Aircraft Sorties and Casualties
3 September 1939–7/8 May 1945

Aircraft Type	Sorties	Lost (% of sorties)	Operational Crashes
Lancaster	156,192	3,431 (2.20)	246 (0.16)
Halifax	82,773	1,884 (2.28)	199 (0.24)
Wellington	47,409	1,386 (2.92)	341 (0.72)
Mosquito	39,795	260 (0.65)	50 (0.13)
Stirling	18,440	625 (3.39)	59 (0.32)
Hampden	16,541	424 (2.56)	209 (1.26)
Blenheim	12,214	442 (3.62)	99 (0.81)
Whitley	9,858	317 (3.22)	141 (1.43)
Boston	1,609	42 (2.61)	4 (0.25)
Fortress	1,340	14 (1.04)	4 (0.30)
Manchester	1,269	64 (5.04)	12 (0.95)
Ventura	997	39 (3.91)	2 (0.20)
Liberator	662	3 (0.45)	nil
Others	710	22 (3.10)	2 (0.28)
Total	389,809	8,953	1,368 (0.35)

Appendix 3   Aircrew Casualties

Approximately 125,000 aircrew served in the squadrons and the operational training and conversion units of Bomber Command during WW2. Nearly 60 per cent of Bomber Command aircrew became casualties. Approximately 85 per cent of these casualties were suffered on operations and 15 per cent in training and accidents.

Killed in action or died while prisoners of war	47,268
Killed in flying or ground accidents	8,195
Killed in ground-battle action	37
Total fatal casualties to aircrew	55,500
Prisoners of war, including many wounded	9,838
Wounded in aircraft which returned from operations	4,200
Wounded in flying or ground accidents in UK	4,203
Total wounded, other than prisoners of war	8,403
Total aircrew casualties	73,741

Appendix 4   Aircrew Casualties by Nationality

Royal Air Force	38,462	(69.2 per cent)
Royal Canadian Air Force	9,919	(17.8 per cent)
Royal Australian Air Force	4,050	(7.3 per cent)
Royal New Zealand Air Force	1,679	(3.0 per cent)
Polish Air Force	929	(1.7 per cent)
Other Allied Air Forces	473	(0.9 per cent)
South African Air Force	34	(0.1 per cent)
Other Dominions	27	

Appendix 5   Casualties by Rank

Officers	27.6 per cent
Warrant Officers	3.3 per cent
Non-commissioned officers	69.1 per cent

Appendix 6   Escapers and Evaders

156 RAF men successfully escaped from German PoW camps in Western Europe.
1,975 men evaded capture after having been shot down in Western Europe.

Appendix 7   Ground Crew

1,479 men and 91 WAAFs died while on duty and 52 male ground staff became
PoWs.

Index

.